ANTICHRIST

AND THE

MILLENNIUM

BOOKS BY E. R. CHAMBERLIN

The Count of Virtue
Everyday Life in Renaissance Times
The Bad Popes
Marguerite of Navarre
The Fall of the House of Borgia
Life in Wartime Britain
Life in Medieval France
Florence at the Time of the Medici

E.R. CHAMBERLIN

ANTICHRIST AND THE MILLENNIUM

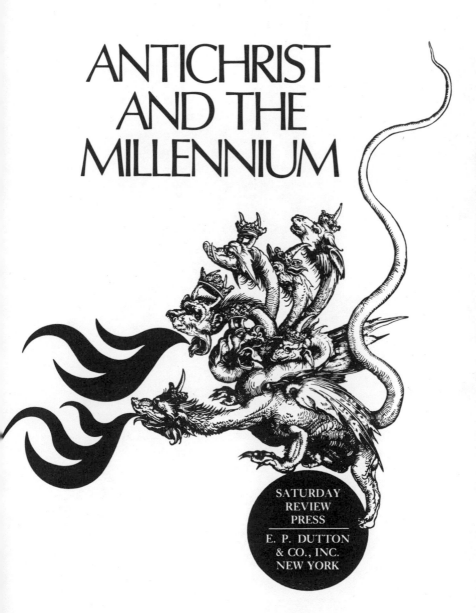

SATURDAY
REVIEW
PRESS

E. P. DUTTON
& CO., INC.
NEW YORK

Grateful acknowledgment is made to the Macmillan Publishing Co. for permission to reprint from "The Second Coming," from *The Collected Poems of William Butler Yeats*, copyright 1924 by Macmillan Publishing Co., renewed 1952 by Bertha Georgie Yeats.

Library of Congress Cataloging in Publication Data

Chamberlin, Eric Russell.
Antichrist and the millennium.

Bibliography: p.
1. Millennialism—History. I. Title.
BT891.C43   1975   236'.3   74–19323

Published simultaneously in Canada by Clarke, Irwin & Company Limited,
Toronto and Vancouver
ISBN: 0-8415-0356-7
Designed by The Etheredges

CONTENTS

●

INTRODUCTION   ix

CHAPTER I

THE SETTING OF THE STAGE   3

i The Vision of Daniel   3

ii The Apocalypse of Saint John   10

iii The Dream of Priscilla   20

iv The Birth of Antichrist   26

CHAPTER II

THE EMPEROR OF THE LAST DAYS   31

i The Boy from Apulia   31

ii The Three Ages of the World   40

iii Stupor Mundi   45

iv Lord of the World   49

CHAPTER III

THE GOTHIC NIGHTMARE   59

CHAPTER IV

THE FIFTH MONARCHY   87
i Thomas Venner   97

CHAPTER V

THE NEPHEW OF GOD   110

CHAPTER VI

THE SIXTH TRUMPETER   131
i The Search for Shiloh   131
ii The Coming of the Trumpeter   135
iii The Ingathering of Israel   146
iv The Coming of Prince Michael   156

CHAPTER VII

OCTOBER 1975   167
i The Invisible Kingdom   167
ii "Millions Now Living Will Never Die"   179
iii Armageddon and After   189

CHAPTER VIII

THE TECHNOLOGICAL DISPENSATION   196

EPILOGUE

THE METAMORPHOSIS OF ANTICHRIST   217
Sources of Quotations   230
Bibliography   232
Index   237

INTRODUCTION

Some time during the second century B.C., the Jewish writer commonly known as Daniel embodied, for purposes of local propaganda and immediate encouragement, a hitherto formless concept into a story that proved to be capable of almost infinite adaptation.

About two centuries later, probably in the year A.D. 90, the Christianized Jew called John, anxious in his turn to provide encouragement for the members of a persecuted religion, recorded a series of supernatural visions, which he claimed to have personally experienced. He called them the Apocalypse, or Revelation of Jesus Christ.

John had transferred his faith from the God of Daniel, but in seeking a literary form for the expression of his vision, he returned instinctively to the wellsprings of his race, drawing upon the same sources that Daniel had drawn. Separated though they were by time and faith and space, between Jewish and Christian writer a dual concept nevertheless came into being.

One part of the concept was an entity who came to be called

Antichrist—a positive, personalized force of evil, who was an emissary and ally of Satan but was quite distinct from him. He would fight the Messiah and persecute the faithful, as prelude to the ending of the world.

The other part of the concept was a time—the Millennium. Etymologically, this was simply the thousand years, preceded by wars and cataclysms and followed by the Last Judgment, during which the Messiah would reign on earth. In practice, it came to be virtually a synonym for the terrestrial paradise—a physically real place, peopled by the Elect and located upon earth.

The dual concept proved to possess an astonishing tenacity. Over the centuries it would change its form again and again. Now one side of the concept would dominate, and now the other: in some eras Antichrist would flicker almost into extinction, in others he would loom balefully, virtually interchangeable with his master. Sometimes paradise would shrink to a mountaintop, expand to embrace the whole world, or sometimes be transferred off the planet altogether to some other wheeling sphere. But though the form might change, it was powered throughout by the same identifiable dynamic—the hope that a physical paradise was about to dawn, and the belief that it would be preceded by a period of woes.

Commentaries on Revelation and Daniel have been appearing steadily over the centuries and presumably will continue to appear so long as men can read and retain interest in the Last Things. In approaching either book, therefore, the layman is faced at the very outset with a jungle of words of appalling luxuriance. One certain point upon which all commentators agree is the necessity to rehearse the whole case upon each occasion, retelling Daniel's or John's story from the first to the last word when remarking upon it. "An exposition of the Revelation is at the same time an argument. And it is one of those arguments in which nothing short of the whole story proves the case." So one modern commentator opens his introduction, going on to say firmly, "the commentary cannot be dipped into here and there by those who have not read it from the beginning."

Such an austere counsel of perfection doubtless holds true for the higher ranges of biblical exegesis. But for those seeking a path through the foothills, anxious to arrive at a concept of the books but reluctant to spend a lifetime at it, it is also a counsel of impossibility. It is, in fact, perfectly possible to follow through strands of thought or subplots in both Daniel and the Apocalypse, much as it is possible to follow through subplots in a novel by Dickens. Such a technique admittedly has to be used with care, for it is precisely because it is possible to detach the images from the overall context that the two books have created such a rich crop of lunacy over the centuries. But given the proposition that both authors were sane, and had a purpose in writing their books, it follows that both books have a ground plan whose main outline, and ultimate purpose, can be detected without minute dissection.

The first chapter of the present book has adopted the technique in order to draw together the major images that have haunted Western consciousness for nearly two millennia. Other biblical books, in particular Ezekiel, Isaiah and Matthew, have contributed richly toward belief in the Millennium and the precise pattern of the Last Days. But it is Daniel and John who form the twin foundations of the extraordinary structure, whose work has been the object of so much devoted and frequently deluded attention and whose interpretation in the present book has been obtained, frankly, by counting heads. Even when there is agreement regarding the overall purpose and pattern of the books, there still remains controversy regarding their parts. The identity of the Beast 666 is today as passionate a subject of debate as when John Napier congratulated himself that his invention of logarithms would speedily solve the problem by accelerating the examination of permutations. The majority of responsible criticism leads overwhelmingly toward the mundane interpretation of the books. But it is perfectly possible to find informed and intelligent argument which seeks, for example, to establish that the Book of Daniel was written not in the second but in the sixth century B.C., thereby transforming its commonplace, if intelligent, historical summary into miraculously detailed foreknowledge. The overall tendency today, however, is to accept that the two books were written by a contemporary for contemporary purposes, the proponents legitimately arguing from thence that their immense moral purpose is, if anything, enhanced with the leaching out of the magical content. It is this lead that the present author has followed.

ANTICHRIST
AND THE
MILLENNIUM

Albrecht Dürer: *Die Geheime Offenbarung Johannis 1498*. Title page: The seven-headed Beast of *Revelation*. The beginning of the Millennium. On the left the Holy City, with its angelic guardian, has descended to Earth; on the right, the Devil is being chained into Hell.

CHAPTER I

•

THE SETTING OF
THE STAGE

(i) The Vision of Daniel

In 168 B.C., the Greek province of Judaea, having known a comparative tranquility for nearly a century, erupted in that most ferocious of all wars, the religious.

Afterwards, it was never wholly clear why Antiochus IV, King of Syria, should throw himself into the sterile, self-defeating business of religious persecution. He was, after all, a Greek—the founder of his dynasty was one of the generals of Alexander the Great—and the Greeks had long since learned that tolerance was a tool vital for the running of empires. His initial error, in fact, was not so very serious; he merely appointed a high priest in Jerusalem, a royal prerogative which most normal people accepted. But in matters of religion the Jews were anything but normal, and there were fierce riots in Jerusalem that challenged the royal dignity.

Antiochus retaliated by striking at the very heart of Judaism. Upon the altar of the great Temple in Jerusalem, he erected or placed something which the Jews could not bring themselves even to name. The "abomination of desolation," they called it, a weird phrase which, even for gentiles, conveyed a sense of horror even while it deepened the sense of mystery. The object was probably a dead pig, sacrificed to an idol placed on or near the altar. Judaism, with its almost passionate addiction to the Law, its almost obsessional regard for the outward forms of religion, was particularly vulnerable to an attack of this nature. Antiochus further ordered that shrines to the gods were to be erected throughout Judaea and that pigs should be sacrificed upon them instead of the canonical lamb. He also ordered that circumcision was to cease forthwith.

After an initial period of shock and confusion, the Jews reacted vigorously. Renegades who sacrificed on the shrines were beaten up, the pagan altars themselves overturned, and the newborn defiantly circumcised. In his turn Antiochus reacted with an escalation of savagery. The mothers of circumcised babies were hanged from crosses, their infants suspended from their necks, while the rest of their families were stoned, crucified, eviscerated. Violence inevitably acted as a catalyst to confirm the hesitant and heighten the fervor of the devout, turning urban riot into national rebellion.

The war was, after all, a local conflict, fierce and bitter to those involved but of little interest outside Judaea. Rome cast its grim shadow over the land at last, prepared to help the patriots—at a price. But Roman help was scarcely needed. A little over a year after the outbreak of hostilities, Antiochus's governor in Judaea was forced to rescind the proscriptions and the altar was triumphantly rededicated to Yahweh in a purified Temple. Antiochus himself died, raving mad, of some loathsome but mysterious disease in the year 164, and the rebellion was over. But sometime during those four years, between the original desecration of the Temple and the death of Antiochus, the commonplace conflict produced an extraordinary result.

Throughout each crisis that marked Israel's reeling course down the centuries, from the triumphant days of her kings to the trauma of the Babylonian exile, the prophets of Israel had appeared to point out the only path. Mystic guardians who claimed to be ap-

pointed by and responsible to no one but their God, each contributed something unique to the body of the Jewish religion. The first
of them was Amos, the shepherd who reluctantly left the harsh,
pure hills to upbraid the fatly prosperous city-dwellers and re-
mind them of their austere heritage. Then came Isaiah, the aristo-
crat who, during yet another period of tribulation, spoke of the
coming of the Messiah who would lead them to triumph over their
enemies. Ezekiel, dragged with his fellow Jews as captive to Babylon, dreamed his mystic dream of the New Jerusalem which would
be a literal heaven on earth. Joel sang of the great Day of the Lord,
the ending of all things. One after another these prophets had come
forward, sometimes two or three in the same generation, to push
language to the very bounds of meaning, straining to describe the
indescribable, and in so doing seeming to transcend the barriers of
past, present, and future.

But the last of the great prophets had stridden off the stage in
the fifth century, over two hundred years earlier, and there had
been silence during the long rule of alien kings. Until now, in the
year 165. To the outsider, the struggle between Antiochus and the
Jews was an event drearily familiar in Asia Minor. To the Jews,
this—the first of all religious persecutions—was aimed at their very
existence, for there could be no Judaism without observance of the
Law. Under that threat and pressure an unknown man of genius
took parchment and pen and, sometime during the years 165–164,
produced one of the masterpieces of the world's literature.

"In the third year of the reign of Jehoiakim king of Juda,
Nebuchadnezzar king of Babylon came to Jerusalem and besieged
it." In that manner the writer began his Book of Daniel, taking the
reader back over four centuries into the past to that day when
Israel was taken into captivity, Jerusalem deserted, the Temple
abandoned, the sacrifices ended. The writer had two closely related
purposes in his mind when he chose to set his story in the remote
past instead of the present day. He wanted to show his compa-
triots of the second century B.C. that their sufferings were not
without precedent, that even as the Temple now was desecrated,

so in the past it had been totally deserted; yet the faith had survived, and Yahweh had returned to the altar. He wanted also to
show how even the raging Antiochus was part of the divine plan,
that all was a majestic working out over the centuries of a scenario
whose parts were foreknown to an all-seeing God.

It was no simple task to show the present as something viewed
from the distant past. The story had to be self-supporting, each
part substantiating the other so that what was, in fact, more than
four hundred years of history between the writer's day and the
period in which he set his story could be shown as a series of
prophecies rising to a great climax "at the end of the days." Daniel,
the eponymous hero of the book, is an epic figure who, from the
very beginning, is shown as one who will be faithful to the Law at
no matter what cost. He, and three young Jewish companions—
Shadrach, Meshach and Abednego—are being trained as pages at
the royal court and are fed from the royal table by Nebuchadnezzar's express command. But despite the honor Daniel refuses to eat
the ritually impure food and, after a tussel with the major-domo,
gets his way. His companions are equally steadfast: Later, they
refuse to worship Nebuchadnezzar's golden image and are cast into
the burning fiery furnace as punishment but are there saved by the
superior power of Daniel's God. Daniel similarly survives his own
ordeal in the lions' den, prophesies Nebuchadnezzar's madness,
and survives into the next reign long enough to read the writing on
the wall at Belshazzar's feast on the very last day of the kingdom of
Babylon.

So the legend of Daniel in Babylon is told with great verve
and skill. But all these details, though colorful and contributing to
the air of verisimilitude, are mere garnishes—trappings for the cosmic prophecies, cast in the form of visions, which are the whole
reason for the existence of the book. In interpreting the first vision,
Daniel triumphs over his rivals, the Chaldean soothsayers, and so
gains the all-important patronage of the king—an incident vividly
reminding the reader of that other Jew in exile who interpreted a
dream and so gained the favor of Pharaoh. Nebuchadnezzar had also
dreamed but, with the caprice of the tyrant, he refused to describe

the dream to his soothsayers while demanding that they interpret it. When they, naturally, failed, Daniel came forward. The king, he said, had dreamed of a fearsome statue or idol whose head was of gold, with a torso of silver, belly of bronze, and legs and feet of a mixture of clay and iron. And while, in the dream, Nebuchadnezzar looked upon the statue in awe, a supernatural stone was hurled at it, shattering it into tiny pieces which were carried away by the summer wind. In the place where the statue had been, the stone grew and grew until it filled the whole earth.

Such was indeed his dream, Nebuchadnezzar admitted, and even by describing it the Hebrew magician had shown his superiority over the Chaldeans. But could he interpret it? Daniel could and did. The four divisions of the statue were four empires: Nebuchadnezzar was himself the head of gold, and the three beneath were those who would come after. The supernatural stone was the Kingdom of God which would destroy all earthly kingdoms and thereafter endure without end. The answer apparently satisfied Nebuchadnezzar who, somewhat uncharacteristically, fell onto his face and did homage to his Jewish servant. He did not think to enquire, and neither did Daniel volunteer, the names of the three kingdoms which were to follow the Babylonian, an omission productive of much luxuriant speculation over the coming centuries. But for those for whom the book was intended—the writer's contemporaries of the second century B.C.—the meaning was clear enough. The empires which were to follow were the empire of the Medes, the empire of the Persians and the present empire of the Greeks now expending its energy in violence. When the Greek empire should pass, as pass it must under the onslaught of the Maccabees, then the Kingdom of God would at last be established on earth.

But there was more, much more, to be uttered through the mouthpiece of Daniel for the great design had to be filled in with details of time and place and person. The symbols used to tell the story were the symbols of Babylon itself, the strange monsters that roared and writhed their way through the myths and then, captured in clay and glazed in brilliant primary colors, decorated the

walls of the vast city. Daniel's creator and manipulator perhaps actually visited Babylon, seeing it in the second century as that "vast
solitude" which Strabo later described, a melancholy desert of
crumbling brick where the brilliant tiles with their heraldic beasts
still survived to produce an impact upon a Jew born centuries after
the fall of the city. The Book of Daniel re-created the weird hy-
brids, investing them with a new significance, ensuring them a
species of immortality: the lion with the wings of an eagle and the
mind of a man; the bear munching human flesh; the winged leopard with four heads; the awesome animal with ten horns and iron
teeth and claws; the battling ram and goat—the phantasmagoria
had a precise purpose, for each nightmare creature stood for some
historic person or institution that was Israel's aid or scourge. Domi-
nating all was the foreshadowing of Antiochus IV, who appears as
a little horn on the ten-horned beast—a little horn that uprooted
others for space in which it grew and grew until at last it over-
shadowed the earth. Endowed with malevolent eyes and a voice uttering blasphemies and threats, the Little Horn persecuted the
children of God until, in the fullness of time, the entire hideous
beast of which it was a part was itself slain and thrown into the
flames.

But it was not enough to predict what was going to happen—
this was known well enough, once the fiction of prophecy was
dropped. In these terrible days of the Greek persecution, when the
outcome was still uncertain, people desperately wanted to know
when the persecution would cease, when the abomination of desolation would be removed. The writer comes back to the problem
again and again, eagerly but gingerly, like a man walking on very
thin ice. First his prophet Daniel overhears two angels discussing
the question; one remarks that "the transgression that makes desolate would last 2,300 evening and morning sacrifices"—1,150 days.
Daniel himself asks one of the terrible shining Beings who have
been conducting the divine fantasia, and the angel swears "by him
who lives for ever that it would be for a time, two times and a half
a time"—three and a half years by Daniel's own scheme of reckoning. It was an accurate enough estimation of the period which actu-

ally elapsed between the first desecration of the Temple and the triumph of the Maccabees, but the author of Daniel, unable to leave well enough alone, embarked upon what was to be a disastrous precedent—the juggling of scriptural prophecies after the fact to fit what actually had happened. At the time of the fall of Jerusalem nearly five hundred years before, the great prophet Jeremiah had prophesied that the Exile would last for seventy years. It had, in fact, lasted for not quite fifty. But Jeremiah could not be wrong, Daniel's creator insisted: he had meant seventy weeks of years (seventy times seven) during which Israel would be in spiritual exile. Those 490 years were now coming to an end and with them the end of all things.

In his persona as Daniel, the writer brings his story to a noble close, debating with one of the Beings the significance of what he has seen and being instructed to seal up the book "until the time of the end" and go in peace to his own grave, "and you shall rest and shall stand in your allotted place at the end of the days." The writer had discharged his self-appointed task brilliantly. It had bristled with problems. It would not have been enough simply to weave a story and father some legendary figure with it, as primitive storytellers did. People were sophisticated, many of them literate and capable of pulling holes in any fabric that was not wholly woven. He had made some mistakes, for it was asking much to expect a writer in second-century Jerusalem to re-create daily life in fifth-century Babylon. But the errors in his story detracted nothing from its force and purpose. Doubtless his contemporaries accepted it for the allegory it was, but when that generation had descended to the grave it took with it the firsthand knowledge of the origin of these prophecies. Succeeding generations, ever obedient to the human preference for the miraculous instead of the mundane, discarded still more of the props that held up the story until, in the first century A.D., the Jewish historian Josephus could say of his own contemporaries, "We believe Daniel conversed with God, for he did not only prophesy of future events, but also determined the time of their accomplishment." [1]

With that, the Book of Daniel was launched upon its secondary—and far more successful—career as a magical key which could open the door of the future if a few minor adjustments were made from time to time. The author's identity was taken over completely by his creation, so that ever after men spoke of Daniel as being not only the hero, but the writer of the story. In return, however, his work was granted literary immortality, for he had created something capable of infinite adaptation. It was an intellectual, somewhat bloodless work; the monsters that prowled through it lacked any real personality or sense of identity. But other prophets would take them up and give them pulsing, horrific life. The first and greatest of these successive prophets was the man known simply as John.

(ii) The Apocalypse of Saint John

The identity of the author of the Christian Apocalypse is almost as mysterious as the identity of the author of Daniel. John was probably a Jew by birth; he was certainly a leading figure in one of the little churches of Asia Minor and was probably known to all of them, for his Revelation was, in effect, a letter of exhortation intended for them all. Beyond that is a mist of uncertainties, of hesitant negatives. He is unlikely to be the Apostle particularly beloved of Christ, for he refers to the Twelve with the reverence of an outsider; he is unlikely to have been the author of the Gosepl of Saint John, although he was perhaps living at the same time, for his own fiercely revengeful work breathes a wholly different spirit from the tranquil philosophy of the Fourth Gospel.

But whatever he was not, he was indubitably one of the world's high masters of language. Over the following centuries, generation after generation of scholars were to deplore his "barbarous Greek," at best seeking to excuse his style as the product of a man thinking in one language while writing in another. But his very limitations became a strength: Struggling to express the emotions of one culture in the intellect of another, he produced something which could transcend the barriers erected by time and interpreters alike.

John and the author of Daniel had very similar purposes. Both men believed that their faith was about to encounter a moment of supreme crisis and were concerned to prepare the faithful. The threat to the Jews had come from the Greeks, the threat to the Christians from the Romans. Ever since the death of Nero in A.D. 68, Christians had been lulled into a sense of tranquility. The terrible persecutions, it seemed, were behind them; their fellow citizens were accepting them as ordinary members of society. Then trouble broke out again about 80 A.D. when the reigning emperor Domitian decreed that he was to be accorded divine honors.

Domitian was, admittedly, mentally unbalanced. But though the decree emanated from a crazy young man, drunk with the knowledge of absolute power, most accepted it calmly enough, and responsible officials implemented it because it had a real social value. The vast empire, sprawling from the forests of Germany to the deserts of Africa, badly needed a symbol of unity, some object or ceremony that would have the same significance for Britons and Parthians, Libyans and Gauls. Caesar-worship ideally filled that need. The more primitive peoples simply accepted the divine Caesar as yet another god in an ever expanding pantheon, while the more sophisticated honored him as the personification of a system that had brought law and tranquility into barbarous places. Some care was taken not to offend religious or national sentiments unnecessarily. The Jews protested, and Rome—vividly aware of the price these people were prepared to pay to maintain the purity of their religion—sensibly dispensed them from the formal sacrifice. The Christians, too, protested, but that was another matter again. They did not, after all, form a coherent national body. They had little social influence, being recruited from the lower levels of society. Above all, there was a singularly disturbing element about their curious faith. Ever since their founder's crucifixion there had arisen a strong and growing belief among the ranks of his followers that he would return again—not in some vague, indefinite period in the distant future but now, in the present generation—to comfort and reward the faithful, chastise the wicked, and bring the world to its appointed end. So strongly rooted was the belief that some of the faithful grew impatient at the delay, and Paul of Tarsus had to turn his mind momentarily from giving an intellectual impress to the new faith to explain, with a touch of irritation, that of course Christ would return in their day, but not until certain circumstances prevailed.

At the very heart of the empire, therefore, at the center of a state founded on the concept of total civic obedience, there was a large and growing body of anarchists, people not so much in opposition to the state as totally indifferent to it. They considered it wholly illogical to compromise even outwardly, to offer even a pinch of incense to the emperor today, when tomorrow, or by the end of the week, or the beginning of next month, the Emperor of Emperors would again be on earth to scatter the enemies of the Christians.

Pressure began to build up against the Christians. It was still a civilized pressure, unlike the delirious cruelty of the persecutions under Nero; at the beginning the recalcitrant were more likely to find themselves threatened with exile than death. But it was a firm pressure, and more and more stubborn Christians found themselves stripped of their goods and thrown into prison or exiled to some remote island in the Mediterranean. About the year 90 A.D., the man known as John was put on board one of the prison ships bound for the island of Patmos in the Sporades. The well-wooded little island with its flourishing town was by no means a rigorous place of exile, and John's residence was in any case brief, for he was released after eighteen months. But during that period of enforced seclusion, he wrote his great work.

The blasphemous demands of Caesar-worship appeared to John as the first gusts of a great storm. His purpose was to exhort his fellow Christians to hold on. The end was not now far removed, but before Christ could return in triumph it was necessary for the faithful to be tested by Satan to the utmost of his diabolic strength and cunning. John was a Christian to the core of his being: He called his book the Revelation of Jesus Christ; the Lamb dominates throughout and is triumphant at the end. But he was also a Jew, instinctively drawing upon a culture that was itself deeply imbued with the exotic imagery of the cultures that surrounded and dominated it. As Israel had been threatened in one crisis after another after the collapse of Antiochus—crises that culminated in the destruction of Jerusalem in A.D. 70, other Jewish writers had followed "Daniel's" lead, transforming Israel's local agony into a cosmic battle of universal significance, telling their tale in a series of apocalypses—revelations in the form of symbolism. It was natural that John should adopt the same medium for the same purpose. But where the symbolism of the Jewish apocalypses had been limited, John's imagination seems inexhaustible as he pours out an astonishing cornucopia of imagery—thunder that speaks with human voice; locust demons; harlots; goddesses; trumpets; seals; bowls; demons with lion's head and scorpion tails; Leviathan; Behemoth; the Lamb; Satan himself—all preparing the way to a stupendous city that is itself supernatural. The richness of the imagery swamps the imagination even as the argument dizzily spirals beyond the reach of intellect.

But behind the imagery and beneath the spiral there can be discerned a plan, a drama showing the battle between good and evil, the subjection at last of the wicked, and the triumph of the faithful. Much of it he drew from ancient sources, much from the astonishing new witness that had begun on the shores of Galilee, but much, too, sprang from his own mind, the product of fusion, different from, though related to, the elements that had produced it.

The vision begins in heaven, before the throne of the Omnipotent who holds out a scroll sealed with seven seals. John weeps as he realizes that no one is worthy to break the seals and so reveal the destiny of man. But a great cry goes up from the myriads assembled around the throne: "Worthy is the Lamb that was slain." The Lamb comes forward to break each seal, one by one. As each seal is broken, a new horror is precipitated upon mankind, beginning with the four terrible Horsemen. A man of John's age would have had excellent reason to believe that all the signs of the end had been made apparent over the preceding thirty years: the earthquakes of A.D. 60; the fire of Rome and the persecutions that followed; the obscene horror of the Jewish war which ended in that forest of crosses above Jerusalem; the eruption of Vesuvius; the famine of A.D. 92; and behind all, the growing unrest within the empire, that organization which all men had come to look upon as an eternal monolith.

Mankind screams with agony under the hooves of the demonic beasts and unavailingly seeks shelter from earthquake and volcano. The slaughter is temporarily suspended by an angel ordering the sealing of the Elect—144,000 human beings, twelve thousand from each of the Tribes, receive the seal upon their forehead which marks them out as the specially favored of the Lord who will survive the coming terror. The Lamb then breaks the seventh seal, but this act, instead of precipitating the end, is followed by an extraordinarily effective dramatic device: "There was silence in heaven for what seemed half an hour." After the pouring out of horrors, after the noise and terror and violent activity, there is the silence almost of an indrawn breath, as though Creation is waiting in numbness for what is to come. And the horror which follows overshadows by far that which has been. Seven angels appear, each with a trumpet: as each of the first four blows his trumpet, the earth is afflicted with natural disasters—plagues, flood, hail, and poison, in turn. There is again a pause, broken by the scream of an eagle, and the earth is smitten by supernatural terrors. Hell opens, and arising out of it in clouds of smoke are demonic locusts with human faces and scorpion stings, while from beyond the Euphrates, two hundred million mounted demons are released and charged to slaughter one-third of mankind.

Still the ghastly scenario does not come to an end for the seventh angel announces, with the seventh trumpet, seven more angels each with a bowl from which more punishment is poured upon an earth already parched, riven, poisoned. The overkilling, though confusing, is never ludicrous, for the enormous power of the language infuses the action. The woes of seals, trumpets, and bowls at last come to an end and at the same time it becomes apparent that they are at once prelude and background, prelude to the true purpose of the vision—the demonstration of the triumph of the faithful—and background to a drama played out by a small number of figures.

An angel appears to John, giving him a measuring rod, telling him to measure the Temple. "But leave the outer court of the Temple exposed and do not measure it for it has been given over to the heathen and they will trample the holy city underfoot for forty-two months." Here John the Christian remembers John the Jew, venerates the Temple that was profaned yet again in his own life-time, and then, drawing upon another Jew, Daniel's own, "time, two times and half a time" predicts that the present tribulation will last forty-two months or three and a half years. Two witnesses appear in a great but unidentified city; they are killed by a monster, and their bodies lie unburied in the streets for three and a half days, when they are resurrected and a tenth of the city destroyed. At this stage the monster, which has been hinted at again and again, comes into focus. It will waver into and out of being, change its identity, but remain recognizable until the end of time—a great red dragon with seven heads and ten horns and a golden crown upon each head, indubitably Daniel's monster, but a monster charged with high and demonic power, pitiless and terrifying, Satan himself.

The monster comes on stage about halfway through the drama. A woman appears in the sky, "robed with the sun, with the moon as her footstool, and a crown of twelve stars on her head." She labors to give birth, and the dragon coils itself to seize and devour the child. The child—the Messiah—is born and promptly caught up to heaven, and the dragon turns its frustrated rage upon the woman. She flees into the desert and remains there for three and a half years while the dragon storms off to destroy the rest of her children. But even Satan needs an ally; he goes down to the shore of a desolate sea, and in obedience to his call Something arises out of that sea—a monster also with seven heads, but one of the heads has been killed and brought to life again. A crowned monster uttering blasphemies, second in power only to Satan himself: Satan's emissary and consort—Antichrist, who was also the emperor Nero.

The concept of a power boundlessly evil yet distinct from the ultimate source of evil was abroad long before John, long before Christianity itself, and probably long before even the oldest Hebrew records. Even the Babylonians, who gave the concept form, probably shaped their dragon myth of Tiamat, the monster of chaos, from materials left behind by the aboriginal dwellers in the great plain. It was the author of Daniel who anthropomorphized the monster, endowing it with the characteristics of Antiochus IV. When Antiochus—a pinchbeck demon at best—disappeared from the stage of history, the dragon skin was ready to be worn by a genuinely evil man. A mediocre man whose pretensions under other circumstances would merely have attracted derision, dead by his own hands at the age of thirty-one, there was yet some quality about Nero, his crimes, or the manner in which he left the world that branded his image in the minds both of contemporaries and posterity. Christians in particular, for whom the slaughter in the Circus was now a sacred epic, endowed him with superhuman characteristics. For the first few years after his death, they believed that he was merely in hiding, but even when they were convinced of his physical death they were not reassured, believing now that he had supernatural powers to perform his evil and would return to earth as a mocking, diabolical parody of Christ's own return. For even as the dragon myth, the legend of the monster of chaos, had given the memory of Nero an extra dimension of horror, so Nero himself gave human identity to the concept of Antichrist. It was no longer the cardboard figure that "Daniel" had created, but a real creature, weird and doomed though he might be. Paul of Tarsus, unwittingly, perhaps, contributed to that personalization. Writing to the impatient Thessalonians he reminded them again that Christ could not return until Antichrist had worked his evil will. The Day of the Lord, the Second Advent could not come about "before the final rebellion against God when wickedness will be revealed in human form, the man doomed to perdition."

All this John remembered when he created his monster rising out of the sea at the summons of Satan. The head that was dead yet lived was Nero, dead by his own hand yet resurrected by the power of evil. And to make that identification certain beyond a doubt, the author created another beast rising from the land who paid homage to the seven-headed monster and branded all men with "the number of its name. Anyone with intelligence may calculate the number of the monster, for it is a man's number and the number is 666"—Nero Caesar.* Both beast and monster played dual roles in John's scenario. Superficially, the beast was the imperial priesthood, brought into being to administer the new cult of Caesar-worship. But it was also the false prophet which comes to proclaim the false Christ. The seven-headed monster was that seven-hilled Rome which John viewed with an extraordinary self-torturing admixture of revulsion and attraction. But it was also the Antichrist, the very real, personal counterpart of the crucified Savior. It mocked and parodied the Christ at every turn, for it, too, was born of a nonhuman father and formed, with the beast and with Satan, a diabolic trinity. It had great powers, as Christ had, but they were powers wholly of illusion. The fire it conjured up neither warmed nor gave light; the food it created gave no nourishment; the dead who walked at its command were automatons, zombies with motion but not life.

For forty-two months—the three and a half years of Daniel's vision—the monster and its attendant beast were allowed dominion while the horrors continued to rain from heaven. But they were mounting now to a climax, approaching that end which John hastens toward with a quivering eagerness that could be triumph, terror, or even lamentation: the destruction of Rome. An angel takes him up and bears him away to a desert, and in this desolate place he receives a vision of something whose images, under the terrible stress of his emotion, seem to shift and change, one following the other in rich and tumbling confusion, melting, crystalizing—now a woman, now a city, now a whore, now a goddess, now Rome in its own right, now Babylon, that titanic place upon its canals which

* John was using the curious punning device known as *gematria*, a system which takes advantage of the fact that the letters of both the Greek and Hebrew alphabets were used as numerals. He added an extra complication by translating Nero Caesar into Greek, Neron Kaisar, and then transliterating the result into Hebrew letters to obtain the necessary numbers.

is, for John the Jew, an inalienable part of his race's memory. It has, in fact, long since been surpassed in sheer size and wealth by other cities but Babylon is still the symbol of all that is enormous in size and wealth and infinitely corrupt. "I will show you the passing of sentence on the great whore, enthroned on many waters," the angel tells him, and John sees again that scarlet monster with seven heads and ten horns which is at once the historical, physical Rome, persecutor of the faithful, and the ancient dragon, Satan himself. On its back is seated a woman, "robed in purple and scarlet and bejeweled with gold and precious stones and pearls," holding in her hand a great golden cup, and even through the violent language of John's revulsion and detestation it is possible to detect the terrible attraction that the great city on the Tiber, the queen of the world, "Babylon the great, mother of all whores and of all the obscenity on earth," holds for him.

The woman and the monster become the physical city, a city collapsing with the smoke of its destruction visible for miles around. Overhead an angel flies, calling out in a terrible voice: "Fallen, fallen is Babylon the great who has made the nations of the earth drink of the wine of the wrath of her fornication." And now it was that John, the Christian Jew, who as both Jew and as Christian had deep and bitter reason to hate the great city, pronounced its epitaph in a lamentation all the more poignant because it was drawn out unwilling from him and mixed with a savage exaltation.

> The kings of the earth weep and wail over her as they watch the smoke from her burning. They will stand far off in terror at her agony and say "Alas, alas! for the great city, the mighty city of Babylon. In one hour your doom has come." The merchants who made their fortunes from her will stand far off in terror at her agony saying, "Alas for the great city that was robed in linen and purple and scarlet, bejeweled with gold and precious stones and pearls." Then every ship's captain and seafaring man, sailors and all who made a living from the sea stood far off and cried out as they watch the smoke from her burning, "Was there ever a city like the great city?" They threw dust on their heads and cried out as they wept and

mourned "Alas! Alas! for the great city, where all who had ships at sea grew rich on her wealth. In one hour she has been laid waste." [2]

With the destruction of Rome, the ending of the vast Empire that was virtually coterminous with the planet itself, John reached the high point of his narrative and thereafter had to make a change. of pace and emphasis. Up to this point he had been, in effect, allegorizing either history or current belief; now he begins to prophesy in the sense of foretelling, groping in unknown regions, striving to give form to the unthinkable and map out the sequence of events that would follow the fall of Rome and the consequent destruction of the known world. The forces of good are now overwhelmingly powerful, and an angel swoops up into the face of the sun, calling upon all winged creatures to gorge themselves upon the carcasses of the slain, those who have been deluded by Satan, the monster, and his attendant beast. Curiously, the defeated monster and the beast are thrown alive into a lake of fire, but Satan, their master and the author of all the terrors and agonies, is merely bound in chains for a thousand years. It is during this Millennium that the 144,000 who have been sealed come forward to reign in the physical, earthly paradise with the returned Christ. John gives no reason as to why this period should last for one thousand years, no more and no less; he gives no reason as to why Satan should merely be bound, while his underlings suffer unimaginable torment, or why the author of all evil should deliberately be released at the end of the Millennium to war with God's people.

The actual, final battle between good and evil is dismissed perfunctorily as though the author were anxious to hasten forward and describe the good things awaiting the faithful. The virtuous dead are resurrected to join the 144,000 who have survived through the Millennium and the New Jerusalem descends from heaven. Here for the first time the author's pen falters, threatening to descend into the bathetic. He turned to Ezekiel for the concept of the heavenly Jerusalem that descends to earth and forms upon the physical globe an actual oasis or enclave of heaven itself. But, unwisely, perhaps, he attempted a physical description. It was natural enough that he should make the city a titanic cube, each side measuring twelve thousand furlongs, for the cube was a sign of perfection and twelve thousand was a mystic number related to the twelve tribes. But the cube shape was to provide a fruitful hunting ground for mystics and miracle mongers, for how were the vertical sides to be interpreted? The description of the city itself, with twelve gates each made from a single pearl, streets of gold so pure as to be transparent as glass, and walls of jasper, emerald, topaz, amethyst and other gaudy if precious stones, was to provide a chilly and somewhat tawdry stereotype for heaven for generations. It seems as though he realized the impossibility of description, for he stops the cheap catalog in midstride and effortlessly picks up the organ notes of the opening of the great vision so that at last the cry is that of an effable yearning, putting in the mouth of the Lamb the ultimate promise repeated again and again in the final chapter: "Behold, I come quickly . . . Surely I come quickly . . . Amen. Amen, Come, Lord Jesus."

There the Revelation ended in the belief and hope of an imminent Return, and as the world turned, the mounting score of years obscured but could never quench that hope. The power of the writer's art was such that men reading his message in languages that would have been unthinkable to him, among nations yet unborn, could react with the same passionate hope. Men living beneath the rule of tyrants, men rotting in industrial cities, men lost and wandering beneath the great skies of prairies and steppes gulped the words like wine. And like alcohol upon an empty stomach, the powerful words produced stranger and yet stranger visions before them.

(iii) The Dream of Priscilla

"A man among us named John . . . prophesied in a Revelation that they who have believed in Christ will spend one thousand years in Jerusalem and that afterwards the universal and eternal resurrection of all at once will take place, and also the judgement." [3] So, about the year 155, a Christian convert vigorously defended his

faith, putting on record for the first time the belief that the Apocalypse of John was more—much more—than an allegory: Those
who had faith would in sober fact spend a millennium in a new and
glorified Jerusalem, a little piece of actual heaven here on the time-
wearied earth.

The writer was a man called Justin. Although born in Pales-
tine, he was no Hebrew with a mind naturally tuned to the mystical, but a pragmatic Latin. Once he had convinced himself of the
truth of Christianity, he devoted the rest of his life to erecting an
intellectual framework for it and acting as missionary. Backwards
and forwards he wandered over Asia Minor, arguing with whomever would listen. At Ephesus, the great city whose glowing
Temple of Diana seemed the epitome of all that was rich and en-
durable in pagan religion, he met his most formidable opponent,
Trypho the Jew. To be fair, posterity knows of the very existence
of Trypho only through Justin himself, in his work called *Dialogue
with Trypho*. Nevertheless, despite the fact that he himself is erecting the objections which he will knock down, the reader is occasionally aware of a note of embarrassment, an occasional overem-
phasis as though Justin's practical Latin mind, aware of an inherent
improbability, is seeking to distract attention from it.

Trypho the Jew lives on in the *Dialogue*, briefly but vividly, in
the lift of an eyebrow, a voice raised in sudden shrill incredulity.
Yes, Christ was God, and yes, he is the Messiah, Justin affirms
with no sense of strain and with dignity, for this is central to all
belief, the very foundation of the universe. With dignity, too, he
defends his fellow Christians as being no rebels but honorable
citizens. The self-defensive note creeps in elsewhere, in particular when he touches on later developments of the Christian theme.
Yes, Christians do believe that Jerusalem will be rebuilt—that same
Jerusalem which the Romans tore apart nearly a century before,
decorating it with the crucified bodies of its defenders, will arise
more glorious than ever. And in it the Elect will live for a thousand
years, enjoying immortality while still in the flesh. How does he
know? Why John, the Apostle, said so, for he was granted a revelation on Patmos.

Trypho the Jew goes on his way unconvinced, and Justin

takes his own path to the martyr's crown that awaits him; but between them they have brought something into being, a recorded statement of belief in the reality of the Millennium.

Justin was writing sometime between the year 155 and 160 and that statement of his pious hope might have been wrung from him by Trypho's skeptical expression, or perhaps by news of the extraordinary events which were taking place in the hinterland of Asia Minor, in the haunted and haunting land of Phrygia. Tales were circulating as to how tiny Christian communities—a farm here, a hamlet there—were being abandoned by their owners, who were making their way to Pepuza. Pepuza! To the critical eye nothing but a poor little township, scarcely more than a village but, to the eye of faith, the most exciting, most important place on the planet. For it was here that the New Jerusalem would descend, as promised by Christ himself to his prophetess Priscilla.

It was not surprising that such news should come out of Phrygia, for there among the towering Taurus Mountains, by the vast green lakes set so improbably among the primeval crags, the extraordinary was the ordinary, the miraculous the everyday. Here Midas of the golden touch had ruled a people who claimed that they were the oldest of mankind and their tongue the first spoken by men. Near Hierapolis the traveler was shown an awful chasm and went away full of awe, confident, if fearful, that he had looked into the mouth of hell itself. But near that unimpressive little township of Pepuza was the most sacred spot of all, Mount Didymus, swelling up from the plain like the symbol and promise of all-fruitfulness, home of the Great Mother, Cybele herself. Here, tumbling down, came the wild processions of her devotees among the shrilling of their pipes, the clashing of their cymbals, the bone-rattling of their sistra, orgiastic, drunk with words and music as well as wine. The little bands of Christians and the more sedate pagans deplored this disreputable Mother, this nurse of Bacchus with her attendant panthers and leopards, her wildly leaping priests who, in fanatical paradox, castrated themselves in the name of fecundity.

And did not one of those priests, the man called Montanus, make the wildest, widest leap of all, from the cave of Cybele to the temple of Christ? So some said. For it was Montanus who was the founder of the new Christian cult and the manner in which he prophesied in the name of Christ differed not at all from the manner in which the priests of Cybele honored their Mother. First there was the terror, the stark fear as the Unknown advanced upon him; then a quietness, a passivity, as the Unknown possessed him and held him, the kind of quietness and passivity that sometimes fell upon the sacrificial ox as the priest raised the knife. Then came the whirling dance of seeming madness and out of it a voice speaking not in the name of God, but as God, admonishing, exhorting, reproaching the listeners as their creator. It would be blasphemy were it not madness, the orthodox cried and drew aside in horror. But there were others who claimed that love and warmth and passion had gone from the Church, squeezed out by the administration. Montanus was speaking as the first Apostles spoke, as Christ himself must have spoken, they said, and they flocked to Pepuza to hear him.

Among the crowds who came were two women, ladies both, Maximilla and Priscilla. Most of posterity's knowledge of this first wave of Christian fanaticism was to be preserved through the pens of enemies; the personalities of Montanus himself and his two priestesses remain shadowy and enigmatic, although the message they proclaimed was unequivocal enough. Maximilla seems to have been a virgin or at least unmarried; Priscilla was rumored to have abandoned her husband, obeying this higher call. The spectacle of these three, the respectable matrons and the priest who was perhaps not wholly a man, whirling in their dervish dance of prophecy was, for most, unequivocal demonstration of possession. But whether that possession was diabolical or divine was the point at argument, an argument that escalated into ferocity when Priscilla announced that she had had a dream or vision. As she lay in her bed Christ had descended and lay beside her. But there was no question of impropriety, for Christ had taken on the form of a woman clad in the most brilliant garments and announced to Priscilla that soon, soon now, that heavenly Jerusalem of which John had spoken, that Jerusalem of gleaming gold, chrysoprase, emerald, and cornelian whose gates were vast and misty pearls, would come into being in the three-dimensional physical world. It was so vast that Pepuza would be swallowed up in it, as well as the plain around as far as the village of Ardabau where Montanus had first prophesied. All who came now, immediately, and entered through these gates of pearl would escape the sting of death for a thousand years under the rule of Christ.

The believers began to arrive—little people for the most part, farmers and craftsmen wearied of urging a niggardly return at the expense of so much labor, ready to clutch at any miracle that promised a break in the dusty, arid cycle. Had not Christ promised in so many words that he would return? The years had slipped into decades, the decades into a century, but God's time was not man's time. Why should this not be the time, and Pepuza the place, for which the world had been waiting? Simultaneously the orthodox, led by the bishop of Hierapolis, mounted their attack. Predictably, the attack was pressed home against the motives and morals of the prophetesses and their priest. They were deluded by the devil; they were in it for money; they were seeking to transmit their own corruption. "Tell me, does a prophet dye his hair? Does he pencil his eyelids? Does he love ornaments? Does he gamble and dice? Does he lend money?" [4] the bishop demanded rhetorically. There was no answer. Or, if there was an answer, the orthodox saw no fit reason to include it in their account of the curious affair.

The dusty streets of Pepuza remained dusty streets; the grayish-yellow stones that formed its houses remained stones; Death continued his appointed task as though no prophecy had been made. At some point the ebbing of belief must have begun; at some point disillusioned eyes must have exchanged a glance with disillusioned eyes and the exodus begun from the city on the plain, a dreary exodus contrasting with the vivacity and hope of the arrival. Montanus, his two lady prophets, and the inner core of his followers stepped off the stage into obscurity and legend. Priscilla disappeared totally. Rumor spread that the steward of the cult, Thomison, was carried up into the air by a devil and let fall from a great height, that Montanus and Maximilla left the earth as finally, if more prosaically, for they hanged themselves. Maximilla, before she died, uttered her last prophecy. "After me there shall be no more prophets, but the end," an end heralded by all the wars and horrors predicted in the Apocalypse. There might have been some unease during the first few weeks following her death, but gradually that unease disappeared and derisive merriment took its place, among the orthodox, at least. "Has it not been made obvious that this is another lie? For it is more than thirteen years today since the woman died and there has been in the world neither local nor universal war but rather, by the mercy of God, continuous peace for all Christians." [5]

The cult survived the death of its founders; it survived even that bitter disappointment which Christians had already learned to endure and would be forced to endure again and again over the coming centuries, the disappointment of yet another postponement of the Second Coming. The cult not merely survived but flourished, invading Rome itself with its message that the Paraclete had spoken, that after the dispensations of Father and Son, there was now the dispensation of the Holy Spirit which would achieve what had not been achieved before. Its final flowering was in the exotic atmosphere of Carthage where for a space it challenged the orthodox, while Authority indifferently executed Montanist or Catholic alike as disturbers of the peace. But after that flowering, its life ebbed back to its roots, to Phrygia where little groups of eccentrics clung to their dusty hope while the world outside turned inexorably toward orthodoxy with its proclamation that councils were preferable to prophets, bishops preferable to ecstatics. The end of these little groups was tragic when Christianity at last triumphed. At the close of the fourth century, the emperor Justinian formally proscribed them, but rather than abandon their hope that Christ's advent was imminent, they went forward to meet him, locking themselves—men, women, and children—in their little churches and burning themselves to death. The dream was ended, but it left an imperishable residue, for belief in the Millennium had been watered with blood, most potent of all fertilizers.

(iv) The Birth of Antichrist

It was not only the Second Coming of Christ that men awaited with impatience and increasing bewilderment. The Parousia, the Return, was the essential precondition for the Millennium, but before the Parousia could happen Christ's supernatural Enemy must work his will upon mankind. Saint Paul had made that very clear in his letter to the little band of Christians in Thessalonica.

> Now we do implore you, by the very certainty of Christ's coming, and of our meeting Him together, to keep your heads and not be thrown off your balance by any prediction or message or letter purporting to come from us, and saying that the day of Christ is almost here. Don't let anyone deceive you by any means whatsoever. That day will not come before there arises a definite rejection of God and the appearance of the Lawless Man. You will remember how I used to talk about a 'restraining power' which would operate until the time should come for the emergence of this Man. Evil activities are restricted until what I have called the 'restraining power' is removed. When that happens the Lawless Man will be plainly seen . . . to those involved in this dying world he will come with evil's undiluted power to deceive . . .[6]

Paul had not specifically identified this Lawless Man with the evil figure of Antichrist, but John the Apostle did so confidently, and later the writer of Revelation molded it into the form of Nero. It was not, perhaps, the Nero that history might easily recognize, but a wholly supernatural figure, "a python, a wrath-breathing dragon, a weird, ghostlike demoniac being wafted through the air by the Fates." [7] There might be academic debates among the more sophisticated Christians as to whether this figure was an actual demon or a species of automaton under the control of Satan, and whether that "restraining power" was God, Fate, or even Satan for his own obscure and diabolic ends. But during the years of sporadic persecution, there was no doubt among Christians regarding Antichrist's earthly nature. He was the personification of Rome, that irresistible, all-pervading power whose titanic and evil energies were directed now to one, sole end—the destruction of the saints of God.

No matter that the Roman Empire, in sober fact, more often reacted against the Christians like a man reacting against the irritation of gnats rather than the Bad reacting against the Good. Responsible officials were perfectly well aware that these extraordinary people seemed actually to be stimulated by the prospect of shedding their own blood: The proconsul of Asia, Arrius Antoninus, declined to execute the Christians who presented themselves to him, declaring that if they were so eager to leave the world they could find their own way via rope or cliff. But the blood spilt during the occasional organized persecutions richly fertilized the ground out of which the hagiographies grew, and they, in their turn, propagated the image of Rome as the penultimate Enemy, subordinate only to Satan. Yet paradoxically, it was a necessary—even welcome—enemy, for each decapitation, crucifixion, burning, and impalement added to the sum total of the evil that must precede the passionately desired end. The famished lions who pounced upon their helpless prey in the arenas were unwitting outriders of the Messiah; the stolid men who performed their routine work of slaughter were heralds of that satanic Herald who must precede Christ's coming. Even Rome must come to an end— for had not John seen this in his divine Apocalypse, a supernatural revelation substantiating men's own experience in the natural world? All things ended, and when the power of Rome collapsed under the weight of its own evil, the Millennium would dawn.

Then abruptly the hard but clear-cut pattern became blurred when, in A.D. 313, the Edict of Milan established freedom of religion throughout the Empire. Under Constantine's benevolent eye the proscribed, derided religion of Christ became first the favored, and then the official cult of the Empire. Rome the persecutor was now Rome the protector, the ghost of Nero fading at last into nothingness. The earlier almost mystical reverence in which the great city had been held returned again, infused with the Christian spirit. When the Ostrogoth Totila threatened to level Rome to the ground, his noble enemy Belisarius warned him that such an act would brand his memory eternally with disgrace: "Beyond all cities on Earth, Rome is the greatest and most wonderful. For neither has she been built by the energy of a single man nor has she attained to such greatness and beauty in a short time for countless years of wealth, and artists from every quarter have been required to bring together all the treasures she contains." [8] If Totila destroys Rome, he destroys his own city for Rome belongs to all the world. Impressed by such an argument from a Byzantine general for whom Italy was, after all, only a province, Totila stayed his hand after a ritual destruction of the walls. Later, when history added its own ironical comment to Rome's endless story and the Christian city displayed a corruption as great as that of the pagan city, the memory of Rome as the enemy of God was revived. But even so, men came to believe that the incredible city could be destroyed only by God, acting through nature. "Rome will not be destroyed by the barbarians but by storms and lightning," St. Benedict prophesied in the fourth century. "Scourged by whirlwind and earthquake, the city will putrefy in itself." [9]

But if Rome and the Christian emperors could no longer be identified confidently as Antichrist, where then were the faithful to look for this necessary monster? Gradually, a composite substitute emerged, drawing upon scattered traditions, Jewish and pagan as well as Christian, combining without embarrassment wholly contradictory factors. Antichrist would be a Jew, born of the tribe of Dan. Alternatively, it was as confidently expected that he would be born of a nun. Some witnesses were content to leave only vague descriptions of him couched in conventional epithets—a dragon, a monster—or purely allegorical. Others were generously specific if dramatically contradictory: "He shall be bald-headed, with a small and a large eye: his right arm shall be a span long but his left two and a half ells. On his brow shall be a scab, his right ear stopped, but the other open." [10] So one group saw him, cheerfully unconcerned that this scarred, deformed, deaf, bald creature was totally at variance with the glowing Luciferian image of a fallen angel which others as confidently described as the image of Antichrist.

Like Christ, he must enter the world as a baby, and again and again there sped through Christendom the thrilling rumor that he had been born. In the year 380, Saint Martin of Tours announced that Antichrist had actually been in the world for some years and was now a boy approaching manhood. Over the following centuries this or that high prelate confidently announced that they had private but certain information that Antichrist had just been conceived, was a baby, a boy, or a young man about to plan the final battle. As with the monster of Revelation, he was a master of illusion, a talent which conveniently explained his widely varying appearance. He worked wonders "to deceive and astonish, not healing for conversion and salvation." At his word statues walked, stones became bread, the dead were given an obscene illusion of life. And just as his advent was the necessary precursor to the sacred Second Coming, so there were signs and portents that marked his own Parousia. The sun would rise by night and the moon by day; there would be a universal drought accompanied by a terrible famine; the very seas would dry up, the birds fall dead from the air. Even here, however, there was a basic contradiction: Other sources firmly maintained that his advent would be marked by a brief but incredible fruitfulness on the earth.

The personality of Antichrist might have changed but the scenario remained essentially unaltered with his rule lasting three and a half years—or multiples of three and a half years—with legions of demons ready to obey his call, and with that small core of the Elect who would escape a physical death for a thousand years. But there now appeared on the stage a new figure—the Christian emperor who would be the general of the earthly armies of the good. The myth of the Emperor of the Last Days probably came into being as a result of the meteoric rise of Islam, providing a counterweight to Mohammed. It was certainly influenced by the magic of Virgil's so-called prophecy in his Fourth Eclogue. Virgil was probably doing nothing more than was expected—for even a poet must eat—when he wrote his praise of his patron's newborn son, foretelling that the child in manhood would rule as king in an age of gold, bringing peace to a tortured earth. The Christians marveled at the exactness with which a pagan prophesied the birth of their Savior, promoted Virgil to the status of honorary Christian, and when it became evident that the golden age was still to come, projected the prophecy forward in time to create the picture of the omnipotent earthly monarch. He was seen at his clearest, perhaps, in the poignant story of Prester John, a ruler so enormously powerful that he despised the title of king and styled himself simply "priest"—Presbyter John. His palace was located somewhere in Africa, behind the arrogant ranks of Islam. Perpetual peace reigned throughout his vast kingdom; before his palace there hung a marvelous mirror in which he could see every detail of what was happening in his realm and the world beyond. Someday, when he judged the time to be ripe, he would move and sweep Islam into the sea and bring all the nations of the earth under the rule of Christ.

And then? Theories varied according to the taste of the theorist. But in general it was agreed that the last Christian emperor, whatever his name or race, would journey to Jerusalem after defeating the hordes of human enemies. There, in the cleansed and sanctified city, he would lay down his crown on the Mount of Olives. The Millennium would follow. The tribes of Gog Magog would arise in the East, bursting out of the mountains where Alexander the Great had by his magic chained them, battle would be joined, and the end of all things would ensue.

Early in the thirteenth century, it seemed that some of the preconditions were being met. In 1227 a Brother Peter of Boreth sent word to the world from Acre that Antichrist was already in the world and, in March, would be ten years old. That was a common enough announcement, but those with long memories recalled a story of how, in the town of Jesi in Italy, a boy was supposed to have been born of a nun just after Christmas in 1194.

CHAPTER II
•
THE EMPEROR OF
THE LAST DAYS

(i) The Boy from Apulia

He was born in a tent set up in the marketplace of Jesi on December 26, 1194. Despite the bitter cold, the tent flaps were looped back, allowing passers-by to look within. A herald, moreover, announced that any matron of the town could approach even closer and watch the woman in labor until the child should arrive. The mother was forty years old—matriarchal in a society where most women were dead by the time they were thirty-five. This child was, in addition, her first after ten years of marriage, and so she had good reason to fear those malicious tongues that would whisper that the birth was suppositious because the mother was too old. Witnesses were needed, the more the better; hence the staging of this undignified, uncomfortable spectacle.

There were witnesses in plenty, for it was not every day that the stolid matrons of Jesi had the opportunity of seeing an empress in labor. They passed in and out of the tent, and some time during that gray day they noted and duly propagated the fact that the big, fair-haired, comely woman had given birth to a boy and ritually suckled him. She was a conscientious queen rather than an ideal mother, for having proclaimed to the world that there was a legitimate heir to the Hohenstaufen throne, she left the child in Jesi and continued her interrupted journey to join her husband in Sicily.

So much was in the records, undisputed fact. His mother was Constance, Queen of Sicily in her own right, for she was a descendant of those Norman adventurers who had hacked their way to power in the island kingdom just seventy years before. His father was the grim Henry VI, supreme ruler of the Holy Roman Empire. His grandfather was the already legendary Emperor Frederick Barbarossa. His stem was the house of Hohenstaufen, the German dynasty which claimed sovereignty over all the lands of the West as heirs of Charlemagne. His name was Frederick, the same whom men were later to call Stupor Mundi, the Wonder of the World.

Such were the facts. But even before his first wail of protest ascended from the cold marketplace, legend attended him, wrapping around him in the womb, heralding his arrival. His mother's story was the stuff of legend: The beautiful, cold daughter of a brilliant king, born upon that voluptuous island of Sicily which most Europeans regarded half enviously, half horrified, as the island of Circe. There was a world of sensuous delights open to her, but she turned her back upon them and took her coldness into a nunnery from which she was removed for dynastic reasons and married to a man she grew slowly to hate. Her pregnancy brought her no warmth, no happiness. Her confessor, Abbot Joachim, gave as his considered opinion that she must have coupled with a demon to have achieved so late and so delayed an event. She herself dreamed that she gave birth to a blazing torch. In distant Brittany, the wizard Merlin pondered the results of her unexpected pregnancy and announced from his cave that the child would be both lamb and lion, rending and being rended, and that the world would perhaps be better without his birth. But there were flatterers, too—such as the poet Peter of Eboli, who took as his theme the Virgilian prophecy that the coming child would be the long awaited king of the golden age, a conceit echoed by the scholarly pedant Godfrey of Viterbo, who was also the Emperor's tutor.

Henry, the Emperor, listened, heard all, said nothing. A warmer man might perhaps have melted the cold at Constance's heart, but he was the Frost King to her Queen, bestriding Europe like a blast from the North, warmth and light and joy dying at his touch, clamping the western world in an iron grip. He gave orders that the newborn child should be given the solid German name of Frederick, contemptuously obliterating the fanciful Sicilian name of Constantine that Constance had bestowed upon him. He planned, too, to send the boy into Germany and briefly inspected the foster parents who had charge of him in Italy. But meanwhile there was a rebellion of Sicilians to be put down; the Sicilians objected loudly to being subject to an uncouth German merely because their queen had taken him in marriage. He crushed that rebellion with a sickening cruelty, forcing his wife to watch the revolting tortures by which he finally established his will over her childhood friends and kinsmen. She watched and made no plea or protest, but waited.

And swiftly she had her revenge, though she enjoyed it for but a short time. The iron German fell victim to those debilitating fevers with which Sicily had often eliminated its enemies from the North. Scarcely was the breath out of his body, and even before the swift corruption of the South had set in when she gave orders that her son was to be brought home. She placed the handsome little lad, now just three years old, on the carved throne of his Norman–Sicilian ancestors and spelled out their glory to him in child's language. Over the next year, she did everything to make him forget his German blood, even at the cost of forfeiting the high crown of empire on his behalf. She might have succeeded; she might have turned Frederick Hohenstaufen into a Sicilian king, given time. But death came for her just fourteen months after it had come for her husband; in November 1198, her small child was left alone in Palermo, to survive as best he might in a disintegrating society.

The navel of all the kingdoms of the world—so the great Pope Innocent III described Sicily in a momentary flight of fancy. Ever since the great days of Athens, the beautiful island had been at once lure and prize to be fought for or bought, but always coveted, so that by the thirteenth century six distinct races formed the social mosaic: Greek, Saracen, Lombard, Jew, Italian, and Norman. Under the rule of the Norman kings, each was equal to the others, distinct in racial personality, but also fusing to form a whole, creating a unique civilization. The kingdom was unique not only in its social structure but in its physical form, for it was composed of two quite distinct sections: the island of Sicily itself and the whole of the Italian mainland from the toe of Italy almost up to the gates of Rome. A strong central monarchy had held the parts together, enforced peace upon the variegated national elements, and kept the outside world at bay. But with the death of Constance, the vital catalyst was removed and the society collapsed into its components. Simultaneously adventurers poured in from outside—Germans, Frenchmen, Italians, Spaniards, all eager for plunder, hurling themselves upon the resident Greeks, Normans, Jews, Saracens, and Lombards.

In the midst of this lethal chaos, the baby Frederick became a boy. Posterity is provided with only one glimpse of him during this vital formative period, but it is wholly characteristic. One of the battling factions tried to lay hands on him, presumably as hostage. They found him in one of the rooms of the palace in Palermo and attempted to drag him out. He fought back, hysterical with rage, biting, scratching, kicking, rending his own garments and tearing his own flesh with his nails. Appalled at his violence, his would-be captors retreated. The spotlight passed on, leaving in mysterious darkness the child who would not suffer his royal person to be touched. And for five years he remained in that darkness. Not the least mysterious aspect of those five years was how he survived at all, for his easily arranged removal would have suited the convenience of a number of parties.

He not only survived, however, but flourished, drawing a unique education from the polyglot, multiracial society around him. For five years the handsome, bronzed, fair-haired boy wandered the streets and harbor of Palermo unsupervised, unprotected, his body fed by casual acts of charity, his mind absorbing experience direct from a phantasmagoria that could have been produced in no other city of the world. Not Rome, not Naples, not even great Constantinople itself presented such a variegated tapestry to the dazzled eye. The outward sign of the city's richness was perhaps best displayed in its incredible churches where Byzantine mosaics clothed the gloomy strength of Norman arches, and classic pillars soared up to a roofbeam on which Saracen workmen had carved God's praises in Arabic. Outside in the narrow streets, that amiable heterogeneity was continued through the people themselves. Here was almost every human shade from gold to ebony; here the shapeless, heavily veiled bundles that were the women of Islam gave an added dignity, by contrast to the simple, stately lines of the costume of Christian women. Here were men dressed in caftans and in armor, their heads covered in turbans, cowls, or the extravaganza of peacock hats; merchants from every Mediterranean country and most European lands; slaves from Tunis, the Caucasus, Syria; rabbis, imam, priests jostled shoulders with soldiers speaking a dozen tongues. Through them all the boy threaded his way.

Sometimes, it seemed, he stopped and talked at length with a seaman, full of tales of strange lands and beasts and stranger men. Or it might be a huntsman who spoke to the boy, talking of the flight of birds, how the boar charges, and what the dance of gnats betokened. The Jongleurs would have had something to give him—those lean, hungry-looking men dressed in rather tawdry, travel-stained finery, working their way down through Europe and bringing to this island of the sun songs wrought in the mists of the North. Later, men would marvel at the depth and breadth of his education, his command of languages and science, and his familiarity alike with the movements of the moon and the falcon, and elaborate theories were erected to account for his accomplishments with this or that wise man cast as his teacher. But if, during those five vital years, he had any one teacher, the man was unusually modest, for he has never been identified. The boy had a naturally eclectic mind, an ability to absorb and relate disparate items that amounted to genius. The very fact that that growing mind was never forced into a procrustean mold accounted in very large part for the wayward, questing brilliance of the adult man. Nowhere was the effect so clear as in the field of religion: The boy took what he wanted when he wanted, indifferent whether the source was Jewish, Moslem, or Christian so that, inevitably, the man's bright unwinking gaze could detect no difference between Christ, Mohammed, and Moses, causing scandal to his less experimental contemporaries.

When he was fourteen, the spotlight of history returned to the lad; he ascended the throne, king of Sicily in his own right. A bride was found for him, an unattractive woman ten years his senior. He accepted her almost joyfully, for part of her dowry consisted of her personal bodyguard of five hundred Spanish knights, and Frederick II Hohenstaufen, who had yet to shave, had resolved to impose his will upon the murderous chaos that was Sicily; five hundred knights was a weapon that made the bride's lack of charm irrelevant. But they were unseasoned men who rapidly fell victim to the Sicilian climate, leaving Frederick in a worse position than during his minority; worse—because in the world outside, the world that had largely ignored him and his kingdom, there had arisen a sudden threat that could deprive him not only of his uncertain crown but of liberty and life itself.

As she lay dying, his mother had entrusted the care of her orphan son to the Pope. The fact that the boy survived at all argued that Pope Innocent III had discharged at least part of his trust. But it also lay within his power to ensure that the legitimate Hohenstaufen heir should succeed to the imperial crown, as well as to the Sicilian, and Innocent III, kingmaker and kingbreaker, had no intention whatsoever of again allowing the crowns of Sicily and the Empire to be united and so draw a ring of steel around Rome. Instead, he supported the claims of a distant usurper, Otto of Brunswick.

Innocent made a mistake, the kind of mistake that kingmakers invariably made: His creature grew independent, arrogant. The new emperor Otto—a crude, unpolished man, built like a bull and with a bull's delicacy of approach—marched down into Italy, trampling over his sworn promises to defend and honor the papacy, and announced his intention of descending upon Sicily where he would simultaneously extinguish the last ruling Hohenstaufen remnant and the last trace of papal influence. "It repenteth me that I have made man," Innocent sighed and set about weaving a net to catch the bull.

He worked almost too subtly, too slowly. In Sicily, young King Frederick could do nothing but wait as his imperial rival charged down the Italian peninsula. Italians might mock Otto's pretensions and naïveté, but there was always profit to be made out of such a situation, and many cities supported him, filling his war chest, waiting to see what would happen. He crossed the mainland frontier of the Sicilian kingdom, and city after city fell to him: He stood at last upon the seashore, looking toward the island kingdom and planning the crossing that would be a simple prelude to triumph. Losing his nerve at the very peak and pinnacle of success, however, he turned about and blundered back to the North.

That was the first of the miracles which studded the life of Frederick. The explanation was prosaic enough: Innocent's intrigues abroad had weakened support for the emperor, and Otto had sensibly decided to protect his base. But though Frederick entirely owed his political—and possibly his personal—survival to his late guardian's talent for international intrigue, to the world at large the sudden destruction of the looming threat was sure evidence of divine favor. Success bred success: Scarcely had Otto retreated when a German nobleman appeared in Palermo to announce that the Germans had elected Frederick to his father's and his grandfather's throne. His wife and his more sober counselors tried to bring him down to earth by reminding him that this was a favorite game of the Germans, pitting one "emperor" against another. He wavered momentarily on examining the depleted treasury—so depleted that it could not even provide him with a change of wardrobe. But hesitation ended when Pope Innocent sent word that he would back young Frederick with all the powers of the Keys of Peter, declaring excommunicate the so-called Emperor Otto. In March 1212, three months after his seventeenth birthday, Frederick left his wife and baby son and the island that had nurtured him and began his journey to the springs of his race.

The journey took seven months, seven months during which he laid the foundation of an enduring legend with tales of hair-breadth escape from thronging enemies, hardship borne with laughter and song, fierce loyalties and equally fierce hatreds engendered by the magical name Hohenstaufen, trust and betrayal. The journey began with a confrontation in Rome, the first and only meeting between the king and his priestly guardian, between Innocent III, perhaps the greatest of all the papal monarchs, the Augustus of the popes who looked upon himself and his office as the pinnacle of the physical universe, and a beardless stripling.

Each held for the other an almost equal fascination and repulsion. Frederick saw a pale, plump man with a smooth, impassive face, an administrator rather than a thinker, who had made him and could perhaps yet break him. Innocent saw two persons—first, the Hohenstaufen heir, living continuation of a brilliant, erratic house who, tamed, could be the papacy's most formidable weapon, but who might not consent to be tamed and so would have to be destroyed. The youth himself, Innocent could not help noting, was an unusually attractive human being—gracefully built but, infusing the grace, fire and steel; of medium height, golden-haired, bronze-skinned, the hands beautifully fashioned, almost delicate but immensely strong; the glance even then somewhat unnerving, for it was direct, unwavering.

The priest gave the eager young man his blessing and little else. The crown of empire was his for the taking—if he could take it. Frederick left, weaving a complex path through Italy to avoid enemies and seek the support of equivocal friends. At Genoa he replenished his frugal supplies by scattering IOU's payable "on the day when I am emperor." He also learned that the Milanese were out hunting him. An escort of knights from Pavia took him, in the gray predawn hours, onto the next stage of his journey, seeing him safe across the River Lambro, but at cost of their own lives; a large force of Milanese fell upon the party and Frederick alone escaped across the river. So, painfully, from Cremona to Mantua to Verona, coming at last under the great wall of the Alps. The Brenner Pass was closed to him, so he had to stumble, with a few companions, over the high peaks themselves before swinging down into the Engadine and arriving at last before the walls of Constance on its beautiful lake. The gates were shut, the town gaily decorated, and a banquet was laid for the emperor—Emperor Otto, who was expected hourly.

The Germans had never wholly forgotten the Hohenstaufen heir on his enchanted island in the southern sea. More than any other northern race, they—set among their goblin-haunted, mist-wreathed forests—cherished a hunger for the South, transforming a natural desire for sun and flowers and fruit into a mystic relationship. Frederick as an absent monarch might have been discounted in the realm of practical politics (although the Germans were never very good at practical politics), but when he appeared as the golden boy touched with the splendor of the Hohenstaufen name and carrying still the aura of the South, he won the first, vital, battle by the simple magic of his presence. Barbarossa's grandson, spirited over from the isles of Circe, was standing outside Constance, asking for entry—precisely the kind of situation that appealed to a German. The gates were thrown open and the youth brought joyfully in; when Otto arrived a few hours later, he had lost both his meal and his crown.

For all that came after was a foregone conclusion. It was perhaps Frederick's youth to which the Germans responded, that bubbling, fresh enthusiasm which came like a draught of spring water after an arid and bitter period. "The lad from Apulia," they called him, and later he inscribed it among his high titles—*Puer Apuliae*, as though youth would sit, for him at least, eternally upon his shoulders. Otto crumbled, declining into bitterness and failure, reaching out for his own death at last: In an agony of abasement and remorse he called upon his confessors to beat him, urging them to strike harder and harder until his life ebbed out in a pool of penitential blood, the darker side of that same German impulse that produced the golden boy. His passing was scarcely noticed. Frederick entered the sacred town of Aachen where Charlemagne lay buried, drove a silver nail into the new shrine where the giant's bones rested, took Charlemagne's crown, and seated himself on Charlemagne's throne in July 1215, his twenty-first year. And in the heady confidence of that moment, he swore a great oath that he would take the cross and wrench the holy places from the infidels' defiling grasp. Never was a generous impulse to be more regretted.

(ii) The Three Ages of the World

Europe was on tiptoe waiting a miracle, a revelation regarding it knew not what. A few months before Frederick rode down the Engadine, the great valley had echoed with the voices of children raised not in laughter but in hymns, thousands upon thousands of children, flooding down toward southern Europe, confident that the sea would open for them so that they could walk dryshod to the Holy Land and there, in the innocence of childhood, achieve what had been denied to sinful maturity. The fortunate ones died on the way: At Marseille two canny merchants, Hugh the Iron and William the Pig, enticed the survivors onto ships and sold them at a fine profit. Men shook their heads over the tragedy, but their faith remained unshaken; plainly it was the Devil's doing. They continued their search for prophets and miracles. Astrology, which for centuries had been in decline, enjoyed an astonishing resurrection; in a few years' time, it would enjoy the even more astonishing approval of no less a person than Thomas Aquinas himself. Responsibility for human action being transferred to the stars, it was entirely logical to assume that when the stars were in favorable conjunction, there would instantaneously occur a regeneration of the human spirit. The heavens were anxiously scanned for the certain indications of the fullness of days that must, soon now, appear.

Frederick had been a boy of eight when there died, in the wild fastnesses of Calabria, an aged abbot who, more than any one man, drew together the wide-ranging hopes and fears of this troubled era, fusing the legends into one intellectual system and obtaining for it the blessing of the Church. Frederick would have known the old man personally, for he was Abbot Joachim of Flora, who had been confessor to Frederick's mother and had delivered himself of the opinion that she had involuntarily coupled with a demon to produce a child so late in life. Joachim claimed that in his youth he had received, on the sacred Mount Tabor in the Holy Land, a vision which laid bare to him all the secrets of the Old and New Testaments—above all, of the interpretation of the Apocalypse. It was the kind of personal revelation of which Authority had already learned to be extremely wary; a century earlier or later, Joachim would probably have found himself in a penitential cell. But in the effervescence of the twelfth century, an effervescence alike of the emotions and of the mind, expressed as much through minnesingers as through theologians, the claim did not seem to be particularly extravagant. Moreover, Joachim was a devout man of demonstrable virtue. In vain he declined the title of prophet, saying that he worked by intuition only. His followers knew better, insisting that God had drawn aside the veil of the future for him so that he could look down the perspective of time to the end of things.

Joachim's revelation was based on that mysterious period of "time, two times and half a time" which Daniel had first enunciated, John had developed further in his Apocalypse, and Joachim claimed now to have resolved. The Creator had decreed that there were to be three states of the world, he announced. The first—that of the Father—ran from the time of Adam to that of Christ; the second—that of the Son—was from Christ to the present day; the third and last phase—that of the Holy Ghost—was almost at hand. He even gave a date to the beginning of this final Dispensation. There were to be forty-two generations from the time of Christ to the time of the Holy Ghost, each generation consisting of exactly thirty years. The forty-first generation would begin in the year

1201, "and it was to be expected with great dread"; thereafter it was simple enough to calculate that the final Dispensation would begin in the year 1260. Upon this structure Joachim erected the now familiar details—but with one disturbing novelty. Antichrist was already in the world, he proclaimed, and would, in due course, occupy the papal throne for the three and a half years ("time, two times and half a time") immediately preceding the Second Coming. Antipapists nodded their heads approvingly, but traditionalists were disconcerted: Had it not always been taught that Antichrist would occupy the throne of David in Jerusalem and there crown himself? That, too, would take place, Joachim affirmed, leaving it to his disciples to disentangle his meaning.

The old man died in 1202, drawing his last breath in his damp Calabrian cell at about the same time that Frederick Hohenstaufen was roaming the streets of Palermo. Already their lives had touched, even while Frederick had been in the womb; now Joachim's teachings and Frederick's destiny were to be inextricably intertwined, the one giving substance and justification to the other.

Joachim's interpretations of the Apocalypse did not die with him; far from it, they grew ever more detailed and lurid. His pious disciples wrote their own prophecies, foisted them onto their distinguished master, and gained for him much posthumous glory regarding those prophecies' exactness, for they took the precaution of writing them after, rather than before, the event of which they treated. The so-called Joachimite prophecies entered deep and enduring into the European consciousness: The coming of Francis of Assisi was identified with the breaking of the Sixth Seal; a papal bull opened with the sonorous, unequivocal phrase, "Since the evening of the world is now declining." The vague feeling of impending doom was codified. The Church itself now accepted that the great play of the ending of things had begun. By the time that the young emperor Frederick strode upon the world stage, intent only upon his own affairs, two roles had, in fact, been already prepared for him. He merely had to choose whether to be Antichrist—or Messiah.

It was the papacy which ensured that it was he, Frederick Hohenstaufen, who made that choice.

For twelve years, ever since becoming emperor, there had hung over him the spontaneous vow he had made to go on crusade. The procrastination was not altogether his fault, for it had been necessary to restore order to the Empire after nearly a generation's anarchy. In doing so, he created two images: The Germans would remember him as the golden boy, ruling with laughter and charm. But to the Sicilians and Italians, he was a terrible, avenging demiurge, for his southern kingdom had almost disintegrated, and terror was the only tool that could weld it again into one. His wife died and he took another, and it was as though there were a movement in the veil of time, for her name was Isabella of Jerusalem and she brought her husband the crown of Jerusalem as dowry.

It was a hollow enough gift, for Jerusalem was in the hands of the infidel and her title to it was derived from one of the Frankish conquerors of the first crusades. But it was impossible not to be stirred by such a title, and it was now, perhaps, that the legend of Frederick Hohenstaufen truly began. In 1227 he went on crusade at last to redeem his vow but chose the lethal month of August to assemble the great fleet at Brindisi, and they had scarcely put to sea before the plague struck. The corpse-laden ships drifted helplessly, and he put back into harbor—at which, with a yell of triumph, the Pope excommunicated him.

For ten years, three popes in succession had been irritably reminding him of his vow and reluctantly accepting his excuses. But in 1227 an old man possessed of a petty mind but an iron will ascended the throne and took the name of Gregory IX. And he, the small-minded, more clearly divined the threat that the risen star of Hohenstaufen presented to the papacy than even his great predecessor Innocent. An excommunicated emperor was shorn of all power: With spite, but also with skill, Pope Gregory gave a turn to the screw that should have eliminated the Hohenstaufen permanently. The Emperor had been excommunicated for failing to go on crusade; he could not go on crusade until absolved of the sin of failing to go on crusade. Frederick went on crusade, grimly ignoring the two black-robed friars who accompanied him everywhere, loudly cursing him, calling on all Christians to disavow the accursed of Christ. And having arrived in the Holy Land he compounded his fault, for instead of plunging into the blood of infidels, he entered into converse with them, exchanging embassies with the Sultan al Kamil, ruler of Egypt.

They had much in common: Both were intellectuals, ceaselessly, passionately curious; both were orthodox in their religious beliefs, but a critical eye could detect a certain lukewarmness in their orthodoxy. Each was interested in the other as a person. They never met, but by that exchange of envoys, carried out at first in secret, they came to know the workings of each other's mind to a remarkable degree. Frederick assured his Oriental counterpart that he had no desire to spill blood; all he wanted was to claim Jerusalem which was his by right of his wife's inheritance. Considering that Christian and Moslem had been battling for Jerusalem ever since Saladin had captured it forty years before, Frederick's polite request seemed almost an effrontery. Astonishingly, al Kamil agreed, receiving nothing of any real value in return. It might have been that he fell victim, even at long distance, to the Hohenstaufen charm; more likely he was concerned to shorten his lines of communication as there came, from the depths of Asia, the first gusts of the Mongol storm. Whatever the cause, in the spring of 1229, Frederick added one more to his dazzling collection of crowns.

On Sunday, March 17, the Emperor entered the Church of the Holy Sepulchre. Despite the crowds, his entry into the most sacred church in Christendom was made in total silence; there was no clattering of welcoming bells, no solemn chanting, no prayers to sanctify. The Pope had forbidden any such ceremony. But the prohibition reacted against him, for in the profound silence Frederick's slow, deliberate actions took on an almost eerie significance. In the rich gloom he seemed to float rather than walk up to the altar. There he picked up the crown, turned and faced the congregation. Slowly, deliberately, and with immense dignity, he placed the crown upon his own head, shattering a centuries-long precedent: Never before had a Christian sovereign received a crown except from the hands of a priest. In crowning himself, Frederick Hohenstaufen was proclaiming his subordinacy to God alone.

Three days later the Emperor sailed for home. Despite his delight in the things of the East, there was nothing further to keep him there, no act that would not be an anticlimax after the ceremony in Jerusalem. At home his base was being eroded by papal propagandists, who spread, with considerable skill, the tale that he was dead, or had at last turned Moslem, or in general was no longer to be reckoned with.

But not for the first time had Pope Gregory overreached himself. At about the time that Frederick's kingdom was reluctantly beginning to accept that their monarch was indeed dead or an apostate, the monarch himself sailed in out of the sunrise, bronzed, confident, indestructible. The cities that had reluctantly fallen to the rule of priests now joyously threw off that rule, welcoming back the man who so unexpectedly appeared among them, much as he had appeared in Germany twenty years earlier, to establish the enduring legend of the golden boy.

(iii) Stupor Mundi

Although the whole pattern and bent of Frederick's nature was southern, it was not in the mature and voluptuous beauty of Sicily that he established his court, but at Foggia, in the center of a vast plain on the Italian mainland. In so doing, he shrugged off the comparative parochialism of his Norman and German ancestors. For Foggia was on the high road of the Empire, not on its limits, and he was proclaiming thereby that all the West was his nation, not this or that country whose crown he happened to possess.

There was not much at Foggia when Frederick's eye first fell upon it. A Norman church and a handful of gloomy, well-fortified mansions gave a certain dignity to what was little more than a cattle town. Even after the imperial court was established there, each autumn the town would be clamorous with the bleating of sheep as thousands passed through to winter pastures from their summer grazing on the hills of the Abruzzi. Frederick began building the palace in 1223, his twenty-ninth year, and continued to expand and embellish it virtually throughout his life; architecture, with its combined need for mathematician's precision and artist's flair, exactly appealed to him. The great building, like so much else that he created, was destined to fall into ruin, but the picture of it was dyed deep in the memory of the poets, chroniclers, *jongleurs* and diplomats who passed through Apulia and tasted the lavish, half-Oriental philosophy. They remembered it as a place of coolness and depth, courtyard within courtyard offering elegant shelter from the brazen sun, the floors of many-colored, softly shining rare marble, slender towering pillars breaking out into Corinthian capitals supporting a roof that hinted Saracen. Richard Earl of Cornwall and later, improbably, to be himself emperor, passed through Foggia on his way back from crusade and left such an account of it with the English chroniclers that they turned it, at last, into the magic palace of a fairy-tale person as potent and as insubstantial as Haroun's Baghdad. Everywhere was music, Richard marveled; music filled with the languor and plangency of the East, filling the cool halls like an intangible liquid. And through it swam figures of a scarcely human beauty and grace, the Saracen maidens who were a gift from the Sultan to the Emperor and who entertained their new master decorously enough, for they were dancers and acrobats, though the uncharitable loudly proclaimed otherwise. The visitor, indeed, was as likely to encounter Saracens as Christians at Frederick's court. The slender, fierce, mailed soldiers who guarded throne room and imperial quarters were Saracen; hundreds were billeted in the palace and thousands established not far away. Frederick had killed their Emir in Sicily and transported the entire community to Italy. Perversely, they regarded him as a kind of god and were ready to die for him.

Outside the palace, in cages, stables, and fenced-in paddocks, there crawled or lumbered or strutted representatives, it seemed, of every kind of animal that had come off the ark. Frederick had acquired some as part of a systematic zoological collection; others were the magnificent gifts of fellow potentates. The elephant, whose fame spread throughout Europe, was another gift of the Sultan. So, too, was the giraffe, the first to be seen in medieval Europe. The camels and dromedaries were used quite casually as transport; the panthers, leopards, and lions were simply for display. Most of this extraordinary menagerie traveled with the Emperor during his endless journeys through his realm, creating considerable problems for his hosts and leaving an indelible impression on the minds of those who saw the procession pass by. This, too, added to the legendary aura around the Emperor's name. There was still a folk memory in Europe of that thrilling god, Dionysus, who also traveled in a chariot with panthers and leopards in attendance. Accompanied by his bodyguard of gorgeously dressed Saracens, preceded by panthers, riding to the shrilling of horns and the clash of cymbals, Frederick's appearance abroad took on an epic, other-worldly quality to a people already predisposed to prefer the miraculous to the mundane.

But all this—the strange animals, the exotic followers, the huge journeys wheeling through Europe—were only the outward expression of an endlessly curious, endlessly working mind. His probing, restless intelligence formed the major component of his legend. For most people, there were only two kinds of knowledge, the divine and the demonic. Frederick showed little interest in the divine, at least as it was expressed in the dreary logic-chopping of contemporary theology. Therefore he must be dabbling in the demonic, his contemporaries reasoned, and stories that had been abroad for centuries were dusted down and adapted to this newest and most dazzling of magicians.

But there was no need to invent anecdotes to illustrate the extraordinary range and nature of his intellect. Michael Scott, his chief astrologer and scientist-in-waiting, recorded an immense list of questions "concerning the foundations of the Earth and the marvels within" that Frederick put to him. They included:

How many heavens are there and who are their rulers and principal inhabitants?
How is the earth established over the abyss?

Does one soul in the next world know another, and can it return to this life to speak and show itself?

How many are the pains of hell?

How does it happen that the waters of the sea are so bitter?

What is the measure of the earth by thickness and length?

Does the earth have empty spaces within it, or is it solid like a living stone?

What do the angels and saints do with their time?

Concerning the wind which issues from many parts of the earth, and the fire which bursts from plains and mountains: What causes its blasts as seen in the region of Sicily and Messina, as Etna, Vulcano, Lipari?

Why is it that the soul of a living man which has passed away to another life cannot be induced to return by love—or even by hate?[11]

Subjects that most of his contemporaries held to be axiomatic, unquestionable, he dissected, holding them up to the cold light of day. It was a dangerous gift, this ability to examine the cause and roots of things. "Our intent is to set forth the things which are as they are," he announced in the preface to his book on the art of hawking, an intent which he applied to other things than hawking, to the dismay of the orthodox. Michael Scott, astrologer and alchemist, part genius, part charlatan, must have been able to give convincing answers to that formidable list of questions, for he continued in Frederick's favor until his death. He described how the Emperor once tested him by secretly lowering the floor of a room from which he had taken a trigonometric measurement of a planet's height and then making him take the measurement again. "Either the heavens have receded or we have sunk a palm's breadth," Scott announced, and Frederick embraced him.

Scott was essentially the companion of Frederick's leisure hours. The man who put his policies into action, who interpreted even his half-formed intentions and desires, was Piero della Vigna. Judge, scholar, poet, and diplomat, Piero was also friend, counselor, and most loyal servant. "I was the one who held both the keys of Frederick's heart," he told Dante in hell later, for it was his tragedy to fall victim to the autocrat's suspicion, and he ended his life by his own hand. But in the long years of his ascendancy, he shaped the image of the Emperor that the outside world saw, wearing himself out in that demanding service so that, as he said wryly, he grew swiftly older while his master remained young.

Singularly blessed among men, Frederick Hohenstaufen appeared to be—blessed in person with charm, good looks, and excellent health; blessed in the devotion that he could inspire in widely varying people, from Saracen soldiers and German nuns to Jewish scholars and Italian merchants; blessed in his time, a world awaking briefly from a long, dark sleep; blessed even in his locale, for his Kingdom of the Two Sicilies had a rare stability, a fact he recognized when he created his own species of Iron Curtain, controlling all the means of entry and exit of his fortress kingdom. But it seems as though the scales of fortune have to be adjusted as precisely as the scales of justice, and to counterbalance this wealth of blessings was the dark misfortune that enveloped all other members of his family: the tragedy of his three young wives, all dead by their twenties; the tragedy of his children—a lurid or premature end awaited them all, legitimate and illegitimate alike, from his eldest son, Henry, who led a clumsy rebellion against his father and rode his horse over a cliff to escape life-long imprisonment, to the golden-haired, noble bastard, Enzio, who was not so fortunate. During one of the Emperor's campaigns in Italy, the citizens of Bologna captured Enzio, locked him in a room, and kept him there despite his father's frantic offer of all the gold that even the merchants of Bologna could desire. The Emperor's son as hostage was even more valuable than the Emperor's gold, and in prison Enzio remained until death released him after twenty-three years. Caged, he was to survive all his family and so watched, impotent, while his father's reign proceeded from its bright morning to golden afternoon and then to a gray and storm-wracked evening.

(iv) The Lord of the World

I am Frederick the Hammer, the Doom of the World
Rome, tottering, at last to destruction is hurled
And never again shall be Lord of the World

It was a battle song, a full-bodied chant of threat and defiance, and in Rome the Pope heard it, trembled with rage, and looked to his own weapons. They were spiritual weapons of interdict, anathema, and malediction, for the looming battle between Empire and papacy was a battle for the soul of Europe, and ideas gave far more lethal wounds than steel. There had been conventional battles aplenty: In the north, Frederick had unleashed his son-in-law, the terrifying Ezzelino da Romano whom men believed, quite soberly, to be an incarnate demon—it was said that his entire body was covered in hair, an infallible indication of his origins. Ezzelino, in concert with Enzio before his capture, ranged Lombardy, and the cities upon which his baleful glance fell seemed hypnotized into subservience. But here and there the imperial armies suffered inglorious defeat—at Parma where the Emperor injudiciously went hunting and the citizens fell upon the briefly leaderless besiegers, and again at Viterbo where, urged on by the papal legate, the people revolted and slaughtered the imperial garrison. But that had been by an act of treachery, and a papal propagandist recorded the Emperor's enraged reaction to that treachery half in exultation, half in awe: "He leaped like a lioness robbed of her young or a she bear bereft of her cubs. Clothed in the fire of his wrath he rushed like a midnight tornado to punish the town; like a courier for speed he rode, and with no royal pomp. Mounted on a red horse he came to snatch peace from the earth." [12]

The rider on the red horse—memory stirred, stimulated by the name that Frederick bestowed upon the horse: Dragon. Deliberately, it seems, he now assumed a forbidden mantel—forbidden, certainly, to any lesser person than the Emperor of the World. What was a good Catholic to make of that extraordinary letter he wrote to his birthplace, Jesi: "Noble town of the March, where Our Divine Mother brought us into the world, where our radiant cradle stood—thou, Our Bethlehem, birthplace of the Caesar, shall remain deep-rooted in Our heart. Thou, o Bethlehem, are not least among the cities of our race, for out of thee the Leader is come . . ." [13] Bethlehem? Divine Mother? Leader? Men had been burned for claiming far less. Was Frederick, in his turn, falling victim to the stress of power?

Tracking the psychic evolution of Frederick Stupor Mundi down to the moment when he was deposed is a virtually insuperable problem. The shimmering myth that he wove, as a conscious part of politics or otherwise, mixed and melted in with the greater myth of the coming of the Messiah that was flourishing wildly. Christians and Jews alike fed the fevered dream. In 1233 the "great hallelujah" burst over Italy; in city after city ecstatics cried out a new rule of love, and their religious dementia spread like an epidemic: "All were drunk with heavenly love, for they had quaffed the wine of the spirit of God after tasting which all flesh begins to rave." It was a common enough phenomenon, this sudden outburst of a people goaded beyond endurance by war or plague or famine. Sometimes it would take a sinister turn, as with the flagellants and the dancing mania, sometimes a gentle ceremonial as with the Bianchi and their processions of love.

But the great hallelujah was given an extra potency by news of the great captain who had arisen in the East and was now marching inexorably toward Europe. Was he the Antichrist whose coming John had long since prophesied, coming from the East at the head of hundreds of millions of demons? Or was he, as the Jews insisted, the Messiah? A.D. 1240 was the Hebrew year 5000, and it was prophesied that the Messiah would come at the beginning of the fifth millennium. Some of the more impressionable Jews sold their belongings and began to travel eastward in order to welcome the Messiah and join his entourage. Most of them were beaten up and thrown into prison by indignant Christians and could count themselves as fortunate in their treatment, for the grand captain in the East was Genghis Khan. In England, safely distant, the chronicler Matthew Paris recorded, appalled, the eruption of the Mongols, and speculated whether this terrifying people might not, after all, be the tribes of Gog and Magog who would come to the aid of Antichrist:

An immense horde of that detestable race of Satan, rushed forth like demons loosed from Tartarus (so that they are well called Tartars), as if it were inhabitants of Tartarus: and overrunning the country, covering the face of the earth like locusts, they ravaged the eastern countries with lamentable destruction. The men are inhuman and of the nature of beasts, thirsting after and drinking blood and tearing and devouring the flesh of dogs and human beings. They have no human laws, know no mercy, know no other country's language except their own. They are short in stature and thickset, compact in their bodies and of great strength: invincible in battle, indefatigable in labour.

Paris noted that the Saracen "the memory of whom is detestable" actually combined forces with the Christians to resist the horrifying invaders.[14]

It was against this background of messianic hope, very real military threat, and social unrest that Frederick began to prepare for his battle with the papacy. Old Gregory IX had gone down to his grave still spitting curses. He was believed to have been at least a hundred years old when he died, but to the end he had defied the Emperor, defied the Romans; chased from Rome by his supposed subjects, he had returned and still sought to impose his will on the world, in particular on that "limb of Antichrist, Frederick." But with his death, Frederick found that he was not fighting a pope but the Pope. The new pope, as a cardinal, had been a good friend of the Emperor's, but as Innocent IV his policy became indistinguishable from that of his predecessor. He and his antagonist could have given a score of excellent reasons for their enmity—the violation of this or that treaty, the insolence of an official, some strategic necessity or other. In reality there was only one point at issue: Was the Lord of the World to be a priest or a king? It was the shattering of that dangerous, ludicrous, noble vision of the Holy Roman Empire in which Christ's priest and Christ's general worked in harmony, ruling all men in Christ's name.

The war was carried on in the name of Pope Innocent IV; the true instrument of vengeance, the man who saw himself as the sword of the Lord, was a cardinal, Rainer of Viterbo. He had inherited the almost lunatic hatred of old Gregory IX, deplored the relative mildness of the new pope, and set himself to the holy task of rousing the world against the monster who wore the imperial crown. Like so much papal propaganda, the very virulence of the attack recoiled upon the propagandists, for it was Rainer of Viterbo who first sketched out a superhuman—a supernatural—role for Frederick Hohenstaufen. He was not content to attack the Emperor as a sinful man; he had to be a monster, something of titanic evil that threatened the very existence of the Chair of Peter. In his venomous pamphlets he rehearsed, subtly twisting, each aspect of the Emperor's life and character that upset the devout: The Saracen dancing girls again made their bow as a harem; the friendship with the Moslem leaders and the exchanging of presents with them; his lax attitude toward heresy—though that was a libel, for Frederick burned heretics as enthusiastically as any priest, on the sound ground that a heretic was a potential rebel; his own casual approach to religion; his shocking remark that Christ, Mohammed and Moses were all of a kind—all charges the world had heard many times before. Rainer added to them, making Frederick the murderer of his own wives and of his rebellious son Henry. And then the Cardinal, drunk with his own words, rushed on to create a figure credible only in mythological terms:

> He carried the war further against the saints and constrained them. Lifting himself up against heaven he flung the holy ones of the Most High down from the firmament and from the stars and tore them in pieces. He hath three rows of teeth in his jaws for the monks and the clerks and the innocent laity, and mighty claws of iron hath he . . . Hellhound shall he be called like Herod: Crueller than Nero shall he be known . . . a new Nimrod, a raging hunter before the Lord. Like Lucifer he essayed to scale the heavens to establish his thrones above the stars . . . He hath in his forehead the horn of power and a mouth that bringeth forth monstrous things. . . .

On and on the tirade went, rising at last to a shriek of hatred, the very voice of fanatic possession as Rainer demanded excommunication and all that followed: "Have no pity for the ruthless one! Cast him to the ground before the face of the kings that they may see and fear to follow his footsteps. Cast him forth out of the Holy Place of God! Destroy the name and fame, the seed and sapling of this Babylonian! Let mercy forget him." [15]

The sentence of excommunication and deposition, when it came, was almost an anticlimax, but it did something to Frederick, making a very real change in his nature. "I have been the hammer, now I will be the anvil." The Englishman Matthew Paris reported a dramatic scene that has the sound of truth about it. On receiving news of his deposition, Frederick ordered the cases containing his imperial regalia to be brought to him.

> And on their being unlocked before him he said, "See if my crowns are lost now." Then finding one he placed it on his head and, being thus crowned, he stood up and with threatening eye and a dreadful voice unrestrainable from passion he said aloud: "I have not yet lost my crown, nor will I be deprived of it by any attacks of the pope without a bloody struggle. I am now released from all ties of affection and from the obligation of any kind of peace with him." [16]

The papacy had cast Frederick into a superhuman role; he accepted it, merely changing the name. Antichrist and Messiah—the attributes of each were necessarily the same and both the enemies and devoted followers of Frederick Hohenstaufen could look back down the vistas of his life and see the awesome marks: the scientists he cherished, obviously the magicians that attended on both Messiah and Antichrist; the self-crowning in Jerusalem; the outlandish creatures that accompanied him on his processional tours; the exotic men who served him as soldiers or scholars or statesmen; the very color of the horses he rode—each was read as a symbol. His courtiers took up the tale, elaborating, exaggerating as was the habit of courtiers until they perhaps believed their exaggerations. Imperator, Caesar Romanorum Semper Augustus, Felix Victor ac Triumphator—these were the normal titles, almost the small change of empire. But they added more: Stupor quoque Mundi et Immutator Mirabilis, Scourge of the World: he who ruleth over earth and sea; he whose might tramples the mountains and bends them—so sounded the drum roll of flattery.

Papal progaganda unequivocally shaped out the figure of a superhuman, if malign, person; imperial propaganda changed the attributes only, maintaining and indeed elaborating the superhuman concept. It was therefore unsurprising that those who took no direct part in the war of words, those for whom the emperor Frederick was a real, tangible, if distant, source of immense energy and power, should come to accept both propaganda pictures and out of the turbulence and the contrasts create their own almost supernatural figure. And did Frederick himself accept that picture? In assessing the sincerity and motives of the central figure of any cult, the observer is again and again brought to an uncertain standstill. It is easy to accept the sincerity of the disciples and believers for whom the leader provides a desperately needed foundation, but there is no known way of testing the subjective reality of the leader's own convictions. Frederick acted as though he were, indeed, the divinely appointed Scourge of God. He had always possessed an indifference to suffering at best, if not an active cruelty—he could not otherwise have undertaken that famed investigation into human digestion. Now men went to their deaths at a nod; severed hands and heads, the shrieks of the disemboweled, the agony of the blinded began to build a miasma of fear around what had been all clarity and the pure light of reason. It was now that the death of his veteran counselor, firm friend, and honored fellow scholar, Piero della Vigna, took place among circumstances of macabre horror. There was a rumor that della Vigna had betrayed his master for money—an unlikely tale, that, but no more unlikely than the other rumors that swirled about his end. There was an Othello-like story telling how the Emperor entered his friend's bedroom in search of him. Della Vigna was not there but his wife was, sleeping uncovered. The Emperor gently drew the sheet over her but unwittingly dropped his glove. Della Vigna found it and was thereafter mad for vengeance. It may have been so, but both master and man kept their own counsel. All that the world knew was that Piero della Vigna had been deposed, blinded, and imprisoned, and on being removed from one prison cell to another, took the opportunity to escape altogether by charging at a wall and dashing his head against it.

The twelve months following the suicide of Piero della Vigna was a year of disaster for Frederick with humiliating defeats in Italy and the death of one son—Richard—by disease and the arrest of another—Enzio—by capture. But through the last few months of 1250 the golden glow returned, the Hohenstaufen fortune again swinging above the horizon. The European monarchs who had stood by or actively encouraged the Pope in his assault on the Emperor, now pondered their own relationship with His Holiness. If the Holy See could divert crusade funds for a holy war against the Emperor, might it not act similarly against a recalcitrant king? Saint Louis, King of France, had refused to recognize the Emperor's deposition, and when Louis was captured on crusade, Frederick was able to repay the debt and give himself added prestige by pleading with the Sultan for the king's release.

Suddenly the currents swung in favor of the Emperor, an alliance against the papacy seemed first possible and then probable. If that carping, interfering power were neutralized, what goal could not be achieved by a man such as Frederick Hohenstaufen who, still in his fifties, by legal title and personal magnetism bestrode Europe? At that point, the sardonic fate which ensured that every Hohenstaufen triumph should have a corresponding failure played its penultimate game. Early in December 1250, the Emperor went hunting in Apulia, where he fell ill—too ill to be taken the long, rough road into Foggia. His attendants turned aside at a rural castle, intending to take temporary refuge there until he should be fit to continue the journey. Frederick seems to have been in a coma, for it was not until he was settled in bed that he asked the name of the castle. Castel Fiorentino, he was told, and at that, eyewitnesses say, he resigned himself to death. For years before the infallible astrologer Michael Scott had predicted that the Emperor would die in a place with a name associated with flowers. In consequence, Frederick had all his life avoided Florence, the Flowery City, only to find his fate awaiting him in Castel Fiorentino, the

Flowery Castle. Three days later, on December 11, he died, probably of a perforated ulcer, at the age of fifty-six.

"If Merlin and the Sibyl speak truth, the imperial dignity must come to an end with Frederick. Nevertheless, I do not know whether this applies to his family only, or to the Germans, or altogether," a Florentine wrote.[17] For all over Europe men were looking for the significance behind that wholly unexpected death. Joachim of Flora had prophesied that the Emperor would rule for seventy-two years, and that during his reign the corrupt and tyrannous papacy would be humbled and cleansed. Now the Emperor was dead, after scarcely thirty-five years on the throne, and the papacy brutally triumphant, not scorning to trample on the dead. Let the Church rejoice, Pope Innocent, one-time friend of the dead man decreed, and the Church rejoiced, though the laity pondered another significance of the man's life. The followers of Joachim, who had seen Frederick as playing a major role in the great plan envisaged by their master, began the game of juggling with dates to prove that the Final Dispensation was yet to come.

It was among these Joachimites that there first grew the belief that Frederick, in fact, lived on. It was a legend whose growth was accelerated by the extraordinary fact that the death of Frederick disconcerted both his friends and his enemies. For his enemies, who regarded him as Antichrist, his death was ten years too early. The new order would dawn in 1260, but in order that the scriptural prophecies be fulfilled, it would be immediately preceded by Antichrist rampant and briefly triumphant. Frederick's friends regarded him simply as the Messiah, who would rule in the new world as Christ's immortal general. From those twin roots, the legend drew sustenance and flourished. Frederick could not be dead; therefore he was not dead. Passionate and ingenious minds evolved elaborate theories to explain his temporary absence. The most dramatic of these was that reported by a Franciscan in Sicily. He had been, he said, deep in meditation on the seashore, when he was terrified to see a great host of armed men led by the Emperor riding down into the sea. The water hissed and steamed as they entered, for they were red hot, and one of the horsemen momentarily drew rein to tell the monk that he had been privileged to see "Kaiser Frederick riding into Etna with his men." Over the following years, the legend of the great emperor who would return was developed ever further with a precise though ever-changing time-table for the return, together with a list of great deeds that he would carry out on behalf of a sinful but tormented world.

"The sun of the world has set, the sun which lit up the peoples, the sun of Justice"—so wrote his beloved son Manfred, and in after years, as men looked back while enduring the convulsions of a continent changing its social form, it seemed that they did, indeed, look into a sunset. Against that golden glow, they again saw a figure of grace and power ride out to their aid. False Fredericks became as common as false messiahs once had been, including both self-deluding lunatics who managed, briefly, to delude others before expiating their crime in the flames and charlatans who enjoyed a brief and heady fame before discreetly moving out of the limelight. In the legend, Frederick the Antichrist had become, unequivocally, Frederick the Messiah—but now the man's sardonic fate played its final and permanent trick. The setting of the legend was moved from Sicily and Italy to the high peaks of the Kyffhauser in Thuringia. There, in a cave in the heart of the mountain, far below the great ravens that wheel endlessly in the updraft, a great emperor sleeps. His golden beard grows ever longer while the centuries pass over him. But on the day that the Empire again needs him, he will awake, mount his horse, and ride out into a world crying out for justice. All this the mythopoeic process weaved to make a man immortal—but in the weaving, Frederick was displaced by his grandfather, and it was Barbarossa not Stupor Mundi, who the peasants said was stirring when the thunder muttered and the storm clouds gathered over the mountain.

CHAPTER III

•

THE GOTHIC NIGHTMARE

Frederick Stupor Mundi was the last of the great historical personages to be allotted a leading role in the apocalyptic drama. The discovery that even his stupendous figure was merely mortal and that A.D. 1260 was, after all, merely the year following A.D. 1259 shook even the resilient faith of Europe. The Italian chronicler Salimbene, when mocked for having once shared the belief of Joachim of Flora that a universal savior was imminent, replied sadly, "I was indeed a Joachist. But when Frederick died that was emperor, and the year 1260 passed, I entirely laid aside that doctrine and after this will believe in nothing that I cannot see."

Salimbene spoke for many, in particular that wholly sane and substantial stratum of society for whom the stories of Antichrist, the Messiah, and the millennial dream were simply another facet of the Christian religion, no more miraculous than the promise of resurrection or the threat of hell. It was these balanced and orthodox Christians who were the most shocked by the nonfulfillment of the prophecies and now turned their back on the apocalyptic promise, relegating it to the realm of mythology, leaving its interpretation to ever wilder visionaries.

The old pattern of faith was breaking up in Europe, and some of its fragments were being used to form most bizarre mosaics. The new beliefs were unconsciously based on social protest, but it was impossible to shake off overnight the habits of thought formed over generations, and protest continued to take religious form. Belief in a specific Antichrist or Messiah might be on the wane, but belief in the Millennium and an earthly paradise grew correspondingly stronger as the passionate desire spread for a reformed society. As the Empire itself began to pass into history and the continent broke down into its racial components, so nationalism arose and took on the prevalent religious covering.

In Prague in 1415, John Huss was burned as a heretic, but from the ashes of his sacrificial fire there arose a fanatic nationalist movement. It took its name from Mount Tabor—that same sacred mountain where Christ foretold his return and Joachim of Flora received his revelation. The Taborites proclaimed their faith in the imminent destruction of the world—exactly timed for February 1420—the return of Christ, and the inauguration of the Millennium. That was standard millenarianism. But the Taborites made their own particular contribution to the cult by also proclaiming a savage exclusiveness. It was not sufficient to preach simply that those outside the group would not enjoy salvation; faithfully following the practices of the orthodox majority, the Taborites burnt deviants when they could lay hands upon them.

The imperial forces smashed the Taborites, for they were a military and political nuisance. But while they were being hunted down in the Bohemian hills, in Germany a similar movement took shape under a working-class priest, Thomas Munzer, who took Martin Luther at his word and began to preach the gospel of freedom. And even as each of Luther's actions forced him on to others, setting his feet at last upon a path he had not really intended to tread, so Munzer's beliefs and actions grew ever wilder and wilder as he moved away from the autocratic center of the Church's teaching. He appointed twelve apostles, announced that he was in personal communication with the Holy Spirit, and preached that the Age of Saints—the Millennium—was about to dawn. He was proba-

bly mad in the strictly clinical sense, but he was able to infect his
followers with that madness. In the last battle of his saints, he
declared that he would catch the cannon balls in his cloak. His
wretched army was convinced that it was indeed invincible, invulnerable, and so was wiped out with scarcely a struggle.

By their nature, the millennial cults were foredoomed to failure, for their members either became disillusioned and so fell
away, or were destroyed as dangerous rebels and heretics. But
each contributed something to the common stock of belief, a heritage upon which successive leaders drew, consciously or unconsciously. Until the sixteenth century, all continued to place the
earthly paradise at some point, near or distant, in the future. In
1534 a confident young Dutchman, Jan van Leiden, introduced a
startling new variant: The Millennium had commenced in the small
Westphalian town of Munster, for Munster and the New Jerusalem
were one.

The nightmare began for Munster on the evening before Good
Friday 1531. In the ancient church of Saint Mauritz, just outside
the town walls, a near hysterical mob smashed the altar and images
and defiled what could not be smashed. Urging them on from the
pulpit was their priest and pastor, Bernt Rothmann. "It is the
Devil who builds churches. It is the Devil who ordains pilgrim-
ages, makes distinction in food, institutes holy days. If you are interested in externals you are no better than heathens. Destroy! Destroy!" [18] And they did.

Munster was a solid, comfortable town, not large—its population was scarcely fifteen thousand—but remarkably prosperous for
its size. Within its solid walls the German virtues of industry and
inventiveness had built up a large middle class of merchants and
manufacturers that held the balance between the disfranchised proletariat and the arrogant ecclesiastical nobility. For Munster was
the property of a prince-bishop, the capital of an ecclesiastical principality whose sovereign was frequently not even a priest, but simply a powerful man who had been able to lay hands upon church
property. It was a depressingly familiar pattern throughout Ger-

many. In Munster, as in most such bishoprics, the cathedral chapter and higher clergy were filled hereditarily by insolent young men who sustained their high titles and expensive way of life very largely by legally dipping their hands into the coffers of the Church. The increasing wealth of the burghers and the close-knit mutual-aid system of the guilds exerted some restraining effect upon the clergy, but it was an obvious point of conflict should the city's precarious social balance ever break down.

The balance began to teeter in the 1520's when successive years of crop failure harshly demonstrated the fact that even a manufacturing town ultimately depended upon the natural products of the land. Social unrest followed natural disaster, culminating in the appalling Peasants Rebellion of 1525, when Protestant swords baptized the Reformation with the blood of more than 130,000 wretched serfs who had dared to believe that they, too, had natural-born rights. In Munster increasingly heavy ecclesiastical taxation added a final, intolerable burden to a hungry, fearful people. With the appointment of each new bishop, the distant Vatican demanded a fee, the equivalent of one year's revenue of the bishopric. There had been two such new appointments in under a year and upon each occasion the tax collector, backed by a swaggering escort of *landsknechte*, made their rounds.

Through all this, while hunger stalked, the tide of Lutheranism lapped around the walls, and Rome demanded an ever greater share of German gold, Munster had been unusually unfortunate in its bishops. Of the two previous incumbents, the first sold his office to the second, and the second drank himself to death during his inaugural celebrations. The third, Franz von Waldeck, was a deplorable example of a regrettable species, an arrogant, avaricious man perfectly prepared to make common cause with the Protestants if there was a profit to be shown, but on the whole preferring to maintain orthodoxy by the traditional means of fire and ax. He wielded both energetically during the first months of his episcopacy for the bitter discontent in the town made itself concrete by taking on the form of the heretical new teaching. Bishop Franz von Waldeck forcibly tried to lead the straying sheep back into virtuous pastures by hurling a force of mercenaries against the town. But the citizens had by then had all they intended to take from their shepherd. The militia flashed into action, the astonished mercenaries retreated, and an enraged von Waldeck was obliged to negotiate with the citizens: Munster was to continue to recognize his sovereignty—but as a Lutheran, not a Catholic town.

So far events in Munster followed the standard pattern that had prevailed throughout Germany since Luther's rebellion, with social revolt proceeding under the cloak of religious reform. But in every town, every city, that threw off papal authoritarianism, there was a tendency to fly off by a species of centrifugal power toward a corresponding Protestant authoritarianism and then, in turn, to fragment into dissenting sects, each loudly demanding freedom of conscience and as loudly refusing it to all others. The headsman's ax swung as readily in Protestant as in Catholic cities, the stench of burning flesh testified to the new rule of love as frequently as it had testified to the necessity of Catholic orthodoxy in the unregenerate cities. At Munster, the tendency toward bizarre fragmentation accelerated under the eccentric but formidable ex-priest, Bernt Rothmann. The comparatively moderate town council grew alarmed at the antics of their supposed co-religionist. They had drawn the claws of their raging bishop but now, it seemed, the town was to become the prey of fanatics urged on by a man rapidly losing touch with reality. "His teaching is eccentric and variable," an alarmed observer reported. "He is constantly altering it. Today he preaches one thing, tomorrow just the opposite, so that no intelligent people any longer believe in him at all. His followers are a wretched, impecunious lot of people, and I do not know one among them who is not so heavily burdened with debts that it would be difficult to pay up 200 florins." [19] The report sounded that authentic note of contempt and alarm that was heard increasingly in all cities that had thrown off Catholic rule. The prosperous burghers, who had led the revolt for strictly limited purposes, had no desire whatsoever to see the wheel continue to turn, bringing the rabble up from the depths.

But Rothmann was not simply a social refomer; he was a

religious fanatic. Indeed, while he was probably not insane in any clinical sense, it is equally probable that he, like so many of the Munster leaders over the succeeding few months, was unbalanced while still retaining the ability to sway masses. Not content with preaching his own extreme form of Protestantism, he went out of his way to deride and degrade the ancient faith held by a large minority of his fellow citizens. He began with the ritual desecration of the consecrated wafers, crumbling them and throwing them to the ground with the standard jeer that, if they were truly the flesh and blood of God, God would defend his own and strike down the blasphemer. From there Rothmann progressed to what was described as a "comic" Mass which, to any outside, must have seemed deeply sinister, imbued with the darker urges of the German. Animals—including cats, rats, dogs, and bats—were sacrificed, draining out their lives amid the roars of laughter of the congregation. "All Masses all over the world are as much a mockery as this," Rothmann proclaimed.

But, even now, most Protestants in Munster tended to regard Rothmann as an extremist rather than a member of a new sect, the Anabaptists, whose name had been heard with increasing frequency in Germany over the past few years. Kerssenbroek, the Munster scholar who was to write a pejorative history of the movement, described them as

> . . . people who had run through the fortunes of their parents and had earned nothing by their own industry: people who, from their youth upwards, had been given over to idleness, who had lived on credit, till, weary of poverty, it had occurred to them to plunder and rob the clergy and well-to-do burghers: people who disliked the clergy not on account of their religion but because they coveted their wealth and were anxious to introduce community of goods. . . .[20]

It was by no means a wholly inaccurate description of the motives which drove thousands to adopt the bizarre tenets of the new faith, but it grossly oversimplified the meaning of the faith itself. "Anabaptism" was a protean term indiscriminately applied to dozens of dissenting sects which had come into being with the Reformation, and which had little in common save a rejection of infant baptism and a thoroughgoing refusal to allow Protestant authoritarianism to take the place of Catholic authoritarianism. As a result, Anabaptists were burnt, beheaded, and hanged with as much fervor in Protestant as in Catholic towns. In its purest form, Anabaptism was merely another echo of that cry heard continually down the centuries in the Church—the yearning for a return to the primitive origins of Christianity when love was the only law and the little communities dwelt in a state of holy communism and anarchy, uncorrupted by possessions and power. Threaded through the gentle philosophy was an obstinate belief in the imminent return of Christ, who would seat himself on the throne that had purposely been kept vacant for him and administer the world as its sole loved and loving King.

This was the Anabaptism destined, against all probability, to survive even into the twentieth century. But the reverse side of this virtuous communism and gentle millenarianism was a ferocious attack upon all forms of established authority with the idea of placing, in their stead, a species of holy regency—a Rule of Saints, who would guide and guard the sinful world until the Master was ready to take up the reins himself. Initially, Rothmann had preached as venomously against Anabaptism as he had against Catholicism, but as his own mind led him further and further down the bizarre path, so he modified his attacks, and then openly joined the movement. His own conversion was doubtless influenced by the fact that Anabaptism was now established in the heart of the town council. This moderate body was normally composed of successful burghers, solid citizens drawn from that part of the community which was as opposed to extreme Protestantism as to extreme Catholicism. But on February 23, 1534—three years after Rothmann launched his attack on moderation—a wealthy clothier, Bernhard Knipperdolling, became burgomaster. And Knipperdolling was an Anabaptist of the same outrageous species as was Rothmann himself. What appears to be, in retrospect, one of the most extraordinary cases of progressive mass hallucination was now in being.

In January 1534, a few weeks before the council elections placed a fanatic in control of Munster, a handsome, well-built young Dutchman, unobtrusively arrived in the town. Variously known as Jan Bockelson, Jan Bockels, or Jan van Leiden, he was an Anabaptist "apostle," and he judged, accurately, that Munster was ripe for his peculiar talents. By the end of January, he was the acknowledged leader of the Munster Anabaptists with Knipperdolling as his eager lieutenant—testimony enough to the newcomer's talents of persuasion, for he was a penniless young man of unknown background.

The social misfit endowed with oratorical talents and seeking personal salvation via revolution—the twentieth century is perhaps more familiar with Bockelson's type than was the sixteenth. He was about twenty-five years old when he stepped out of obscurity, and his blond good looks, eloquence, and magnetic charm constituted his sole stock in trade. He was illegitimate by birth and had been apprenticed to a tailor; that was the only certain knowledge about him. Later he spun a brilliant, deceptive web about that obscure background, but it seems probable that he went to England and joined a wandering band of players. Certainly he had a highly developed dramatic flair which had something professional about it, and which proved to be of great value in the brief but lurid drama he staged in Munster.

On his return to the Low Countries from England, he came under the influence of Jan Matthys, one of the scores of dissenting preachers who mushroomed in the fertile ground provided by the collapsing Catholic Church. Matthys, baker turned prophet, was an Old Testament figure preaching of blood and fire, the archetypal religious fanatic prepared to drown the whole world in blood—including his own—in pursuit of the chimera of godliness. Following Master Luther's example, he had married a nun, a remarkably beautiful girl known as Divara, who had as powerful an effect upon young Bockelson as did her husband's preaching. It was with a very confused and potent admixture of motives that Bockelson agreed to act as John the Baptist to Matthys and go to Munster, so temptingly ripe for plucking. The Master would follow, just as soon as the disciple had prepared Munster for his coming.

With the arrival of Bockelson in Munster, the character of the revolution changed. Hitherto it had been uncertain, hesitant, fragmented. There were still large numbers of solid Catholic burghers, thoroughly disliking the Protestant trend but with no wish whatsoever to return to the narrow tyranny of Bishop Franz. Forming an uneasy alliance with them were ordinary Protestant burghers, contemptuous of their neighbors' addiction to popery and, under other circumstances, quite prepared to dissuade them by ax or rope, but now far more frightened of their own lunatic fringe. Scattered throughout the community was every form of dissenting belief, ranging from a sober Lutheranism which was simply popery without the pope to a feverish belief that, with the overturn of the Great Whore of Babylon, the Kingdom of the Saints was at hand. Within days of Bockelson's arrival, the dissenting leaven was purged of its moderate elements and drawn into one fiercely effervescent entity.

There is little doubt that Bockelson acted as a catalyst, but in assessing his character and motivation, posterity is again badly hampered by the fact that there is no known method of testing the reality of a mystagogue's visions. The tendency is to apply a double standard: to accept, or at least not question too closely, the experience of respectable mystics such as Catherine of Siena or Joan of Arc, while dismissing as obscene or ludicrous fabrications the visions of a Joanna Southcott, an Aleister Crowley or a Jan Bockelson. Judging by the influence Bockelson wielded, and the fortitude with which he met his appalling death, the almost inescapable conjecture is that he personally believed in the objective reality of his visions. The very fact that at his trial he admitted fabricating some of his visions—and bitterly regretted doing so—argues forcefully that he believed in the rest. Yet, like a good actor, even while he was carried away on the flood of his own eloquence, he was able to note its effect upon his audience and modify his style to obtain the most effective reaction.

Rothmann and Bockelson both had, as it were, professional reasons to urge on the populace to ever greater flights of fancy. But confronted by the enigmatic figure of Bernhard Knipperdolling, the observer is forced to abandon the ordinary tools of criticism and grope blindly for an answer. Knipperdolling belonged to a type which was to become increasingly common—the plain, blunt man who amassed a large fortune by plain, blunt methods and then fell easy victim to a smooth-talking metaphysician. Overwhelmingly, the impression left by Burgomaster Knipperdolling is of a man who desperately wants to believe. Rothmann could talk himself into belief, Bockelson seemed capable of sliding into a paranormal condition, but Knipperdolling seemed able to obtain the blessed state only by closing his eyes firmly to reality and throwing himself with violence into the task of convincing others.

Throughout January Bockelson and Knipperdolling were in the streets, rushing up and down, preaching, admonishing. Women in particular flocked by the hundreds to the handsome young Dutchman's open-air meetings, stolid German housewives screaming in ecstasy, throwing themselves upon the ground in convulsions, running through the streets half dressed and crying his name. "People jumped into the air, as if they wished to fly away into space. Others rolled about in the mud. Many foamed at the mouth." Mass hallucination became commonplace. "Some cried out that they beheld the Eternal Father, surrounded by many thousands of angels, standing, rod in hand, to punish the godless. Others adored a brazen weathercock upon which the sun was shining, and fancied that God the Father was sitting on the house, while others ran like wild up and down the streets, shrieking that at any moment Christ might come again." [21] Knipperdolling excelled himself as a grotesque in these early days, wallowing in the mud like a hog, foaming at the mouth, shrieking that he must die and rise again, that he would give sight to the blind. Bockelson seems to have been more dignified, but immensely effective.

Then, temporarily, Bockelson was eclipsed by the arrival of his master, the Prophet Jan Matthys himself. A grim, hate-filled figure, mad for blood, Matthys achieves a certain dignity because of his awful sincerity. In him, religion had upset its delicate balance and become madness. In the depths of his clouded mind there flickered something that had once been a noble concept, the belief that man's highest happiness and duty was to enter into communication with his God. Nothing was left of that concept now except the Procrustean passion to force the infinite channels of communication into one, that favored by Jan Matthys. He swept into the town like a sulphurous cloud, bringing a smell of hell itself, reviewed what his lieutenants had done, pronounced it good but not drastic enough, and began to evolve the nightmare scenario.

Munster was to be the New Jerusalem, the same that John had seen descending from the sky above Patmos—the titanic cube of precious stones and metals which would provide the only sure asylum during the imminent destruction of things. Therefore let all godly brethren come to Munster, Matthys proclaimed, and a summons went out to the world. The converted, the saved, the godly, wrote ecstatically to their friends outside the town, describing the ideal conditions that prevailed—anticipating a little, perhaps, but not sinfully, for what the prophet had foretold could be said to be virtually in existence. "Come, for here you will have enough to satisfy all your needs. The poorest of the poor who are here among us, and who were formerly despised as beggars, now go dressed like the highest and the noblest of the land. And there are many poor people who, by the grace of God, have become as rich as the burgomaster and the wealthiest inhabitants of the town." [22]

"And so they came, the Dutch and the Frieslanders and the good for nothing characters from all parts of the world who were not wanted anywhere else, flocked to Munster and overflowed the town." [23] So wrote Heinrich Gresbeck, cabinetmaker and renegade Anabaptist himself.

Gresbeck was accurate in his assessment of the swarms of newcomers. They were, for the most part, the defeated: hungry peasant farmers tired of trying to earn a living from the soil;

members of the new urban proletariat, possessing neither the rights of a guildman nor the tools of a farmer; sturdy beggars, criminals, fanatics, all come with ambition and hope into the plump and prosperous town. And as more and more of them arrived, so more and more of the sober citizens, Catholics and Protestants alike, packed up their goods and left. Once they had had the option to call in the bishop and at least restore the status quo, for Franz von Waldeck was prowling hungrily outside, eager to sweep the plump town into his net again. But he had been unable to do so without the aid of the citizens, and the sober leaders, believing the upheaval to be merely transient, had left it too late. Almost until the end they hoped that the new town ordinance decreeing freedom of conscience for all meant what it said. But Matthys the Prophet was faithfully following that drearily inevitable evolution whereby the oppressed religious minority, once it achieved power, promptly became the oppressing majority. It was not sufficient for Matthys that the Anabaptist power should now be supreme in Munster; every citizen of the town had to belong, overtly and specifically, to the new faith, abjuring their old, "godless" ways. Matthys was, with difficulty, dissuaded from ordering the liquidation of all the godless—those who harbored the faintest doubt that Jan Matthys, baker, might not perhaps be the authentic Voice of the Lord. Instead, all Catholics and Lutherans within the town were given until February 27 either to be rebaptized within the Anabaptist faith or to leave the town. Thereafter all nonconformers would be executed.

While the wretched moderates debated whether they should sacrifice home and living for a theological tenet, or risk living in a community apparently headed for insanity, more and more of the hungry and landless flocked into the town, attracted by such propaganda as Bockelson's letter to his Anabaptist fellow countrymen: "Redemption is at hand. Let all get ready to come to the New Jerusalem, the city of the Saints, for God is about to punish the world. Let no man fail to join the march, lest he tempt God. Flee from Babylon, that each may keep his soul. Let each man remember Lot's wife . . . let none regard an unbelieving husband or wife, nor take them with him, nor children that are unbelieving or disobedient. . . ." The believer was not to worry about material things: "Goods there are in plenty for the Saints: therefore bring nothing save money, clothes and provender for the journey. He who hath a knife, a halberd or a handgun, let him bring them and if he lack them, let him buy them. . . ." [24] The thoughtful might perhaps have paused awhile to ponder that injunction to bring arms, but the promise that they would be made free of the goods of a wealthy German town was a heady attraction for poor Dutchmen, and they, too, came in the hundreds.

In Munster, Bockelson, Rothmann, Matthys, and Knipperdolling worked hour by hour in the marketplace, baptizing those citizens who had elected to remain rather than trust themselves to the charity of the open countryside. But the period of choice ended on February 27. It was a bitterly cold day of sleet and snow, Gresbeck remembered: "A dog should not have been turned out on a day like this." Nevertheless, the surviving Catholics and Lutherans—men, women, and children, aged and infirm as well as the healthy—were dragged out of their homes and, urged by the blows and jeers of the godly, made their way out of the town. Bockelson held an emotional prayer meeting in the marketplace, where he fell into a trance. He may have been irritated by the comparatively minor role he had been forced to play and was seeking again the heady delight of crowd manipulation; equally, he may have been genuinely hallucinated. The Father appeared to him, commanding that "the holy city of the saints must be purged of the sons of Esau. All, all must go, or die." The mob broke up and fell upon the unbaptized. None were killed, but the violence manifested was so extreme, so obviously unbalanced, as to confirm the waverers that almost any situation would be better than continued residence in Munster. By nightfall of that cold, dark day the city was inhabited entirely by the Saints; including immigrants and those who had accepted forcible baptism, the population of the New Jerusalem was about eleven thousand.

Meanwhile, Bishop Franz had been frantically trying to convince his fellow sovereigns, both lay and ecclesiastical, that it was to their mutual good that the Anabaptist rabble be suppressed in

Munster and the city returned to the fatherly care of its bishop. The response he received was cold. The landgrave of Hess, the archbishop of Cologne, and the burghers of Cleves were sufficiently impressed to supply him with token contingents of troops with which he mounted a siege. But the mercenaries were of inferior quality, badly paid, badly led, and badly armed; they contrived to spend their nights in carousal and their days in yawning indolence, rallying themselves only when their personal safety might be threatened. Their presence, in fact, was far more valuable to the besieged Anabaptist leaders than to the bishop, for they provided concrete, unequivocal evidence that the hosts of Satan were in arms against the Saints. Any lingering doubts on that score were promptly extinguished by the bishop himself on February 28, the day after the wretched Catholics and Lutherans had been expelled from the town. The bishop had not raised a finger to help them, but he did take vengeance on their behalf, bloodily hunting down every Anabaptist he could find outside Munster. The most lukewarm Saint, no matter how dull his imagination, knew exactly what was now in store for him should the city fall.

Matthys and his lieutenants were therefore able to exact the most extreme obedience from the citizens. Immediately, a rigorous form of communal ownership was enforced. The gathering together of all food, clothing, heating materials, and money was in part the natural and sensible action of a garrison commander preparing for a long siege. But the military effect was only a byproduct of a passionate religious belief that there should be—could be—no private property in the New Jerusalem. Similarly, there could be no sin in the city that was awaiting the coming of Christ. Sin was crime, and crime was now punishable by death, so that within hours of the beginning of the siege, the Saints of Munster could be beheaded for drunkenness, for the possession of gold, silver, or food, or for querying the sacred nature of their leaders. The first victim fell at the beginning of March, a citizen who criticized the regime and was publicly executed by Jan Matthys. The situation developed from there onward with grim logic, the headsman's ax or Matthys's personal dagger ready to ensure joyful acceptance of the pious measures.

Matthys had little time to enjoy his rule of the holy city: He was killed at Easter, testament to his sincerity if not his good sense. At a public banquet, he suddenly fell silent, then arose and in a great voice announced that the Lord had made a revelation to him. He was the new Gideon and, like Gideon, was to hurl himself upon the ungodly with only a token force. Men jostled each other for the honor; he chose about a dozen and announced that the following day they would make a sortie. The mad little group did so. They got a few yards beyond the gate, the landsknechts outside being for a few moments wholly astounded. But then they rallied and slaughtered the fanatics, carefully carving Matthys's body into four quarters and nailing them to the gate. Jan Bockelson (who probably had a hand in the interpretation of his master's last and lethal vision) was now sole and undisputed prophet and lord of Munster.

Ever since Bishop Franz had mounted his siege, Munster became, and remained, locked off from the world so that the evidence for the fantastic rule of Jan Bockelson comes from suspect sources. The primary contemporary account is that of the cabinetmaker Heinrich Gresbeck, who was actually living in Munster throughout the vital period after accepting baptism. But Gresbeck was not only a remarkably bad writer, baldly recording superficialities with little apparent awareness of the underlying significance, but also the man who eventually betrayed the town to the besiegers. His otherwise invaluable eyewitness account therefore manages to be at once shallow and biased. A far more competent recorder was Hermann von Kerssenbroek, whose lengthy account has both structure and depth. But von Kerssenbroek was only a schoolboy in the town at the time of the crisis, and his account was not written until nearly forty years later. In his case, faulty memory and a prudent loyalty to Catholicism would inevitably result in distortion. Elsewhere, chroniclers picked up garbled versions of events in Munster and made what they could of them—patchwork accounts that were later padded out by the letters and stories of the victorious besiegers. The observer views the events in Munster uncertainly, as through a kind of distorting glass which grotesquely magnifies some objects and eliminates others while casting a lurid, wavering light over the whole. But even when all due allowances are made for the bias of hostile reporting, and the lack of a corrective supplied by even an objective chronicler, there is little doubt but that Bockelson played out on the Munster stage the classic fantasies of paranoia. Yet there is equally little doubt that he was in conscious control, both of himself and his eleven thousand victims or colleagues, until the end.

He began his reign mildly enough, modestly announcing that the Almighty had, in fact, vouchsafed him a revelation regarding Matthys's end. The Prophet had been punished for his presumption, he announced. There was another, and much greater man, who was to be revealed as the true leader of the Saints. Bernhard Knipperdolling hastened forward to confirm this, adding the interesting information that it would be the people themselves who would recognize and spontaneously acclaim that new leader.

What follows next is reported largely on the testimony of Heinrich Gresbeck, whose bald, laconic style makes it difficult to determine what exactly happened. It appears that Bockelson and Knipperdolling between them sparked off yet another wave of mass hallucination. The two men ran naked through the streets of the town, proclaiming that the hour of judgment was at hand, that the avenging sword of the Lord was even now poised above the town. The crowds reacted immediately and violently. "Father, Father give us thy love, give us thy love," was the general cry as they rushed through the streets, the men brandishing swords, the women screaming. In the absence of unbelievers to massacre, the hysteria turned into a comparatively harmless dancing mania which continued until most inhabitants were involved. At the height of the orgy, Bockelson collapsed and remained in a coma for two days. When he came to, he proclaimed that the Almighty had granted him a revelation regarding the government of the town. The people were no longer citizens of Munster, to be ruled by a sinfully elected town council, but Israelites to be ruled by twelve Elders, presided over by Jan Bockelson. All sinful human laws were abrogated in favor of the law of God as inscribed in His book. Hereafter "everything prescribed or forbidden by Holy Writ is to be observed, on pain of death." Knipperdolling was appointed the sword of the Lord—possibly as compensation for his undeniable downgrading in favor of his young master—and given divine authority to execute offenders at a nod from the prophet. Rothmann became the propagandist, turning his feverish energy to the production of innumerable broadsheets and pamphlets which, hastily printed, were thrown out by the thousand among the besiegers. Their warning that the mercenaries were acting against their own brethren, and their invitation to join the hosts of the godly behind the secure walls of Sion had a considerable effect. Some two thousand ill-paid mercenaries, contrasting their uncomfortable conditions with that of the snug, well-found town, actually abandoned their paymaster and went over to the Anabaptists. They were welcomed and promptly inducted into the army of the Saints where they formed a welcome stiffening with their professional expertise. As soldiers, they did not amount to much, but still they were professionals, armed with professional weapons.

Jan Bockelson possessed an administrative flair that amounted to near genius. He had imbued the whole of Munster with his bizarre ideals—but that was not enough for a city that was an island in a very hostile sea. The first necessity was to provide a military defense and this he did with extraordinary success, bending to his one purpose a handful of mediocre renegade mercenaries and some thousands of courageous, devoted, but quite unskilled men and women. In May, shortly after the establishment of the Elders, he organized a series of vigorous sorties which were totally successful. Hundreds of the enemy were killed, and the rest so thoroughly startled and demoralized that the bishop was unable to rally them for a counterattack. It was not until May 22 that a general attack was made on the city. It was beaten off bloodily. Civilian defenders well supplied with handguns and ammunition and firing from the top of a well-built wall were at least the equal of professionals firing from ground level and with limited ammunition. The raging officers prodded the landsknechts to scale the walls, but the women met the attempt with boiling water and oil, adding their own special contribution to the art of siege warfare: wreaths made of flammable material, soaked in pitch and set alight when they were dropped on the shoulders of the men trying to clamber up.

The Saints were jubilant. Some wanted to follow up the advantage and pursue the demoralized enemy, and conceivably, if the bolder spirits had had their way, the siege would have been broken permanently. But the victory held its own problems for the leaders; once the discipline of fear was removed, there was no certainty that the holy city would continue with such remarkable unanimity toward the goal. Again the Saints were turned in on themselves to learn of the most recent revelation granted to their prophet. It was as well that they had had the euphoria of May to raise their hearts, for Bockelson's decrees now became ever more incredible. In August he called the Elders together and announced that God wanted polygamy to be established in His holy city.

There is no doubt whatsoever that, in this matter, personal desire gave birth to divine revelation. Bockelson was probably already a bigamist; there was rumor of a wife in Leiden, and he had recently married Knipperdolling's daughter. But he had also long had eyes upon the widow of the late prophet—Divara, the beautiful ex-nun. Now, obediently, the preachers began a series of marathon sermons, all designed to prove that, by taking a multiplicity of wives, the Saints—the modern Israelites—were explicitly linking themselves to the patriarchs of the Old Testament. The measure was by no means unpopular among a large number of the Saints. Early in the uprising, while the Catholics still held nominal control of the town, Bockelson and Knipperdolling had hurried from convent to convent, preaching the virtues and joys of the secular life to the nuns. "They were by no means unwilling to renounce their virginity and propagate the race," Kerssenbroek noted drily but, as the female population of Munster seems to have considerably exceeded the male, they were denied the more conventional role of wedded bliss until the Prophet's timely revelation. The womanless landsknechts, too, were glad to identify themselves with Abraham and the rest of the patriarchs, and by the end of August all those women who desired to have a mate, even at the price of sharing him with other women, were duly accommodated.

But it was not enough for some women gladly to accept polygamy. "Everything prescribed or forbidden by Holy Writ is to be observed, on pain of death," the sacred ordinance ran, and those women who preferred to maintain their virginity or state of widowhood were implicitly criticizing both their more generous sisters and Holy Writ itself. The decree went out: *all* women were to attach themselves to a harem. The decree was invitation to mass rape, and mass rape followed; even children who had yet to achieve puberty were forced into grotesque "marriages" with grave mental and physical consequences.

Shortly after the decree was announced and carried out, a band of some two hundred citizens rose in sudden revolt. They were, for the most part, close relatives of women who had been raped—the brothers of widows, the fathers of young girls—men who, even in a population far gone in emotional excess, preserved some element of sanity. They acted swiftly and efficiently, helped by the effect of total surprise; had they been endowed with the ability to murder in cold blood, they could probably have restored Munster to normality. Bockelson, Rothmann, Knipperdolling, and most of the leaders were surprised in their beds, dragged out, and thrust into the cellars beneath the town hall. The counterrevolutionaries intended then to open the town gates to the bishop, but before they could do so they were surrounded by hundreds of the enraged Saints, led by an ex-burgomaster, Herman Tilbreck. After a ferocious hand-to-hand struggle, the insurgents were overcome and the prisoners released. The surviving rebels were then beheaded, Knipperdolling personally wielding the sword of the Lord and so wiping out the blasphemy of the rebellion in blood.

A suppressed counterrevolution is perhaps the revolutionary leader's most valuable asset: Not only can the last suspect elements be legitimately removed, but the faithful are further encouraged in their belief in the leader's mission. Bockelson was further helped by the fact that, outside Munster, von Waldeck heard of the rising and promptly launched an attack to take advantage of the disturbed conditions. The defenders reacted vigorously, Bockelson himself displayed great courage and skill in directing the defence, and by the time that comparative calm returned to the town, the ex-tailor had the unquestioned status of hero.

It was at this stage that Bockelson departed finally from reality, victim of the common delusion that besets the holder of absolute power. He was above and outside the normal run of humanity, and he wanted concrete recognition of that fact. But though he was, by now, an undoubted megalomaniac, he also remained a very shrewd demagogue well aware that an announcement of his new and exalted nature would come better from another party. A prophet of his status needed a prophet of his own. There was one to hand.

Among the many minor prophets who had arisen during the past few months was a goldsmith, Johann Dusentschur. Until now there had been little to distinguish him from all the others, for his stock in trade was the same wild babbling, accompanied by convulsions, rolling eyes, and foaming mouth. However, he possessed the right which all prophets claimed and which the faithful were glad to grant, and that was the right of drawing the Saints together and, with wild and whirling words, further stimulating their faith. In mid-September the faithful were summoned to the marketplace to hear the prophet. They obeyed gladly, as ever, being in ever increasing need of the drug which kept them at their extended peak of ecstasy. Bockelson, Knipperdolling, Rothmann, Tilbreck—all the leaders were there. But the star of the show was the relatively unknown goldsmith. His revelation was indeed astonishing, well earning him his moment of glory. The Almighty had appeared to him, the wholly unworthy goldsmith of Munster, and revealed that Jan van Leiden, otherwise known as Jan Bockelson or Bockels or Bockelszoon, was to take up the scepter of David, seat himself in the long vacant throne of the New Jerusalem, and be forthwith hailed as king of the entire world.

At his trial Bockelson was to admit that the whole scene was of his devising, that Dusentschur had been well rehearsed. But the atmosphere in Munster was now so febrile that the state of self-delusion was almost normal, and Dusentschur gives every impression that he believed, personally, in the revelation implanted in his mind by Bockelson. The crowd was somewhat less impressed, for the immigrant ex-tailor from Leiden seemed to have gone very far, very fast since his arrival in Munster barely nine months before. But Knipperdolling and the other leaders, either far gone in fantasy or acting from a healthy self-interest, loudly proclaimed the new king. Gracefully Bockelson denied his worthiness, observed that the Almightly had, in fact, already revealed the great truth to him, but modesty had forbidden him to publish it, and now reluctantly he took up the burden of royalty.

King Jan, ex-tailor, was in the line of descent of the brilliant Hohenstaufen emperor: He was more—far more—than an ordinary king. He was the Messiah, the person appointed by divine authority to preside over the last days. Such he announced and as such he was accepted. Over the following months, as the siege grew ever more rigorous and famine and death became constant companions, his very arrogance became for his "subjects" a vicarious guerdon for their suffering and a guarantee that they would at last triumph. As he assumed ever richer garments and ever more sumptuous ceremonials, while his ragged, hungry followers looked on with their souls in their eyes, he explained that it was fitting for him to take on such luxury, for he was dead to the world and could not be contaminated by it. But such specious sophistry was barely necessary; a fusion was established by the ex-tailor and his following that many a legitimate monarch might envy.

He began his reign by moving into one of the great aristocratic mansions in the town that had been standing empty, signs of sinful wealth that they had been. His rapidly growing harem of young women, none of them over the age of twenty, was established in the mansion with him and decked out in superb costumes. Dusentschur, the goldsmith, went back to his bench to make for the king of the world a splendid new regalia, ransacking the town of its gold and silver and jewels to make crown and scepter, jeweled sword, rings and golden chains of office. More gold was needed for the newly struck coinage which bore the legend, "One Master, One Faith, One Baptism" together with a bust of the "king." The German genius for portraiture has left posterity at least one authentic portrait of Jan van Leiden as king of Munster—the crayon drawing by Heinrich Aldegrever. The face that Aldegrever immortalized indubitably belongs to a man who could impose his will upon others but who, in his turn, is at the mercy of his imagination. A handsome face, simultaneously strong and sensitive, yet wholly ruthless. The observer needs to be told that it is the face of an illegitimate ex-tailor; without that information it might be concluded that the subject of the portrait was natural-born to the purple and brought up in the expectation of command. The crimes that could be laid at the door of Jan van Leiden were many and bizarre, but it cannot be denied him that he was one of nature's originals, a born leader of men who made the most of a fleeting opportunity.

For the third time Munster's constitution was turned upside down. The Elders, with their implication of equality, went the way of the sinful town council. There was now the priest-king and, far, far below him, the administrators. The customs of the people, the very street names of the town, were changed to signify the new life and the new rule. Sunday ceased to exist; all days were now the Lord's Day. The innumerable feastdays followed Sunday into oblivion, for life was now all happiness. The Sacred City lacked Christ alone; apart from that, it was ready down to the last detail for its thousand-year voyage. Rothmann obediently produced more scholarly arguments, this time to prove that the time of the End was beginning, that the days of tribulation were over. Those whom John on Patmos had seen sealed with the sign of the Lamb were safely gathered now in the little Westphalian town, and soon the great slaughter would begin among the hosts of Satan outside. "I saw an angel standing in the sun and he cried aloud to all the birds that fly in mid-heaven 'Come, gather for God's great feast to eat the carcasses of kings and officers and warriors, of horses and their riders, of free and slave, great and small.' " The enormous words, minted in the Aegean, boomed and thundered again in the cloudy German skies as the summer of 1534 gave place to autumn. Some of the euphoria was beginning to ebb and fade now as food supplies began to fall, disease broke out, and sheer ennui and claustrophobia slackened the will to resist. The king restored the tautness by a dramatic admixture of blood and gold, of terror and entertainment presented with a rich ceremonial.

Three times a week a throne was set up in the marketplace, and to it came, in splendid procession, the king, his generals and ministers, his counselors, orators, and executioner. In solemn state, the ex-tailor then sat in judgment upon his subjects. Sometimes the trials were detailed, the judgments considered, the inevitable execution performed by the correct official. As often, however, the whole process was performed at speed and with a macabre levity. Death being the penalty for every infringement of the laws, no time needed to be wasted on consideration of sentence, no able-bodied man had to be withdrawn from the garrison to act as jailer. Among those whom Gresbeck claimed to have seen pay the penalty in the marketplace were a number of landsknechts who had threatened an innkeeper during a drunken brawl and a woman who was convicted of adultery (monandry was as compulsory for women as polygamy was for men). One of the king's own "wives" was beheaded here. She seems to have repented of being involved in the whole bizarre affair, laid her gorgeous robes at her "husband's" feet, and begged his royal permission to leave the town. Her plea amounted to blasphemy. Bockelson cut off her head with his own hands and then, with his court, danced round the headless trunk singing "Glory to God in the Highest."

But even these bloody displays were in the nature of an entertainment, performed in the certain knowledge that the overwhelming bulk of the population was behind their leader. And though the marketplace was very frequently stained with human blood, just as frequently it echoed to the sound of human laughter and song. It was now that Bockelson displayed that flair for dramatic entertainment that he had perhaps first exercised as a strolling player in England. His own gorgeous processions were themselves a species of

theatrical display, but he organized, too, endless morality plays—
the confounding of Dives and the exaltation of Lazarus was a great
favorite, promising as it did the eventual exaltation of the Saints
and the confounding of the sinners. The plays were usually followed by energetic dancing which went on far into the night, and
in the earlier period when food was plentiful, there would usually
be an enormous banquet for the entire town, apart from the garrison on watch, at which King Jan benignly presided.

It was with a deep instinctive knowledge of crowd psychology
that Bockelson organized these entertainments, in all of which he
took a vigorous part. Daily the realities of the siege were coming
home to the defenders, but a lively dance or an uproarious morality
play not only took their minds off their troubles but gave assur-
ance. Matters could not be in so dire a state as they seemed if the
organizer of the defense could take time off for frivolities. It was
this ability to identify himself with the commonalty, to give them
hope in what even he was beginning to realize was a hopeless future, that enabled him not merely to survive but to dominate.

There was only one more rebellion against his total authority,
and this took so strange a form as seemingly to disconcert him.
Knipperdolling apparently finally went mad, but the madness took
a dangerous form for the man who had displaced him in the civic
hierarchy. Knipperdolling took to capering before Bockelson as the
king made his ceremonial way to the throne, crying out, "Once I
used to dance before my sweetheart, but now the Father commands me to dance before the king." He then jumped upon the
backs of the crowd as they faced the king—such at least is the only
interpretation that can be given to the extraordinary statement that
"he crept with his hands and feet upon the heads of the multitude" [25]—and peering into their faces, breathed into their mouths
with the remark: "The Father sanctifies thee: receive the Holy
Spirit." Both Bockelson and the people endured the undignified,
unpleasant incident, presumably because Knipperdolling was one
of the founding fathers of the New Jerusalem. But he then went
too far. Throughout, he had apparently been brooding over the
fact that he, Bernhard Knipperdolling, the wealthy merchant who

had taken the penniless Jan van Leiden under his protection, was now subordinate to that same young man, glorified though he was. On a morning set aside for the king's levee in the marketplace, Knipperdolling appeared some time before the procession. When Bockelson arrived, it was to find his father-in-law and ex-mentor seated in the throne while the populace looked on open-mouthed. The Father had appeared to him, Knipperdolling announced: There were to be two kings in Munster, one in the flesh and one in the spirit. He, Bernhard Knipperdolling, was the divinely appointed king-in-the-spirit. Such blasphemy coming from any other mouth would have resulted in summary execution. But Knipperdolling was still a power in the town, and after an embarrassed silence, Bockelson merely ordered that the lunatic be taken to prison. Three days confinement were sufficient to bring Knipperdolling back to an orthodox viewpoint.

Meanwhile the siege was growing ever more rigorous. Von Waldeck had at last been able to convince his fellow sovereigns, both ecclesiastical and secular, that it was to the benefit of all that this oddly tenacious ulcer should be cauterized, and with an additional supply of troops, he was at last able to maintain an efficient blockade. But Munster was far more than simply a rebellious city; it was an idea, a most potent idea. Outside Munster, in Germany itself and particularly in the Low Countries, were thousands of people who passionately believed in the reality of the New Jerusalem, a belief made all the stronger because the city was sealed off and faith could not be tested by experience. Rothmann's propaganda continued to get through the lines. Bockelson was even able to send out "apostles," devoted men who eventually rendered up their lives in torment in pursuit of their ideals, for all were captured. One man, Heinrich Grasse, bought his life by turning traitor—and incidentally providing posterity with a priceless indication of the sincerity (or credulity) of the Saints. Still wearing the chains that had shackled him in von Waldeck's dungeon, he appeared at one of the town gates, crying that he had been liberated, like Saint Peter, by the angels. He was brought in triumphantly, spent a few days assessing the military disposition of the defenders, and returned to von Waldeck leaving behind a jeering letter: "All your prophets are exactly like myself." Despite the now heavy odds, a force of some one thousand Anabaptists assembled near Gronigen and began to march to the relief of the sacred city. They were cut down long before they came in sight of the walls.

Now famine struck. Later Bockelson's enemies were to charge him with living not merely well but in luxury while his deluded "subjects" died in agony of hunger. Vigorously he denied the charge, and there is no reason why he should be disbelieved, for he admitted, with every indication of remorse, the truth of other accusations. The probability is that the luxurious style he adoped, which was so very effective in maintaining morale, was based on costume and ceremonial. The splendid velvets and brocades he wore, the gold chains and ornaments clinking at his neck and waist, the flashing jewels, were all so much dross in a besieged and starving city.

By the end of May 1535, some ten months after the beginning of the siege, the city was scraped clean of all normal food. Cows, horses, dogs, and cats had all long since been eaten; the starving population began to chew leather, hunt down rats and bats, eat the weeds and grass that sprang up between the stones. One scientifically minded landsknecht in the besieging force examined the contents of the stomach of a disemboweled defender and reported that the man had eaten only grass in the previous eight hours. A deputation waited upon Bockelson, begging that women, children, and old people should be allowed to leave the town. He agreed, unwontedly resigned and melancholy, and the refugees hastened to leave before he changed his mind. They went merely from probable to certain death. The bishop refused to let them into his lines; a few of the more personable women became the prey of the landsknechts, and the majority of the refugees died—some eating earth—in the no man's land between town wall and camp.

Yet, astonishingly, the will to resist remained as strong as ever in the town. Something more than despair, more than the knowledge that surrender meant death, bound together the starving people. In their now semidelirious state, they were able to regard their agony as the last of the earthly tribulations they would be called upon to endure, those necessary "messianic woes" which had so long before been predicted in the Apocalypse. Bockelson rallied after that brief, uncharacteristic melancholia. He maintained his regular processions and state audiences; the populace were still entertained by moralities and dances and the occasional execution. Their king promised a major sortie backed by secret weapons that the Lord would provide, and they believed him and fought on, singing their hymns though now so feebly that they could scarcely be heard by those outside.

The end was predictable, but treachery precipitated it. In June, one of the landsknechts who had come over to the Anabaptists—a certain Hans von Straten—decided to make his peace with his old employer and escaped with the cabinetmaker and later chronicler, Heinrich Gresbeck. On the night of June 24, Gresbeck led a detachment on a weakly guarded gatehouse. The small garrison, sunk in the torpor of starvation, was easily slaughtered, and the gates were opened without hindrance. The main body of the besiegers stormed in, and for the following four days Munster was given over to an orgy of cruelty, the mercenaries' normal ferocity urged on by the enraged bishop. Most of the town's leaders were killed in that first rush, but only after they had fought with astonishing courage, sometimes outnumbered a dozen to one. Knipperdolling alone fell below the general standard, running into hiding when it became obvious that the town was lost and was betrayed by the woman in whose house he sought refuge. Bockelson surrendered on the promise that his followers would be spared—a promise that was promptly broken. The bald, pedestrian account of his trial manages to preserve a sudden vivid vignette of his meeting with Bishop Franz von Waldeck. "Are you a king?" von Waldeck demanded, presumably not conscious of paraphrasing Pontius Pilate on a similar occasion. "Are you a bishop?" was the contemptuous reply. Stung, von Waldeck retorted that he was legally bishop of Munster, duly elected by chapter. "And I am king by grace of God," Bockelson replied unanswerably.

He and Knipperdolling and the "chancellor," Bernhard

Krechting escaped, for a time, the summary justice of the victorious force. A special fate was planned for the king of the New Jerusalem, the regent of the Messiah: He was placed in a cage and for six months was dragged around the province. Yet naked, filthy, stinking though he was, covered with sores and wounds, still he retained his sanity and—remarkably—his dignity. At the end of the six months, he, Knipperdolling, and Krechting were put on "trial." The prosecutors seem to have been uneasily affected by the prevailing messianic atmosphere, for they were not so much intent on proving that Bockelson was a blasphemer and charlatan and imposter, as a witch, someone who had defied a professional army and bedazzled a city and acted as lure to all of Germany and the Netherlands only through the power of Satan. All three men were condemned to be torn by red-hot pincers and then disemboweled.

The sentence was carried out on January 23, with Bockelson the first to suffer. Some observers reported that he kept silent during the atrocious pain while the executioner took three bites with his tongs, but then howled continuously. Others, no more friendly toward the discredited man, recorded that he kept silent throughout the hour that he survived on the scaffold. These observers had no reason to tell such a tale apart from the fact that it happened, and the likelihood is that theirs was an independent testimony to his astonishing self-control. Knipperdolling and Krechting were then treated in a similar manner, and at the end the three terribly mutilated corpses were placed in three specially constructed cages and hauled to the steeple of the Lamberti church. Even after the wretched remains were at last disposed of, the city of Munster carefully preserved the cages and tongs, as though they might be prophylactic guarantees that, should the Kingdom of God ever be established on earth, it would not be in Westphalia.

CHAPTER IV

●

THE FIFTH
MONARCHY

When, on ·the afternoon of January 30, 1649, the head of King Charles I fell into the straw on the scaffold in front of his Banqueting Hall in Whitehall, it marked precisely a moment of profound change. Here was no symbolism, no elegant allegory, but bloodstained fact. To those crowded in the handsome street curving between Charing Cross and Westminster, to those who could only hear as well as those who could both hear and see, the crunch of the ax as it met the oaken block stated emphatically that the monarchy established six centuries earlier had come to an abrupt and most final halt. Alike, those who cursed Charles Stuart for the arrogant treacheries which had plunged the land into civil war and those who mourned him as a true martyr to a divine ideal believed that a vacuum of power had been created. And that vacuum, if not promptly filled by the Saints of God, would be filled by the emissaries of Satan, above all by Antichrist.

The common people of England seemed to have become somewhat indifferent to the once horrific monster and needed to be whipped up into a proper state of fear and indignation. "Next unto our Lord and Saviour Jesus Christ, there is nothing so necessary as the true and solid knowledge of Antichrist," the schoolmaster Thomas Beard thundered in 1625. One of his pupils was young Oliver Cromwell, so his warning eventually found very fruitful soil, indeed. Over the following decades successive scholars, including such as the caliber of Milton and Newton, did their best to relay the warning. But the coin had become somewhat devalued since the Reformation. At first there had been no doubt whatsoever regarding the new identity of the ancient enemy: It was the pope in Rome "in his Dragonical and Priestly Power," and all those who followed him in the use of the gorgeous rites of Rome. But as Christendom fragmented, so too did Antichrist, until he could be identified with virtually any cause that aroused the writer's ire and disapproval. In England, particularly, even the Reformed Church was labeled Antichrist by those who disapproved of its clinging to its hierarchical structure, expressing their disapproval in the pungent language of the day so that bishops were the tail, parsons the excrement, of Antichrist. Mathematicians of every degree of sobriety seized upon the enduring conundrum of the Beast—666—to belabor a particular enemy. One such victim was William Laud. A judicious juggling of the letters of his name—WILLM LVD—satisfactorily transformed King Charles's archbishop into the ravening beast from the sea.

But while the identification of Antichrist became more and more the cerebral pastime of scholars, or was used as the common change of political abuse, belief in the reality and imminence of the Millennium was charged with a most passionate sincerity. As king and Parliament continued on their collision course and it became evident that the nation was about to be plunged into a chaos from which anything might emerge, a new race of prophets took the stage to call their warnings and exhortations. Central to their preaching was the confident, unchanged belief in the Millennium; what was new were the complex systems for calculating exactly when it would start and what it would be like. The century that produced Archbishop Ussher, Isaac Newton, and the Royal Society had no doubt whatsoever as to its ability to follow up the mathematical clues left by the Almighty in his Book.

It was in 1642, the year King Charles raised his standard at Nottingham and the nation began to slide toward the precipice, that there appeared Henry Archer's little book, *The Personall Reign of Christ Upon Earth*. Archer had been a preacher, and the purpose of his book was to encourage the fainthearted by proving that Jesus Christ "shall visibly possess a Monarchical State and Kingdom in this World," and by pinpointing when this blessed State would commence and its duration. His method was one which proved very popular: combining the books of Daniel and John and filling up any gaps with judicious selections from the other biblical prophets. Basic to the calculations were the two visions of Daniel in which he saw first an idol composed of four contrasting materials and then a fearsome monster with ten horns upon his head. Daniel was quite right in interpreting the vision of the idol as signifying four successive kingdoms, Archer declared, but he identified the last kingdom wrongly. It was not the Greek but the Roman kingdom which immediately preceded the Fifth Monarchy—the Kingdom of God on earth. And in this year of grace 1642, they were witnessing the last convulsions of the fourth kingdom. How did he know? By indubitable signs and seals. First, the ten horns of the monster signified not the ten kings of the Seleucid dynasty as the uninformed supposed, but the ten kingdoms of Europe which had sprung from the dying ashes of the Roman Empire. Then there was that "fearefull little Horne" which sprang up and dominated the ten horns after destroying three of them. This was not Antiochus Epiphanes, but the Roman papacy.

When exactly would the dominance of the little horn end and the Fifty Monarchy begin? For the reply, Archer turned to Revelation, where it was prophesied that the Gentiles would defile the holy city for "forty and two months," with further corroboration in the story of the woman clothed with the sun who fled into the wilderness "for one thousand two hundred and three score days." Having calculated his total of 1,260 days, Archer then turned to

Isaiah and triumphantly plucked out of context the phrase, "I have given thee each day for a year." The followers of Joachim of Flora had come up with the exact same number of years, but A.D. 1260 had come and passed with no great significance. The base date was wrong, Archer proclaimed: The true period from which reckoning should commence was the fall of the Roman Empire and the usurpation of the papacy. "Let us reckon it (A.D.) 406 when it begun, then add to 406 the 1260, and it maketh 1666." Still not satisfied, Archer rummaged ever further in Daniel's mélange of dates, adding and subtracting on some esoteric system of his own, and at last announcing that Christ would return to earth some forty-five years after 1650 or 1656.

The year 1642, in which Archer wrote his book, was a stirring enough year, filled with the clangor of trumpets and the rattle of swords as Parliament and monarch began to jockey for position. Great events were obviously afoot, but even Archer could not guess the unthinkable and look seven years into the future to see the sacred king lying with his neck upon the block. When it happened, there was an air of awesome inevitability about it. Looking down the vista of those seven years, it seemed to the least imaginative that some outside power had directed the steps of Charles Stuart to the foot of the scaffold so that his death had something sacrificial about it. Nor was it the fanatics alone who believed that something splendid as well as terrible had been enacted in Whitehall. Throughout Cromwell's speech, when he arose to address Parliament on July 4, 1553, there sounds the exaltation of the priest and the prophet, rather than the statesman: "Truly you are called by God to rule with Him, and for Him . . . I confess I never looked to see such a day as this . . . when Jesus Christ would be so owned as he is, at this day and in this work." [26] The Kingdom of God had dawned.

But spiritual exaltation, an occasional luxury for the responsible, was the staple diet of an increasing number of those less burdened with the realities of power, a diet which eventually quite turned their brains. The first clear intimation of a new sect came a few days after Charles's execution, when a petition was delivered to General Fairfax from "many Christian people, dispersed abroad throughout the County of Norfolk and the City of Norwich." Characteristic was the complaceny with which the petitioners assumed that "Christianity" and their own narrow viewpoint were wholly synonomous: characteristic, too, was the didactic tone of the petition itself in which Fairfax and his colleagues were urged to set up a godly government that would act as worthy caretaker till Christ arrived and seated Himself in the vacant throne. The petition was courteously received—the euphoria, the sense of a common triumph was still strong in the land—and other pamphleteers hastened forward to shower the government with advice.

Among the loudest of these was John Rogers, destined to survive into the Restoration and slink gratefully, at last, into a safe obscurity after baiting Cromwell almost up to his deathbed. Unlike most of his fellow fanatics, Rogers left enough autobiographical material in his prolix work to enable a background to be constructed for him; from it can be deduced something of his motivation and the motive power that drove his fellows. The ineradicable impression is that of an unbalanced mind. It was not, perhaps, sufficiently unbalanced to make its owner run the risk of incarceration in a Bedlam—throughout, there runs a cold streak of self-awareness and self-interest—but sufficient to make him and those like him unpleasant and dangerous members of a community. He was twenty-two at the time of the king's execution, and a contemporary portrait of him a few years later shows him as a thin, pale, dyspeptic young man with an intense look. Ironically, this archenemy of human royalty was the son of a stout royalist, the Reverend Nehemiah Rogers, who had suffered both for his faith and his king. Young Rogers himself became the victim of religious mania before he was ten years old. He heard a hellfire sermon that so terrified him as to throw him into what appears to have been a wholly compulsory ritual of prayer: He noted that eventually it took him the entire evening to get through his self-imposed cycle of prayers and sermons. He suffered also what he described as "raging fits," during which he had to be tied down in bed to prevent him injuring himself. All this he took as evidence of divine guidance. He became so intolerably godly that his father—a perfectly good Christian himself—threw the young man out.

There followed some months of near starvation, a timely offer of a teaching post, and a journey to London at precisely the right moment. Among the welter of Independent preachers, each with his fragment of eternal truth, the earnest, vociferous, humorless young man from Essex promptly made his mark as a lover of the godly. It was about this period, in April 1652, that he joined the new sect, which had now acquired a name: the Fifth Monarchy Men.

The Fifth Monarchists were by no means all such as Rogers' kidney. Predominant among them was Major General Harrison, who not only managed to combine good looks, good birth, and religious sincerity, but was also a first-class soldier, giving a very good account of himself in the Civil War. The sect attracted a number of earnest, high-ranking soldiers, men who had fought the good fight against the legions of Antichrist and now, puzzled and disillusioned that England was not yet the New Jerusalem, were clutching at almost any means that would enable them to maintain their ideals and their hope. John Rogers spoke for them, turning their inarticulate lamentations and desires into fiery, wordy sermons. In April 1653, he supplied His Excellency the Lord General Cromwell with an exhortation and a blueprint: The former urged the Lord General to appoint only "Lovers of Truth and Justice" to the Sanhedrim of the new state, and in the latter, the twenty-five-year-old theorist supplied the fifty-five-year-old veteran with precise details as to how his state should be constructed and governed. Other Fifth Monarchists trod on his heels in their eagerness to instruct Oliver Cromwell. John Spittlehouse, ex-soldier, came forward with "Certain rules and regulations how to advance the Kingdom of Jesus Christ over the face of the whole earth." William Aspinwall, in *A Brief Description of the Fifth Monarchy*, warned the world that the divine prophecies of Daniel must be taken absolutely literally and encouraged his readers with the certain information that this present, doomed fourth monarchy must end not later than 1673.

So far, relations between the Fifth Monarchists and the army leaders had been courteous enough, if marked on the part of the Saints by a certain asperity and impatience. They had high hopes for the new Parliament which Cromwell addressed so movingly in July 1653, the Parliament which was to reform a corrupt nation and usher in the age of sanctity. But yet again it proved unaccountably difficult to establish heaven upon earth. The ungodly scoffed at the pretensions of the "Barebones Parliament," as they derisively nicknamed it after Praise-God Barbon, one of its more eccentric leaders. The moderates grew alarmed, the extremists wilder as disillusion set in. On December 12, those moderates who were still in control formally divested the assembly of power, rendering it back into the hands of Cromwell, and postponing indefinitely thereby the advent of the Kingdom of God. And from the month of December 1653 onward, the Saints were as implacably opposed to Cromwell as they were to the pope of Rome himself—more so, perhaps; for the pope was a distant, slightly unreal figure, while Cromwell the apostate was here, grown out of their own soil.

John Rogers maintained his position as chief chastiser of the sinful but was most effectively backed up by two men of a very similar turn of mind: Christopher Feake, a minister who had urged on the slaughter of the ungodly from the safety of a pulpit, and a Welshman, Vavasor Powell, who had at least fought in the Civil War as a soldier in the line. The pamphleteering and sermonizing war triggered by these men must rank as among the most virulent, the most unpleasant of all religious polemics. Their attacks were filled with a savage contempt for all who deviated a hairsbreadth from their fantastically narrow interpretation of existence. The earthy imagery which, in the hands of such as Luther, had given a pungent vigor to Protestant argument, became in their lesser hands merely disgusting. As invective it was self-defeating, for the mind eventually revolts against the description of other human beings as ordure, excrement, vomit and the like; and when someone of the stature of Cromwell is attacked in these terms by someone of the stature of Feake or Rogers, then the victim almost automatically gains the sympathy of the observer. "Bastard of Ashdod," "bloody

BEAST," "Satan's excrement," "perjured villain"—so now was Cromwell viewed. The attacks grew to an hysterical climax of virulence when their late hero assumed the style of Protector. Feake discovered that all the prophets had been wrong regarding the identity of the horrific little horn on the ten-horned beast, the horn that had eyes and mouth to utter blasphemies and which made war on the Saints. It was neither Antiochus, Nero, Frederick, nor the pope, but the elderly, tiring squire from Huntingdon.

Not the least extraordinary aspect of the Fifth Monarchy episode was Oliver Cromwell's patience. In addition to the ordinary cares of a head of state, he was burdened with the ever present threat of a royalist rising, and now joined to that was the very real danger of a rising on the left. For the Saints passed rapidly from insult to action, from loading Cromwell's name with obloquy to fomenting rebellion. The Welshman Powell made explicit the suspicion that must hang over the head of any successful revolutionary, the suspicion that Cromwell had been corrupted by those he had sworn to overthrow, that the insidious power of wealth had eroded the early high ideals. "Are they choked with parks, lands and manors?" Powell demanded. "Let us go home and pray and say, Lord, wilt thou have Oliver Cromwell or Jesus Christ to reign over us?" The invitation was blatant. So, too, was Rogers's call for a state of anarchy—for such indubitably was his plea that all power should be placed in the hands of Jesus Christ.

Cromwell at last acted. Rogers, Feake, and Simpson, another hellfire preacher, were arrested. But for every Saint temporarily arrested, two more arose eager to wear the prophet's mantle, and Cromwell opened the Parliament of 1654 to a background of nagging exhortations. He referred specifically, and with an overtone of weary resignation, to this waspish buzzing. They were all united in the hope, he said, that there should be a true Kingdom of God in which dissensions would be at an end, but it was entirely preposterous that a small group of men should think "that they are the only men to rule kingdoms, govern nations and give laws to people. . . . Truly they had need to give clear manifestation of God's presence among them, before wise men will receive or submit to their conclusions." [27]

Yet Cromwell was still burdened by his own conscience. These men, these Fifth Monarchists, might be fanatics of a peculiarly virulent breed, yet they held, after all, merely an exaggerated version of that faith which had destroyed the corrupt old order and was now cleansing England. Cromwell's secretary, John Thurloe, admiringly described how his master kept his temper under extreme provocation: "I doe assure you that his highness is put to exercise every day with the peevishness and wrath of some persons here. But the Lord enables hym with comfort to beare the hard speeches and repoaches which he is loaded with from day to day, and helps hym to return good for evil, and good will for their hatred." [28] But for Cromwell it was not enough merely passively to accept their reproaches; he decided to enter into debate with his more vociferous critics—trying to explain to them what he was doing and the nature of his limitations; trying to find, too, what exactly they believed and wanted.

On February 6, 1655, Rogers was therefore brought to White-hall from his prison. An additional, unofficial record of this extraordinary debate between the careworn head of state and the irresponsible fanatic was later published by one of Rogers's own followers, dedicated in the usual elegant fashion to those who "in this Day of great Rebuke and Blasphemy (are) ingaged against the Beast and his Government." Wholly biased in favor of Rogers though it is, the record is all the more impressive in the picture it conveys of the irreconcilable conflict between reason and emotion, between Cromwell, irritated but striving to be just, and Rogers, contemptuously assured of his God-directed role.

Cromwell went over to the offensive right at the beginning. It was entirely inaccurate and unjust to say that Rogers was in prison because of his faith, he said vehemently. No one in England suffered on such grounds. Rogers was in prison because he was a danger to the state, a man ever engaged in plotting and stirring up sedition. Here Rogers seems to have raised his hands and rolled his eyes in the classically sanctimonius gesture, for Cromwell burst out sharply: "Nay, do not lift up your hands and eyes," and slightly abashed, Rogers allowed the other to finish.

He then took up his own accusations. They were of a kind with which Cromwell had become wearily familiar: The army was betraying the cause of righteousness; Cromwell was an apostate; Rogers and his friends alone were true in the cause of King Jesus; Cromwell had usurped the throne of David and sought to exercise absolute power, in direct violation of the promise that such power should never again be vested in a ruler.

This touched Cromwell on the raw: "Who—hear me—who, who I say hath broken that? Where is an arbitrary or absolute power—Nay, hear me—where is such a Power?"

Rogers waved the question aside with the maddening calm of the man who refuses to let facts change his opinion and swung into a Fifth Monarchy tirade, ending with the cry, "I beseech you, my Lord, consider how near it is to the end of the Beast's dominion, the forty-two months, and what time of day it is now."

"Talk not of that," Cromwell said drily. "I must tell you plainly that they are things I understand not."

That must be so, Rogers retorted, for otherwise he would not dare lay hands upon the sacred witnesses.

The debate had now gone full circle and Cromwell brought it to a close, having achieved nothing. "I tell you, there wants brotherly love," he said suddenly as Rogers and his advisers were leaving. Rogers disdained to reply.[29]

Throughout the spring and early summer of that year, 1655, the Fifth Monarchists continued their sniping by pamphlet and sermon. But at the same time, among the extremists there grew steadily the determination to solve the matter by blood instead of argument, to "pull Babylon down by force," and eject the usurper from Christ's throne.

"I will make my arrows drunk with blood, and my sword shall devour flesh, and that with the blood of the slain and of the captives, from the beginning of revenges upon the enemy." There was never lacking biblical precedent for slaughter, and a ranting Fifth

Monarchist, John Gardiner, found a sufficiently bloody pretext in Deuteronomy. But it was not he, or Feake, or Rogers, or any of those who had so often sworn to inaugurate the millennium of love with a bloodbath, who now turned words into action. The outrider of Christ was Thomas Venner, a man who had never yet ascended a pulpit.

(i) Thomas Venner

A little, dried-up, arid man with an unkempt beard and burning eyes; a man—unlike so many of his fellow sectarians—with little gift for words but with a dogged determination that carried him on plodding to his goal; a man who did not waste his time in invective, for he regarded all those who did not share his beliefs neither with contempt nor with pity but simply with a blankness; a man prepared to kill neither in anger nor in fear, nor even in love, but as a gardener might remove weeds or a ratcatcher kill rats—such was Thomas Venner, winecooper, whose birth was unknown but whose bloody end would be pitilessly observed and recorded by many. He first became known not in England but four thousand miles away, in Salem, New England, where he had a comfortable little property and some reputation in the town. He was a winecooper by trade, but in the frontier tradition of New England, where a man was expected to have a Bible on the table and a musket on the wall, he became a member of the Artillery Company in 1645. It was this seemingly unimportant fact which would gain for him his curious place in history, for it gave him at once a taste and some ability for military organization. Infused with the potent millennial drug—for Thomas Venner, winecooper, was in his secret moments Thomas Venner, Christ's outrider—his military talents practically guaranteed a bizarre adventure when the little tradesman, with thirty other devoted souls, took on a king's army.

Venner returned to England in October 1651, and with his skill at his secondary trade he got himself appointed to a position in the Tower of London. Secretary Thurloe laconically described Venner's short career at the Tower: "He was removed, being ob-

served to be a fellow of desperate and bloody spirit and was suspected to have designs to blow up the Tower with powder . . . He
also spake at the time some very desperate words concerning the
murder of His Highness." [30] It seems truly extraordinary that a
known fanatic, heavily suspected of plotting both the destruction of
the Tower and the murder of Cromwell, should simply have been
allowed to disappear quietly into the teeming streets of London,
there to continue his plotting.

Venner might have lacked the ability to rouse mobs by sermon
and pamphlet, but he nevertheless shared to the full the Puritan
prolixity which, in his case, took the form of a journal minutely
describing the meetings of the conspirators. Most of it was concerned with recording which brother was to do which work, where
they were to meet, what weapons were to be brought, and the like.
But he could not resist the fashionable tendency to blueprint paradise, to lay down laws and constitution for the coming Millennium.
The Fifth Monarchists were perhaps unique among all millenarian sects in their attempts to describe the indescribable. Down
the centuries, those who impatiently awaited the Parousia and the
descent of the Holy City had contented themselves with describing
the physical beauties of the New Jerusalem, together with vague
indications of a thousand years of bliss and a more precise description of the torments to be endured by the infidel. The Fifth Monarchists accepted the challenge of describing what they were actually
going to do through those long, long years. There was some doubt
as to whether Christ would be physically present all the time
and—a graver embarrassment—some controversy as to whether
human beings had the right to enact laws when the Lawgiver Himself was to occupy the throne. Propriety was satisfied by dividing
the Millennium into an Evening and a Morning State. During the
Evening State, the Saints would be acting as regents, and it would
be entirely proper for them to undertake any measure that would
purify the City for the arrival of Christ in the Morning. With that
problem resolved, the Saints enthusiastically set about planning.

The first thing necessary was to disabuse the faithful of any idea that the Millennium was to be one long, carefree state of anarchy. The Millennium was characterized by gravity. Certainly there were to be no jokes, no laughter, though a sedate rejoicing would be permitted when the Ancient of Days seated Himself on the throne. It seemed that the old, old sins of man were to be rampant even during the new age, for provision was made for the punishing of "whoremasters, drunkards, adulterers, thieves," and the rest of a too familiar crew. The faithful, far from living in a state of anarchy, would find themselves far more closely policed than in Cromwell's England: The populace was to be divided into groups of ten, fifty, one hundred and one thousand with a Saint above each, and all would be subject to the holy Sanhedrin that was Christ's regent during the Evening. Curiously little attention was paid to the question of whether people would grow older, or even die, during the thousand years and whether cripples, the blind, and other physically afflicted people would be restored to full health during that period; and considering that the Millennium was a spiritual condition, there was a correspondingly curious interest given to its economic life. That there would be no taxes was natural, but Christ seems to have been cast for the role of customs officer; there was to be a ban on the export of fuller's earth and unwrought leather and any other commodity which would enrich the foreigner as against the native Saint. The position of the Jews in the New Jerusalem was a delicate question. As it happened, most Fifth Monarchists were free of the endemic anti-Semitism, for it was held that the conversion of the Jews was a vital prerequisite.

Venner adopted most of these principles and added his own grandiose plans. Not for nothing was he an ex-member of the Artillery Company. It was not enough to save England—and the parochialism of his fellow Saints with their preoccupation regarding unwrought leather and fuller's earth and the rest struck him not so much as blasphemous as unworthy. Beyond the Channel lay the great world, groaning under the tyranny of priests, corrupted with kings, thirsting for the faith that Thomas Venner bore aloft.

Never shall we sheath our swords until Mount Zion become the joy of the whole earth, untill Rome be in ashes and Babylon become a hissing and a curse. We are not purposed—when the Lord shall have driven forth our enemies here in these nations and when we shall, in holy triumph, have led our captivity captive—to sit down under our vines and fig trees, but to go on to France, Spain, Germany, and Rome to destroy the Beast and Whore, to burn her flesh with fire, to throw her down with violence as a mil-stone in the sea . . .[31]

It was necessary to draw together a great army for this holy work, and the grizzled little man went to and fro, seeking recruits.

But unaccountably the Saints failed to respond. Christopher Feake, who attended so many of the meetings in his capacity of all-purpose plotter, quietly backed out when it became evident that Venner was thinking of swords in more than purely symbolic terms. Major General Harrison and those other members who had actually been on a battlefield, declined to have anything to do with the hairbrained scheme. Venner scornfully dismissed these lukewarm Saints from its calculations, and with about a hundred likeminded men, made his detailed plans to overthrow the Beast, the man who impiously called himself the Lord Protector. The revolutionaries provided themselves with a standard—a lion couchant with the ambiguous motto, "who shall rowze him upp"—divided themselves into three companies, and arranged to rendezvous just outside London, in Epping Forest, on the night of April 9. About twenty of the company had sensible second thoughts before the night, and it was with about eighty men that Venner marched out to overthrow the kingdom of the ungodly. The odds were not particularly dismaying to Venner, for he believed firmly that England lay groaning under a tyrant heel, that the Saints had only to sound their trumpets for the multitudes to rush to them. And even if the people of England proved indifferent, it mattered not at all, for behind the little band as it marched out of the gloom of the forest were the unseen legions of the Lamb, ready to dip their sacred swords into impious blood.

The militant Saints marched straight into a police trap.

Throughout the days of their plotting, government agents had kept Cromwell closely informed of their intentions and movements. It was, indeed, scarcely possible to be unaware that a sedition was in process, so verbose were the plotters, so intent that the world should know just what they were laboring for on its behalf. The whole lot of them could have been swept into the bag long before they marched, but Cromwell had sensibly decided to give them as much rope as possible. By the time they set out for Epping Forest, the government had a very clear idea of the military strength of the movement, and it was probably this knowledge that explained the astonishing clemency shown toward a band of men who had sworn to drown the government of the Beast in its own blood. Twenty men were captured, including Venner himself, and promptly transported to the Tower; the sixty or so who escaped planned another attack a few weeks later, but these, too, were surprised and captured, and the military side of the rebellion was, for the time being, at an end.

But the war of words went on, encouraged by the government's docility. Again Rogers's voice was heard in the land, urging his fellows on to desperate deeds of blood. The gallant effort of Jan van Leiden was recalled: If a humble Dutch tailor could make a true New Jerusalem of a small German town, then surely Englishmen could turn the great city of London into a worthy abode for the coming Christ: "Come come, Sirs, prepare your companies for King Jesus, his Mount Zion musterday is at hand: His Magazine and Artillery—yea—His most excellent Mortar pieces and batteries be ready," the pulpit general proclaimed, until at last even Cromwell's remarkable patience was exhausted and Rogers joined Venner in the Tower.

That was in January of 1658. Although the Saints could not know it, their great adversary, the Beast and Bastard of Ashdod had just nine months more of life and, with him, their freedom to curse their national leaders and plot against them. Those last months of Cromwell's life were rendered burdensome by ill health, family tragedy—he watched his beloved daughter Agnes die a lingering death—and above all by the necessity of struggling alone without the assistance of Parliament. In the country the rising tide of reaction swept the most unlikely groups into harness together, so that Fifth Monarchists, who yearned only for the end of earthly monarchy, joined fervent royalists in execration of the Protector. Yet still he retained his tolerance. Venner and Rogers remained unharmed, almost forgotten, in the Tower; from time to time some of the more vociferous Fifth Monarchists joined them. Inevitably, they were lauded by their fellows as martyrs, but most were street-corner ranters, loud, insolent men usually sentenced for contempt of court rather than for crimes against the state.

Cromwell died in September 1658; for eighteen months his son Richard struggled with the impossible task of stemming the royalist tide before he gratefully retired. The Fifth Monarchists were jubilant. Here, quite clearly, was the finger of God. First the Beast had been removed by death, and then, when his son attempted to continue the usurpation of the sacred throne, he was proven inept. Most of the imprisoned leaders were released, including both Venner and Rogers. Now, cleansed of the dross of Cromwell, England could be shaped into the Holy City so long prophesied.

One year and four days after Richard Cromwell laid down the burdens of office, King Charles II arrived in London.

> *We have sin'd: and therefore for our sin*
> *Frustrate was made that Glorious Design*
> *And we are brought where first we did begin*

So sang an unknown poetaster, his doggerel verse striving to convey the sense of unbelieving shock that assailed those who had confidently awaited the arrival of Christ and found themselves staring into the saturnine face of Charles Stuart. Daniel could not be wrong; John on Patmos could not be wrong, and neither could those labyrinthine calculations erected upon their cryptic visions. Therefore the Restoration of the monarchy was simply another trial, an extension, perhaps, of the expected messianic woes. The Saints had not been strong enough and pure enough; they must be put through the fire again to burn out the dross and anneal them in strength.

Old Rowley, the restored king—urbane, amused, seemingly indifferent to everything outside his comforts and pleasures. Cromwell—steely, principled, bending England by the sheer force of his personality. The contrast was dramatic but misleading, for the man of high principle had been rendered vulnerable by his own conscience, while the man of no principle was restrained only by consideration of what could harm or benefit him. He wanted vengeance on the regicides. The people were prepared to allow him that pleasure, and he took it. The desecration of corpses, even the corpses of such men as Ireton, Cromwell, and Blake, was poor revenge, and his government turned upon the living. First to fall victim was Major General Harrison, that incongruously debonair Puritan with his long curly hair, his lace and silks—and burning, unshakable religious convictions. In him the Fifth Monarchists had their most outstanding proponent: no loveless, humorless, joyless fanatic, but a rounded man, civilized, gay, and courageous, who happened to hold an extraordinary belief and by the sheer force of his personality set a wavering doubt in the mind of the most obstinate enemy of the sect. He could have escaped the country but refused to do so, and on October 10, 1660, he was brought to trial and condemned, as was inevitable. He went to his death with a dancing step. His courage and good heart survived even the spiteful indignity of the hurdle upon which the condemned were bound, securely but uncomfortably, so that they slid uncertainly about as they were dragged along at the feet of the crowd, staring up into jeering and hostile faces. Pepys saw him hanged, drawn and quartered at Charing Cross, "he looking as cheerful as any man could do in that condition. He was presently cut down and his head and heart shown to the people. It is said, that he said he was sure to come shortly at the right hand of Christ to judge them that had now judged him, and that his wife do expect his coming again. Thus it was my chance to see the King beheaded in White Hall, and to see the first blood shed in revenge for the King at Charing Cross," [32] Pepys concluded with the satisfaction of a raconteur

rounding up a tale. But he had not, in fact, seen
the story.

Throughout the last months of the Commonw
been frequent rumors of a Fifth Monarchy uprisin
fanatics who were prepared to do something more
being transformed by heated imagination into thou
men. The story of the Anabaptists at Munster wa
relish, each version a little more richly embroidered
have been safe to say that the majority of those w
King Charles I were at least sympathetic toward
but as the extremists became louder and ever more
the memory of royalist England became tinged w
charm, so the common people began to regard t
chists as cranks, and dangerous cranks at that. Tho
gone underground after Richard Cromwell had
February 1659 and seemed disposed to wait and
happen. But as the current set in toward the r
monarchy, so Venner began to gather again a revo
to defend the throne of David. He had no difficul
exchanging hatred for Oliver Cromwell for hatre
but, as in his previous insurrection, it is almost in
terity to decide what exactly it was he thought h
There can be no doubt whatsoever regarding his
cerity, but the spectacle of one man backed with
porters, hurling himself at a state belongs virtuall
mythology or romance.

Nevertheless, the doomed David went abou
to demolish Goliath with a prosaic attention to de
difference to the magnitude of the task before
impressive. Stores of ammunition were accumu
place arranged. Again Venner counted on a spo
to hurl the monarchy into oblivion, his task b
catalyst to create the explosion. But again, his
military detail overlooked a vital military necessit
his devoted band of Saints got drunk in a sin
manner and, in his cups, blurted out to a compa

the coming rebellion. The companion promptly hastened to a magistrate, and by nightfall the houses of known opponents of the monarchy were being searched. It was an excellent opportunity to eliminate the disaffected, and men who had only the most tenuous connections with the Fifth Monarchists found themselves brought in for questioning.

Venner escaped detection along with his companions; the government agents were interested in high-ranking army officers and were probably unaware of the existence of a dissident body composed of coal heavers, winecoopers, and the like. But Venner decided to bring forward the date of the rebellion, choosing the night of January 6, 1661. The watchword chosen was the bloodthirsty, "King Jesus—and their heads upon the gate."

At about ten o'clock on that cold Sunday night, a Mr. Johnson, bookseller near Saint Paul's, was brought to his door by a thunderous knocking. Outside was a party of men, variously estimated as between thirty and fifty, whose leader demanded from the bookseller the keys to the church, which were in his keeping. Johnson claimed that he did not have them and, rather tamely, the band wandered off to the church where they succeeded in breaking down one of the doors. They then entered, leaving a guard outside. Their purpose in breaking into the church at that hour of night is unclear, and it was later assumed that they had chosen Saint Paul's to be their fortress—a reasonable assumption, for the massive old church could have accommodated hundreds of the people expected to rise in support. Unfortunately, however, the guard left outside was trigger-happy. A passer-by carrying a lantern was halted, and the guard demanded who he was for. The man cautiously replied "King Charles," whereupon the guard replied that he was for King Jesus and shot the wretched man through the head. The shot brought a company of musketeers established at the Exchange doubling to the scene, but the band, displaying that incredible courage which was to astound London over the next two days, beat off the professionals and escaped to the outskirts of the city. There they killed another man—a constable—before retreating to the high open ground four miles to the north of the city.

London was buzzing with excitement, the handful of religious maniacs transformed into unknown hundreds of bloodthirsty desperadoes. Pepys heard that more than forty thousand militia were under arms, and though this was an obvious exaggeration, it was testimony to the fear that the "fantatiques" aroused. News sped round that they were invulnerable to bullets—a garbled version of Venner's exhortation to his followers that the bullets of the enemy could not hurt the Saints. People moving in groups about the streets were halted and rigorously examined while a squadron of cavalry thundered off in pursuit of the band. There was a brief and bloody clash in the woods, as a result of which about twenty-five of the rebels were arrested and dragged back to the city. The rest disappeared.

But not for long. Hidden in the thick woods around Highgate, the surviving members of the band—about fifty men—rested and refurbished themselves during Monday and Tuesday. No record of their conversation was made or published; neither their contemporaries nor posterity could gain even a hint as to their state of mind while they swallowed cold food and drink during the two raw January days and prepared again to attack an entire city. Here perhaps was demonstrated as never before or since the power of fanaticism, for there was nothing to prevent the band from melting into the winter mist instead of undertaking a wholly impossible mission that could end only in disaster and death. Sometime during the small hours of the morning of Wednesday, January 9, they marched silently out of their temporary encampment, evaded the patrols, and erupted again in the heart of London.

Pepys was awakened at six A.M. by people running about the house, crying out that "the Fanatiques were in arms in the city. So I arose and went forth, where in the street I found everybody in arms at the doors. So I returned—though with no good courage at all, but that I might not seem to be afeared—and got my sword and pistol." [33] He walked around rather aimlessly with a companion through streets crowded with excited armed men and with all the shops shuttered as though to withstand a major siege. It was not until the following day that he was able to piece together what had happened and then recorded that, to his astonishment, it was only a handful of men that had caused such fear and excitement:

> . . . not in all above 31. Whereas we did believe them (because they were seen up and down in every place almost in the City and had been in Highgate two or three days) to be at least 500. A thing that was never heard of, that so few men should dare and do so much mischief. Few of them would receive any quarter, but such as were taken by force and kept alive: expecting Jesus to come and reign in the world presently, and will not believe yet. . . .

The last stand of the Fifth Monarchists took place in the heart of the city they were attempting to capture for Christ, in and around Threadneedle Street and Cheapside, a few hundred yards from Saint Paul's where they had raised their standard three days earlier. It was not wholly surprising that they had been able to inflict losses and cause panic in a military force many times their size. The narrow, twisting streets of London before the Fire tended to give an advantage to smaller groups in a street battle, provided the group was energetic and determined. It was almost impossible to attack them from above, for the upper stories of the buildings projected so close to each other that neighbors could reach out and touch hands. A direct charge was useless, for only three or four men could wield swords in the front ranks, and the twisting streets made it possible to fire only random shots instead of a fusillade. Venner and his men were able to advance and retreat as they wished, now suddenly appearing out of an alley to assault an unprotected flank, now circling around to attack from the rear. But gradually the trained bands forced them out of the alleyways into the major thoroughfares where they could be attacked in force. By mid-morning the tough, resilient little band had been broken up and, fiercely attacked by musketeers, part of them sought refuge in an inn, retreating—still fighting—to the upper story. The rest were hunted down in tiny groups, for the city gates were closed and they were trapped. About half of the original force of fifty men were killed in the fighting, and twenty—including a

badly wounded Venner—were captured. An i
rocity with which they fought their hopeless ba
the Blue Anchor Inn where ten sought refuge:
tured, the rest fighting until cut down.

The attempted insurrection of four year
squashed before it got under way, and Cro
been able to treat Venner and his followers wit
most clement government could hardly overlook
twenty-two militiamen had been killed, an
wounded, the life of a great city brought to a
person of the monarch threatened and insulted.
of Charles II was anything but disposed to be cle
Venner and his nineteen surviving companions
week after their capture. Venner denied that
giving that dubious honor to King Jesus Himsel
from fear of the consequences or—more likely b
believed this to be the case, the record of his tria
Three men were found not guilty, the jury acce
they had acted under duress from the rest. It wa
the cohering factor of the Fifth Monarchist extre
who had surrendered at the Blue Anchor Inn cla
their companions would have shot them dow
attempt had been made while they lived.

The remaining sixteen men were sentenced
and quartered, although only Venner and his
suffered the full agonizing punishment, the rest b
of hand. Pepys crossed the path of the Fifth Mo
time on that day, January 19, for he was on his wa
he encountered Venner and three other of the
dragged to their death. He was not particularly
recording the fact in his compulsive manner.

Thomas Venner—who had crossed four
ocean to meet his death a few hundred yards
Stuart had been beheaded—marked the effecti
dream. The government took the opportunit
sweep, hunting down every person who had

nected with the rebellion. In November 1661, ten months after Venner's butchered corpse had been nailed up on the city gates, a wretched coalman, John James, was beheaded at Tyburn for seditious speeches, and not long afterwards, Sir Henry Vane went nonchalantly to the scaffold, proclaiming his faith in the imminence of Christ's coming as best he could above the rolling of drums and the shrilling of trumpets. But these were the last to die violently for their curious faith. Here and there over the country, like the last rumbles of a departing summer storm, came reports of Fifth Monarchist preachers, but in most cases the mere threat of official action was sufficient to damp their ardor. Christopher Feake, the once passionate sermonizer and excoriator of Oliver Cromwell, the man who had declared again and again his longing to shed his blood for the Lamb, was swept up with the others and, after a groveling recantation and promise of good behavior, he was released and disappeared from history. His fellow Saint, John Rogers, escaped to the continent and returned to take up a blameless career of doctoring after the excitement had died down. At the end of December 1663, that skillful survivor General Monk—once a fervent parliamentarian, now so devoted a royalist that he could call himself Duke of Albemarle—was able to announce that "All things here are well. Now and then there are some little designs among the Anabaptists and Fifth Monarchy Men, which are a people who will never be quiett, but their designes are so weak and inconsiderable that I am confident they will nott bee dangerous to his Majesty and Kingdom." [34] It was an accurate estimate. The Fifth Monarchists could never again present a military danger, but their beliefs had merely gone underground to flourish there and blossom out in the most extraordinary of forms.

CHAPTER V

•

THE NEPHEW OF
GOD

"The very loud and unusual kind of Thunder that was heard in the beginning of January, 1791, was the voice of the Angel mentioned in the Eighteenth chapter of the Revelation, proclaiming the Judgement of God and the fall of Babylon the great. It was the loudest that ever was heard since man was created, and shook the whole earth every time the angel spoke." [35]

In that manner—characteristically calm, characteristically confident—Richard Brothers, ex-lieutenant of His Britannic Majesty's navy, nephew of Almighty God and future Prince of the Hebrews, begins his account of the doom which overhung London and which was averted only by his great labor. God, he reported, had become so exceedingly indignant with the iniquity of the city on the Thames that He had turned aside from everything else in the universe that might have distracted His divine attention in order to concentrate on London's destruction. His prophet and relative, Richard Brothers, had been ordered to leave the city for a species of divine conference. "I had, similar to the prophet Daniel at Babylon, an attending Angel to explain all the Visions." It was a long and, for Brothers, distinctly frightening conference, for again and again the Onipotent threatened him for his stubborn defense of a heedless London. But all ended well. At the end of the conference he was carried up to heaven where God, speaking to him from a large white cloud, informed him: "I pardon London and all the people in it for your sake. There is no other man on earth that could stand before me and ask so great a thing." There was an interesting geological postscript to the conference, one presumably supplied by the attending angel. If London had been destroyed in that year 1791, "the place where it stands would have formed a great bay or inlet of the Channel. All the land between Windsor and the Downs would have been sunk, including a distance of eighteen miles on each side, but considerably more towards the sea coast." London itself would have been submerged to a depth of "seventy fathoms or four hundred and twenty feet."

It was this admixture of confident precision and wild claim that partly accounts for Brothers's astonishing success during the 1790's—a brilliant if brief period for him when the carriages of the great drew up outside his dingy lodgings; learned men engaged in polysyllabic battle deriding or defending him; Parliament itself listened to a solemn exposition of his philosophy; and King George, in periods of sanity, frothed with rage at his claims and demanded action against the insolent prophet. But though the prophecies of Richard Brothers made compulsive reading, being couched in an easy, fluent vernacular, they would probably have gone unheard outside a tiny band of devotees had it not been for the time at which they were uttered. Across the Channel the great monarchy of France had collapsed in bloody ruin, the revolutionary soldiers of the Republic were defying the forces of stability, and the dangerous seeds of revolution were being carried throughout Europe. Alike, those who feared the breakup of the old order and those who welcomed it peered into the future seeking to discern the pattern that would emerge. From out of the chaos emerged Lieutenant Richard Brothers with his calm and confident message: The Day of Fulfillment was imminent and the Millennium would commence sometime between the late summer of 1793 and the autumn of 1795.

Brothers was thirty-seven years old when he emerged dramatically, suddenly from obscurity into the deceptive blaze of notoriety. The first the public heard of him was through his *Revealed
Knowledge*, a publication—little more than a pamphlet—which appeared in 1794 and which, in the compass of just sixty-eight pages,
provided a true chronology of the world, corrected errors in the
Bible which had crept in over the centuries, and informed the
world that Richard Brothers was the Prince of the Hebrews whose
coming had been awaited since the Diaspora. But Brothers was not
wholly unknown to the world before 1794, as certain Admiralty officials and the Westminster Board of Guardians could, with some
feeling, testify. Among their papers was recorded the fact that
Lieutenant Richard Brothers had been born in Placentia, New-
foundland, in 1757, came to England to join the Royal Navy and, as
an officer, had performed honorable if undistinguished service until
1783 when he was discharged on half pay. And that, precisely, was
when the trouble started and when the name of Richard Brothers
began to be mentioned with emotion by overworked admiralty bu-
reaucrats.

Officers on half pay were entitled to draw their stipend every
six months—but an inescapable condition was that they had to
swear "voluntarily" that they had not been employed by the
Crown during those six months. A compulsion to swear voluntarily
was a bureaucratic barbarism which could well irritate even those
who had no real objection to swearing an oath, as such. But to
Richard Brothers there was an offense additional to the assault on
English language and liberty. Sometime between 1783 and 1790
the mind of this neat, meticulous naval officer began to teeter on its
balance and to swing towards religious fanaticism. It became more
and more evident to him that it was a sinful act to swear an oath.
There was, as yet, no outward sign of his obsession. Indeed, the
letter which he wrote to the secretary of the Admiralty in September 1790, objecting to the practice, was admirably lucid and
mild in tone: "To avoid the imputation of appearing troublesome,"
he wrote, "I waited a considerable time after the half-pay was advertised, that a very just application should not displease the Admi-

ralty." With gentle skill he goes on to correct the English of those who drafted the clause, ". . . a voluntary act is an avowed freedom of choice . . .", cites William Pitt as one who refused to obtain revenue by oath, points out that indiscriminate oath-taking devalued the currency, and calls on the secretary "as a man of good sense, for the good of the Navy (and) the benefit of your country to attempt the extirpation of a custom dishonourable to God, and reproachable to man." [36]

His lengthy, reasoned letter received exactly the answer that might be expected from a hard-pressed official: The secretary had no authority to dispense Lieutenant Brothers from taking the oath if he wished to receive his pay. Thereupon Lieutenant Brothers resolved the matter by refusing to take the oath and thereby losing his pay.

It was at this point that the next group of officials, the Westminster Guardians, were willy-nilly involved in the affairs of the recalcitrant ex-officer. The half pay was Brothers's sole source of income—not because he was idle but because he was called upon to use his time for greater things. "It was in the year 1790 that the Spirit of God began to visit me—though I had always a presentiment of being some time or other very great." Prayer and meditation and the planning of his great future left no time for the mundane business of earning a living. He was in lodgings and went on automatically eating the food provided by his landlady and enjoying the modest comforts of her house as though they were natural products. And at last the landlady—a Mrs. Green—took action, though reluctantly. There were to be many testimonies to the sincerity and honesty of Richard Brothers, but it is doubtful if there was another one quite so impressive as this reluctance on the part of a hard-bitten London landlady. Mrs. Green, in her time, had had wide and dismal experience of defaulting lodgers. Mr. Brothers was not one of these, she explained to the Guardians; he was a pious, honorable, well-behaved, mild-mannered gentleman—but he did owe her £33, and she was a poor woman, and what were the Guardians going to do about it?

The Guardians, in their turn, provided posterity with an impressive testimony to Richard Brothers's personality. They, like Mrs. Green, had peered too often into the murkier depths of society to be easily moved to spontaneous expression of confidence in the motives of those who came before them. Drunkards, drifters, the unfortunate, the vicious and the plain idle—these were the kind of people who, falling deeper and deeper into the depths, came to them for a grudging assistance. Now they looked with some surprise at the tall, neatly dressed soft-voiced person who stood before them. Gillray's brutal cartoon of Brothers leading the Elect shows a slackmouthed, wild-eyed moron—the Brothers of popular imagination who was to survive in history. But the Brothers who appears in William Sharp's neat engraving seems, if anything, rather a dandy, with the enormous, carefully tied cravat and the fashionable set of the coat. The good-looking face is cast in an introspective, rather melancholy mold, certainly, and there is clearly a hint of the irritation that could burst out when the prophet felt that he was being impertinently questioned. But there is nothing of madness, nothing which could give the puzzled Guardians any real clue to his motives. They questioned him with a most unusual gentleness, asking him what he would live on if he rejected his pension and how he hoped to pay the patient Mrs. Green, who had kept him all these months. Loftily he replied that he had the highest possible expectations, that soon he would come into a sum of money that would amply repay Mrs. Green and leave much more besides. Fortunately for him—and for Mrs. Green—that particular Board of Guardians took their responsibilities seriously. They lodged him in the poorhouse and then began a dogged battle with the board of the admiralty. Six months later they collected nearly three years' back pay on his behalf from the admiralty, paid off Mrs. Green, canceled a number of other debts, and sent him out into the world a solvent man. But again he refused to swear the oath to collect his pay; again his debts mounted, and a few months later he was back in confinement—this time not in the poorhouse, but in Newgate prison, whither he was consigned by an irate landlady who quite lacked Mrs. Green's confidence in him.

Newgate left a scar on him as it left a scar on most of those who felt its inhuman embrace. Here at last his mind began to turn in on itself, creating a megalomania as compensation for the humiliation and sheer physical misery that he endured. Newgate killed or toughened its inmates—or sent them mad as the only means of escape. Brothers's madness still remained under control; to the very end, years later, when he was indubitably insane, he nevertheless still remained capable of complex arithmetical calculations and drew innumerable architectural plans for his New Jerusalem. But it was Newgate that saw his first departure from reality. That was made clearly evident in his book published eighteen months later. The reader is plunged, quite without warning, from a precise exposition of Revelation to an agonized re-creation of the horrors of Newgate. Gratefully he remembers a woman who brought him a three-penny loaf every week—although even here grandiloquence covered the pain of the memory and he discharged his debt in lofty terms: "The Lord God commands me to acknowledge the kindness of a poor woman ISABELLA WAKE . . . Although I am now poor, I shall soon have abundance and be at the Head of the greatest nation on Earth. In my Palace you shall always have an apartment and at my table you shall always have a seat." In a few disjointed phrases the reader has a sudden insight into the reality behind the dreams—the filthy cells without heating, blankets, or beds; the slow starvation; the stinking atmosphere; the sense of utter hopelessness and helplessness. "Therefore be no longer astonished that LONDON in one part of the Revelation is called under the name of the GREAT CITY . . . . : in another she is called SODOM and in a third, she is, as well as ROME spiritually called BABYLON THE GREAT." [37]

But again he aroused compassion; again his pension was collected, his debts paid, and lodging obtained for him in the warrens of Paddington. But now the vision that had so long been in his mind, taking shape in the workhouse, colored by the horrors of Newgate, took him over completely; in his lodgings he scribbled hour after hour and produced at last *A Revealed Knowledge of the Prophecies and Times—wrote under the direction of the Lord God . . . containing, with other great and remarkable things not revealed to any person on Earth, the Restoration of the Hebrews to Jerusalem by the year of*

1798, under their revealed Prophet and Prince. Comprehensive though the title page appeared, it scarcely covered all the marvels within the flimsy pages. The style throughout is lucid and easy, contrasting favorably with the turgid obscurities usually favored by prophets. Brothers explains why this is so: "When I began to write I believed it necessary to adopt the same language as the Scripture does . . . but God spoke to me and said Write in the same manner I always speak to you, write according to the custom of the country you live in. You will be better attended to and what you write will be more easily understood"—altogether, sound literary advice.

The Divinity who spoke through Richard Brothers was not the laconic, bloodthirsty deity of the Old Testament, but a bad-tempered, verbose old man who seemed to have little affection for His prophet but was making the best of a not very impressive job. On one occasion he informed Brothers, abruptly, "You may call yourself my Nephew." It was a title which Brothers's enemies received with joy, even while his disciples anxiously tried to explain that, as Richard Brothers traced his descent from James the brother of the Lord, and as the son of a brother must necessarily be a nephew, it was an entirely proper title. The divine Uncle gave him permission to correct the many inaccuracies of the Bible that seemed to contradict the new prophecies: "There is no man under the whole Heaven that I discover the errors of the Bible to, and reveal a knowledge how to correct them." Casually, while they are discussing one of Daniel's more obscure visions, the Lord remarks, "I passed by this part with Daniel," leaving it to be understood that Brothers now possessed revelation denied even to Daniel. Uncle and nephew together work through the manifold prophecies of the Old and New Testaments which, once enigmatic, are now shown to apply specifically to this newest and last of prophets. His present humble position is touched upon and explained: "My present poverty is no obstacle to my future elevation, neither is it of much concern to myself for the time of my being revealed with power from Heaven is nigh. The certainty of my elevation to the greatest Principality that ever will be in the world cannot be prevented by the rise or fall of any power on Earth." It is impressed upon him that he must remain modest, even though kings come to kiss his feet: "Although I am to be great, far above any Prince on earth and cannot be destroyed by man, I'll not provoke any but endeavour, by a peaceable conduct, civility and fair words to make all men believe."

The high destiny held out to him was to be the Messiah of the Jews, the man who would lead not only the known Jews of Europe, but the mysterious Lost Tribes back to the Holy Land where he would rebuild the Temple of Solomon and reign in splendor until the end of things. With admirable precision he calculated the opening of the Millennium, basing his calculations on the ages of biblical personages as supplied by revelation to him. Unlike so many prophets, he does not place the beginning years or even months away: On July 1, in the following year of 1795, he would be in Constantinople at the head of a huge army, preparing for the final march on Jerusalem. But even this high destiny could be—not frustrated, certainly—but postponed if the present wicked war were not immediately ended. But God cannot allow even this postponement and therefore, unless the combatants make immediate peace, hideous will be the fate that will fall upon the heads of the kings and people of Europe. Here Brothers indulges in the traditional game of identifying the beasts and monsters that prowl and roar and rend in both Daniel and Revelation. And a musty list it is for posterity, since most upon it are simply titles now: the king of Sardinia, the king of Prussia, the Russian emperor—gorgeous robes upon dusty skeletons. Here and there the reader recognizes a figure that momentarily steps out from the background: The head of the ten-headed monster that was killed and brought again to life is the Restoration in the shape of Charles II; Daniel's Lion is poor, mad George III; the Leopard is Louis XVI, whose death on the scaffold Brothers pophesied again and again.

The first edition of *Revealed Knowledge* was an immediate and astonishing success. Those who feared the ravening hunger of the French revolutionaries as well as those who regarded them as the builders of Utopia bought the book and feverishly examined it for portents of the future. Emigrés who waited daily, hourly, in expectation of a return to France together with would-be revolutionaries who longed to set England alight, the usual feather-brained ladies of fashion who eagerly picked up any novelty, together with gaunt-faced Puritans who regarded Brothers as indeed the Lord's prophet—all these found their way to his lodgings in Paddington. All were received in the same somewhat abstracted manner. Brothers seemed wholly unsurprised at the stir he was making; he would perhaps have deemed it blasphemous to be otherwise than calm, for had not the Lord assured him that fame and power and greatness would be his, and that within the twelvemonth? So the callers were brought in and one after the other introduced themselves to the prophet. The interviews followed a set pattern. First Brothers asked if his visitor had read his book. If the answer was negative, the interview terminated immediately. But if the visitor had done his homework—or was wise enough to say that he had—then he was treated to a rambling, somewhat disconnected lecture. It was an entirely one-sided affair. Any attempt at discussion aroused the prophet's irritation, and should the visitor be foolish enough actually to contradict or display incredulity, the gentle manner and soft voice would disappear completely, the monomaniac would peer forth with the pale glare of the fanatic, and the voice would rise, discordant.

By the winter of 1794, Brothers's fame was so widespread, his disciples so many, so bizarre and so enthusiastic, that the great Thunderer itself, the London *Times*, paused in its task of organizing the world and bent a piercing glance on the prophet of Paddington Street. "This extraordinary character, having for some months past been the theme of the public in general, induces us to state some particulars concerning him which, we trust, will gratify the curiosity of our readers," it announced portentously, and went on to give an astonishingly favorable account of the man. Newspaper muckraking was already a fine art in the London of the 1790's but the most dedicated raker could find nothing morally detrimental about Brothers's past except the story of an abandoned wife. And even here he appeared as victim, the subject for sympathetic—or, at worst sardonic—attention. While still in the navy he had married but was obliged to rejoin his ship on the same day; returning to England some years later, he found his wife the mother of a flourishing family. The bawdy laughed and turned to other, more interesting transgressors; the sympathetic agreed that he had shown almost saintlike patience.

The *Times* openly raised the obvious question of Brothers's mental state. Was he simply a lunatic, the same as the poor wretches in Bedlam who thought they were Julius Caesar or the Archangel Gabriel? The question was irrelevant, the *Times* declared. "Let him be a madman, enthusiast or hypocrite, he must be considered as the most extraordinary man this century has produced. To cause the most distinguished divines to hesitate in their opinions, respecting the truth or falsehood of his scriptural expositions, is surely in an untutored man, a most wonderful trait of character." The writer remarked on those aspects of Brothers's character which surprised all who came in contact with him, friends and enemies alike: his calmness, gentleness, and courtesy. "As a madman, there is such an urbanity of manners, such a piety of principle, such forbearance of self-gratification that we think it impossible for all the faculty, versed in all the different kind of manias, to define the nature of Mr. Brothers's madness." He was compared very favorably, indeed, with the usual run of religious fanatics. "Such persons are generally impelled to the most strenuous and even violent of bodily and mental efforts: their faculties are in a state of perpetual agitation: their passions seldom find a quiescent pause from continual excitement. But, contrary to this, Mr. Brothers has appeared to be divested of the common passions of nature—ever calm, ever collected, ever affable and communicative . . ." [38]

Not a madman, not a hypocrite, not a fanatic—the negatives left, it seemed, only one conclusion: that Richard Brothers was the long awaited prophet who would finally unravel the mystery of Revelation, the herald of the Millennium. The press around him increased. His disciples became ever more vociferous, aggressive and confident. And by no means were all of them idle or unbalanced. George Ribeau, a highly successful bookseller in the Strand, came forward to act as his publisher. Brothers had been obliged to pay for the publication of his first revelation. Ribeau took over publication of all the successive pamphlets emanating from the prophet, and was proud to describe himself as "Bookseller to the Prince of Hebrews." From Hull came the plump and prosperous merchant C. Coggan to engage in the pamphlet war on the Prince's behalf. He himself was in the prophecy business, having already warned Prime Minister Pitt, the king, the queen, the Duke of Gloucester, and whoever else would take in his letters, of the dire consequences of England's foreign policy. He, too, knew the mockery of the skeptic: "On the 13th of March 1791 I had a peculiar manifestation of some events, which I knew would have their accomplishment. I communicated the circumstance to some religious acquaintances who treated me and my manifestation with contempt and like swine they turned upon me and rent me." [39] Coggan felt that his espousal of the prophet's cause had even greater weight, since he had at first rejected the *Revealed Knowledge*, ". . . owing, I suppose, to some preconceptions of my own regarding myself." If he, Coggan, could not be the Messiah, he could at least be the Messiah's forerunner, preparing the sinful world for His coming. He developed an ingenious line of argument to substantiate Brothers's claim of divine guidance. The prophet had announced that his Messiahship would begin, and he would be revealed to the Hebrews as their Prince, on the day that, by the power of God, he turned a rosewood staff into a serpent. Those who mocked were denying the Omnipotent's ability to perform such a simple task, Coggan declared, neatly drawing attention away from the question as to whether the Omnipotent had, in fact, granted such a power to his nephew.

But the most outstanding of Richard Brothers's recruits was the great Oriental scholar and member of Parliament, Nathaniel Brassey Halhed, the man who gave the world the immense philological discovery of the common Aryan source of European languages. Regarding the contrast between Halhed's career and that of Brothers, regarding the sorry spectacle of a scholar and intellectual of his standing wallowing in the Gothic extravagances of his master, posterity is granted the clearest possible indication that religious conviction has nothing whatsoever to do with intelligence, that the wildest cult will yet find devotees among men on grounds they would scorn to apply to their most trivial everyday activities. Halhed belonged firmly to that class of men which included Justin Martyr, Joachim of Flora, Knipperdolling, Major General Harrison—men who seemed able to convince themselves of the miraculous by a deliberate suspension of the intellect. The strong romantic streak in Halhed probably predisposed him to accept the Prince of the Hebrews. He had been jilted as a young man—the girl threw him over in favor of his great friend Richard Brinsley Sheridan—and he promptly went off to India. But instead of hunting animals he hunted words and eventually attracted the attention of the great Warren Hastings. It was Hastings who suggested to him the craggiest of intellectual tasks—the translation of the British law code into the vernacular—and before leaving India, Halhed had published a Bengali grammar and even set up the first British press for the printing of Bengali.

Back in England in 1770, this formidable man became M.P. for Lymington. He had been in Parliament for nearly a quarter of a century before he fell under Brothers's influence. The initial contact was understandable, given Halhed's interest in intellectual detective work. Brothers had announced that the Millennium was imminent and, using the figures that he supplied, Halhed set about making his own calculations, ironing out the many inconsistencies to give a logical answer. Basic to his reasoning was that interpretation of biblical time which was to be so popular in the nineteenth and twentieth centuries: "With the Lord one day is like a thousand years and a thousand years like one day," the Second Epistle of Peter had incautiously remarked. Therefore, Halhed argued, the "week" of the Creation had, in fact, lasted seven thousand years, and just as the Creator had rested upon the seventh day, so it was divinely appointed that all mankind must rest at the end of six thousand years of labor and pain. Further abstruse calculations, drawing very freely upon Revelation and Daniel, convinced Halhed that the Millennium "will commence, on the 19th of November next (1795), at or about sunrise, in the latitude of Jerusalem."

It was precisely the kind of meticulous, calm reasoning which distinguished Brothers's own calculations, and whether he would have welcomed it or not, Halhed was henceforth firmly identified in the popular mind with the prophecies of the Prince of the Hebrews. Halhed, in fact, welcomed the identification, throwing himself into the spirited pamphleteering war that broke over the unheeding head of Richard Brothers. In Parliament and out of it, the doughty Member for Lymington defended his master, belaboring his opponents with Greek and Latin, rummaging through the sacred writings to find yet more parallels and foreshadowings that could apply only to Brothers.

Brothers took no part in the war of words. He might, perhaps, have been grateful or warmed by the championship of such as Coggan and Halhed, but such activities were almost an irrelevance—his divine path was clearly set before him, and the carping of pedantic academics could not prevent him from reaching the glittering goal. There was much work to be done in so short a space of time—the work of converting the world, persuading the nations to place their power at the disposal of God's Prophet, and above all, turning the great ones of the earth from their blind paths which could end only in destruction. He went personally to Parliament and handed in a letter for the Speaker, outlining the terrible things in store for mankind if God's word were not obeyed, and waited patiently, calmly, for the answer. "In a few minutes after a messenger returned with my own letter who treated me, in such a public place particularly, with unfeeling contempt and uncivility. The Lord God spoke to me instantly, on being ordered to go about my business, and said—Get away, get away from this place. Be under no concern, it was not you that was despised and ordered away but me in your person that sent you." [40] There, for a moment, the mask drops and the reader shares, vicariously, the cringing sense of shame at the public humiliation—"Get away. Get away from this place"—the frantic speed with which the wounded ego disguised itself as the voice of God.

But the great work went on. There were the visions to be copied down and sent via "the Penny Post, according to the directions I received on that head by Revelation from God," almost certainly the first time in history that the Almighty communicated through the post office. And splendid and terrible were those visions. There was the vision of the Queen of England "coming towards me slow—trembling—afraid"; the vision of her husband, the irascible George, yielding his throne and royal ornaments to Richard Brothers, "not with grief or reluctance to give, but with evident satisfaction." The Lord took him at two P.M. to the Bank of England and there announced that THERE IS ONE OF TWENTY, an enigmatic statement that neither Uncle nor nephew troubled to define. Meanwhile the Thunders roared and had to be interpreted, there were the endless rich confusions of Daniel and John to be explored, and every reference to the Prince of the Hebrews and his great mission to be extracted, noted, and prepared for the second edition of *Revealed Knowledge*. The Lord had a special message relevant to this edition: "He shewed it to me in a vision, ready printed, holding it up by one leaf and shaking all the others open while he pronounced in strong, clear words THERE IS NOTHING IN THIS BOOK THAT THE ENGLISH LAW CAN TAKE HOLD OF—SO says Him that Isaiah the Prophet calls Wonderful Counsellor." [41]

But Richard Brothers, it seemed, had either misunderstood or misheard the divine message, for the English law promptly took a most vigorous hold both on him and on his book. On the morning of March 4, 1795, just three months before the Prince of Hebrews was scheduled to march triumphantly into his heritage, there was a thunderous knocking on the door of number 47 Paddington Street. The alarmed landlady opened the door to disclose two king's messengers, resplendent in the dingy street, bearing a warrant for the arrest of ex-Lieutenant Brothers. The charge? High treason. Despite the presence of a large and threatening crowd which rapidly collected, the messengers took their prisoner away. It was to be eleven years before he regained his freedom, eleven years spent in the living death of a lunatic asylum because the law, in fact, could find him guilty of nothing, but politics demanded his incarceration.

The immediate cause of his arrest was a paragraph which he had inserted in the second edition of his book. "The Lord God commands me to say to you, George III, King of England, that immediately on my being revealed in London to the Hebrews as their Prince and to all nations as their Governor, your crown must be delivered up to me, that all your power and authority may cease." The extent of Brothers's fame or notoriety can be gauged by the fact that it penetrated even into the darkened mind of George III and there touched off a wholly unpredictable explosion. Considering the invective that was continually hurled against the royal family, notably by such satirists as Rowlandson and Gillray, it is curious that the king should be stirred to such depths of rage by Brothers's casual paragraph. That rage was not only sufficient to have the prophet taken up, but was to pursue him with unrelenting malice throughout the years of his imprisonment.

Brothers was taken before the Privy Council the following day. The Lord Chancellor, Loughborough, conducted the trial—for trial it was, carried out in secret, without jury or defending counsel. Brothers was grilled ruthlessly; mockingly his judges asked what life would be like in the Millennium, how he would conduct himself when King of the World. Brothers replied to the charges and questions quietly, courteously, patiently, and the privy councilors went through the same change that the Westminster Guardians had gone through five years earlier: "I see nothing in the words of Mr. Brothers but what is sensible and proper," Loughborough said at last. "He may withdraw."

It was impossible to convict this calm, gentle man of treason, but there was still the intention of removing him from the public. The decision to incarcerate Brothers was by no means undertaken only to placate the king. Throughout the previous months, while the prophet's rocket fame had soared to its brief and brilliant height, Prime Minister William Pitt had grown ever more perturbed at the role that Brothers could play—or be induced to play—in the turmoil of contemporary English politics. Tom Paine and his pernicious *Rights of Man* had been chased out of Britain, but the revolutionary ferment was still working violently throughout the country. There were riots in the great industrial cities of the North, and middle-class intellectuals were singing the praises of republicanism. In the social chaos, with the conventional norms of behavior obscured or shattered, even such a bizarre message as the Prince of Hebrews brought might unexpectedly act as a catalyst. The outbreak of war with France had led to a certain closing of the ranks, but that war promised to be long, hard, and bitter, and Pitt wanted no unnecessary complications in his rear. Richard Brothers, the Prince of the Hebrews who had come to announce the end of all earthly governments, was safer out of the way. A cruder age would have solved the problem with rope or ax; the Privy Council set up a commission *de lunatico inquirendo*, which obligingly found the subject to be insane. On May 5 he was moved to a private asylum.

The choice of a private asylum was probably that of William Pitt, for the prime minister was a humane man, forced to take an unpleasant path only to avoid a possibly greater evil. Certainly the money to pay for Brothers's "treatment" must have come from official sources, for as a lunatic, he automatically lost the naval half pay that was his only source of income. The owner of the asylum had a financial interest in his continued presence, and he was therefore well looked after physically—in marked contrast to the wretched inmates of the public Bedlams. A few years after his own imprisonment, a public inquiry revealed that a certain William Norris, inmate of a Bedlam, had been chained by the throat, waist, and ankles to an iron post for twelve years.

But a private asylum not only assuaged the consciences of those who placed him there; it effectively kept him out of the public eye. The news of his arrest and detention had met with a storm of protest. Brothers's major prophecy—that on July 1, 1795, he would be in Constantinople at the head of a huge army—had still to be fulfilled. There was still time for the thrilling event to come about.

So, at least, thought Halhed. Brothers had promised him that, in the imminent Millennium, he would have the choice of being "Governor-General of India or President of the Board of Control in England," and on March 31, Halhed rose in the House of Commons to pay off his future debt. In an impassioned speech, he sought to clear Brothers both of the charge of lunacy, under which he was now detained, and of the graver charge of treason. In rejecting the latter, he made use of a curious analogy, considering his belief in Brothers's sanity. "If I were to assert that, on some future day, I should ascend to the top of Saint Paul's and from thence fly over London and in sight of all its inhabitants to Westminster Abbey, after which the King must seat me on his throne and kiss my great toe: most people, I allow, would think me mad. But I certainly should not dream of being apprehended for treason." Richard Brothers had propounded an almost identical proposition, Halhed argued. "He has said that he shall be revealed by a sign visible to that of Moses, viz turning a common hazel stick into a serpent—a fact fully as impossible to all human comprehension as my flying from Saint Paul's to Westminster—and that he shall then be accompanied by an angel in the form of a flame of fire: after which the king must do so and so." [42]

Parliament listened in stony silence while Brothers's disciple argued that his master could not be guilty of treason because he could not take over the crown of England until he had performed an impossibility. Halhed was unable even to find a seconder for his motion that a copy of Brothers's book should be placed on the Speaker's table so that Members could at least read what the prophet himself had said. That speech on March 31 virtually ended Halhead's long and honorable career as a politician. Parliament tended to cherish its eccentrics, but by the time of the next election the whole Brothers affair had come to its pitiful end, and Halhed was indelibly branded as the champion of a madman. He never again stood for Parliament.

July 1, 1795, arrived, and Richard Brothers was still in his lunatic cell. The thousands who had breathlessly waited for him to begin his triumphal march to the East underwent the inevitable violent reaction. Halhed was among those who now publicly execrated the one-time hero—but again the human capacity for self-deception proved capable of withstanding the most logical demonstration of error. In Scotland a young lawyer, John Finlayson, heard of the obloquy and mockery that was now heaped upon the

Prince of the Hebrews. Finlayson was a highly successful man—he was able to sell his practice for some £25,000—but even a fine legal brain did not guarantee its owner immunity from the contagion of fanaticism. He had closely followed Brothers's brief career as prophet, had read his books and Halhed's pamphlets, and was convinced that here indeed was the Messiah who would bring about the beginning of the Millennium. The fact that the Messiah was in London and not Constantinople on July 1 was entirely irrelevant to his divine claim: It was the fault of the people who had refused to believe, the fault of the Jews who remained blind to their Prince's advent. Indeed, the very fact that he was in a lunatic asylum immeasurably strengthened his claim. For a lunatic was, for all civil purposes, regarded as dead, and Richard Brothers could therefore, without impiety, be regarded as the slain Lamb of Revelation.

So young Finlayson argued and prepared himself for one of the most astonishingly selfless of roles: At his own cost and almost without hope of return, he was to be the master's mouthpiece for the rest of his life. He sold his practice and came to London in order to be closer to the imprisoned Brothers. He was a religious fanatic—but he was also a canny Scots lawyer, and he was able to make a good living for himself in London, marrying and bringing up a family perfectly successfully. But all his energies were directed to one end: the interpretation of the master's message to the world and, above all, the securing of his master's freedom.

Meanwhile, Brothers in his asylum was probably as happy as he had ever been in his life. His had always been a solitary, inward-turning existence; cut off now from the world, supplied with regular meals and reasonable lodgings, he turned his mind to the development and elaboration of his great mission. Like the Fifth Monarchists, he speculated on the day to day details of the Millennium. But where they had been largely concerned with arid legal concepts, he concentrated—like the author of Revelation before him—on the physical building of the New Jerusalem. All Christendom was to take part in the mighty project, and edicts were drawn up ascribing this or that area of responsibility to the various monarchs. The Scandinavian kings were to provide three hundred shiploads of timber each, together with immense quantities of nails, hammers, and saws. Other monarchs, including those of Russia, Prussia, and Spain, were to provide tents, tens of thousands of shovels and ploughs, seeds, architects, laborers—the latter in particular being required for the demolishment of the pyramids, "idle monuments of ostentation." The Prince reserved to himself the task of actually designing New Jerusalem. Somewhat illogically, the city was to have four cathedrals—presumably with a bishop for each, 20 colleges, 320 streets, 47 private palaces, and 56 squares, the largest being the Garden of Eden at the center. The plans for the New Jerusalem were not theoretical, but a very concrete reality, being engraved on nine large sheets and offered to the public at £38 the set. It was the devoted John Finlayson who arranged the humdrum details of engraving and publishing the massive project, all at his own expense.

Two years after his incarceration in Doctor Fisher's private asylum, Brothers suffered the last and most poignant intrusion of reality. On a spring morning in 1797, there appeared at the breakfast table a young and pretty girl, a Miss Frances Cott, daughter of a clergyman. She had tried to commit suicide in a momentary fit of depression and had been discreetly hustled away. Brothers was a few months short of his fortieth birthday when what appears to have been the first real love of his life almost succeeded in dispelling the clouds gathering ever thicker around his mind. Almost—but not quite: Frances Cott could not be the pretty but otherwise thoroughly ordinary girl she appeared to be. A suitable bride for the Prince of the Hebrews—and already his eager mind had leaped over all intervening difficulties—could not but have the very highest antecedents. The daughter of an Essex clergyman was "the recorded daughter of David and Solomon," she who had been promised to him from all eternity, the future Queen of the Hebrews. The fantasy was spun within his own mind in richer and ever more exotic colors—but not a word of it was uttered to Miss Cott. He feared, perhaps, a rebuff; more likely, he was impatiently awaiting that moment when the girl would see her own manifest destiny and throw herself at his feet. Meanwhile he smiled and bowed, listened to the small talk, and awaited the moment of revelation. It must have been with a sickening sense of failure and loss that he learned one day, quite casually, that her family had come and fetched her away. She was to be married. In something like despair, the Prince of the Hebrews sat down and wrote her a series of passionate letters, one of which Finlayson published out of an indiscreet sense of loyalty. It is doubtful if little Miss Cott ever received the letters, ever knew what fantasies concerning her had been boiling and bubbling in the mind of the solemn man in early middle age who had stared at her across the dining table. The pathetic affair was added to the legend; he protested to the Privy Council, vehemently complained to all who would listen of this, the greatest evil that had ever been done in the history of the earth, an evil that would propagate greater evil still, for who could calculate the effect of breaking the foredoomed tie between the Prince and Princess of the Hebrews.

Then, as suddenly as it had begun, the whole thing was over. Miss Cott vanished into the lumber of the past, and his attention turned to the New Jerusalem. Edicts and prescriptions were dispatched to the loyal Finlayson specifying what headgear was to be worn in the New Age, designing the flag of "God's Kingdom" in minute detail, enunciating the final truth about astronomy. Calmness and order returned to his life, which was certainly preferable to that of poor Finlayson, proclaiming the kingdom while harassed by ever increasing debts, torn between loyalty to his family and loyalty to the Messiah. But there was no real doubt but that working for the New Jerusalem took precedence over all. William Pitt died in 1806 and Finlayson promptly petitioned Pitt's successor. The warrant for treason was withdrawn and, encouraged, Finlayson approached his fellow countryman, the lord chancellor Erskine, petitioning for Brothers's release and the withdrawal of the lunacy verdict. Erskine was embarrassed. He agreed that Mr. Brothers could indeed be safely released, but he would not—could not—suppress the lunacy charge, virtually pleading with Finlayson "as his countryman" not to press the point, because there were "still some scruples in high quarters." The anger of King George

III was as hot now as it had been eleven years ago, and while he lived, there was no likelihood of the lunacy charge being dropped. Erskine admitted that Brothers would be unable to draw his half pay while still legally a lunatic, and he therefore proposed a pension of £300 per year as an act of grace. Finlayson, aware of the mounting burden of debts, aware that the cost of supporting the master would now fall almost exclusively upon him, agreed. Triumphantly, he hastened to the asylum bearing the order of release, and shortly afterward Richard Brothers stood blinking in the April sunshine, a free man after eleven years imprisonment.

Brothers was to live for another seventeen years. He continued to spin his fantasies, and the faithful Finlayson arranged their publication and defended his master in the intervals between attempts to extract money from the government. Bitterly, he regretted that gentleman's agreement with his fellow Scotsman; for a matter of weeks later, the government fell and the new chancellor, Lord Eldon, declined to honor a personal arrangement made by his predecessor. Nine years after Brothers's release, his debt to Finlayson amounted to over £2,000.

The Prince of the Hebrews died in 1823, and Finlayson was with him at the end. Late at night, Brothers summoned this most faithful of disciples, took his right hand in his, and asked him to swear that his sword and hammer were ready to defend and build the New Jerusalem. And Finlayson, as steadfastly loyal to the man as that man was loyal to an idea, so swore. "He seemed pleased and, a few moments after, about ten o'clock at night, breathed his last, no one being present but myself." As his last gesture, Finlayson buried his Master at his own expense—and then continued his attempt to get the promised money out of the government. His claim on Brothers's estate now amounted to £5,710; after four years of battling he received some £300 and promise of more. He never received more, although, in 1900, fifty-six years after his own death, his heirs claimed that the government debt now amounted to £80,000 with compound interest. That money was to prove fairy gold, as substantial as the dream of Richard Brothers.

CHAPTER VI

●

THE SIXTH
TRUMPETER

(i) *The Search for Shiloh*

In pondering his divine role as Prince of the Hebrews and speculating on the mystery of how he, an undoubted Anglo-Saxon, could inherit a Semitic throne, Richard Brothers evolved a complex theory regarding the movements of the Jews after their dispersal in the first century. The two tribes of Judah had distributed themselves throughout Europe, he argued, and it was from these that modern Jews were descended. But the ten tribes from the northern Kingdom of Israel had made their way to Britain. These ten tribes were the true "children of Israel" with whom Jehovah had originally made his covenant, and because that covenant was eternal, it extended to the descendants of those tribes—who were now known as Saxons, or sons of Isaac.

Much of Brothers's energy was expended in awakening the Saxons to the nature of their Israelite heritage, and others followed him, developing ever more ingenious ways of identifying the lost ten tribes with the inhabitants of the British Isles. Later, by natural extension, all descendants of the Anglo-Saxons overseas were included in the heritage, not least the breakaway descendants known as Americans—a fact that was to have profound future effect. But in the early nineteenth century, Brothers's theory remained in the domain of scholars, appealing to those who liked juggling with semantics, maps, and chronologies. Left to such as these, the Christian Israelite movement, as it came to be called, would have remained an arid academic exercise. The fact that it did not was due entirely to the Devonshire prophetess, Joanna Southcott, who picked up Brothers's cerebral creation and infused it with her own ebullient personality.

Joanna Southcott was the working model of a psychiatrist's theorem. From the story of her first love affair down to the grotesque phantom pregnancy that set a seal on her cult and cost her her life, sexual frustration was an obvious factor. But frustrated maiden ladies are common enough, while founders of religion are rare—and Joanna founded a genuine religion. It was irrelevant whether her frustrated desires drove her to fashion a camouflage, much as Richard Brothers's did, or whether a genuine religious impulse found expression in sexuality. The result was the creation of a unique complex of belief that possessed a powerful magnetism and proved to have great powers of endurance, for it retained its essence while changing its form again and again.

Joanna was born in 1750, the daughter of an unsuccessful Devonshire farmer. She went into domestic service, working hard and cheerfully for a number of employers. Nothing in the slightest distinguished her during the first forty-odd years of her life, except perhaps her inability to establish a normal relationship with men. There was no reason why she should not have done so, for she was a bustling, buxom, cheery soul, predestined, it would seem, to preside over the hearth and board of some fortunate man. But every timid move on the part of herself or some potential swain, was blocked by hesitances and inhibitions which came at last to be taken for religious emotion.

She was in her midforties when her talent began to manifest itself. She found that she had the ability to produce an endless stream of doggerel verse of a quasi-religious nature. The subject matter was, for the most part, political—an unusual interest for a semi-educated domestic servant—interspersed with local affairs. Gradually the verses took on a prophetic nature, and the sheer mass of them ensured that an impressive number hit, or at least approached, the target. She was in service in Exeter at the time, and in the claustrophobic provincial society of the day, she began to gain a considerable reputation. She became convinced that she was a woman out of the ordinary and began to hunger for official, ecclesiastical recognition. The voluminous prophecies were parceled off and submitted to the clergy—up to and including the august bench of bishops—with the demand that they should pronounce, one way or the other, upon their authenticity. Most of the clergy refused to have anything to do with the matter, but a few of them were sufficiently impressed—or at least had the honesty to admit uncertainty regarding the nature of her gift—to give a respectable ecclesiastic background to her work. Again, as with Brothers, the cataclysmic events in France served to give purpose and fire to her mission. In a collapsing society, people hungered for guidance, and just as Richard Brothers's books were snatched up, so were Joanna's effusions, achieving the equivalent of best-seller status. Buried within her otherwise commonplace mind was the genuine skill of the seer, the same skill that allowed such as the Delphic Oracle or Nostradamus to wrap up their enigmatic pronouncements in a form that favored almost any interpretation.

In May 1802, Joanna began the great work of "sealing" the faithful. The Millennium was imminent, she announced, and only those 144,000 who were sealed in the manner prescribed in Revelation would enjoy the thousand years of earthly paradise. The seal she adopted consisted of a piece of paper, inscribed with a mystic verse and signed by Joanna, to which the believer put his own signature. The paper was then folded over and sealed on the back with a brass stamp, bearing the letters IC and two stars. Joanna had found the stamp while sweeping out a house, and believed it had been brought to her supernaturally.

Over the following six years, thousands were sealed—probably many, many more than prescribed in Revelation. The great work was eventually brought to a sudden and rather embarrassing stop when one of those so sealed to salvation—a certain Mary Bateman—was taken by the authorities and hanged for forgery. But already the work of prophecy and sealing was becoming less important as there dawned in Joanna's mind the intimation that she had a far greater role to play in the cosmic drama. The Almighty now spoke to her direct, and it was from this unimpeachable source that she learned that she was the "woman clothed with the sun" identified in Revelation, the same who gave birth to a child which was snatched up to heaven out of reach of the Dragon. Was this child, perhaps, to be purely symbolical? Not so, she announced triumphantly in her book, *The Third Book of Wonders.* Her divine Instructor had informed her that "This year (1814) in the sixty-sixth year of thy age, thou shalt have a son by the power of the Most High, which if the Jews receive as their Prophet, Priest and King then I will restore them to their own land, and cast out the heathen for their sakes." [43] The child was to be called Shiloh, after an enigmatic statement in the Old Testament that the days of the Gentiles would not commence "until Shiloh comes."

Throughout the summer and winter of 1814, the imminent coming of Shiloh was a dominant topic in England. The religious were indignant, the bawdy delighted. The *Times* hurled its thunders at "this deluded, elderly virgin" who had dared, quite specifically, to equate her condition with that of the Mother of God. There was talk of having her prosecuted. Crowds began to gather regularly outside her London home when news spread that the sixty-five-year-old virgin was, in fact, pregnant. Not the least astonishing aspect of Joanna's ministry was that she had, first, been able to find respectable ecclesiastics to testify to her divine role and now found a number of eminently respectable physicians to testify to the physical reality of her pregnancy.

The end had an aspect of macabre comedy. A few days before, reality seems to have broken through and, weeping, she told the disciples thronging her room that it was all, perhaps, a delusion. The pathetic, hidden plea to be allowed to return to the real world was swept aside with robust assurances that she was suffering the reaction usual to any woman near childbirth. By the evening of December 26, it was evident that she was dying, but the faithful even now were undismayed. Had she not assured them, years before, that she would take on the appearance of death for three days?

She died early on the following morning, but the disciples refused to allow the body to be taken away until the three days had passed. The doctors were called in again—not to preside over a death, but to prepare for a birth, and it was not until the body was opened to disclose an empty womb that the brutal fact of delusion was accepted.

But not for long. Joanna Southcott's body was taken, unhonored, to its grave, but Joanna Southcott's creation marched triumphantly on to immortality. Belatedly, the faithful remembered that the divine child in Revelation had been snatched up to heaven to save him from the Dragon. This, of course, was what had happened to Shiloh, mystic child of Joanna. He, too, had been wafted to the safety of heaven and would, sooner rather than later, return to gather in the faithful and lead them to Jerusalem. Over the next generation, successive Southcottian prophets arose to proclaim the message that Shiloh was about to return, that the children of Israel (Anglo-Saxon branch) were about to be led back into Jerusalem and so open the Millennium.

The Southcottian sect flourished but was no more immune to heresy and schism than the established religions. Each heresy that was strong enough to survive created its own orthodoxy, adapted what was required from the central stock of concepts, and drew apart from the rest. In the 1870's one of these fragments rooted itself in the port of Chatham, Kent, gave itself the exotic title of the New House of Israel, and quietly awaited the coming of a Leader.

(ii) The Coming of the Trumpeter

Late in the evening of October 13, 1875, a well-built, good-looking young man in the uniform of a private of the 16th Foot (the

Bedfordshire regiment) knocked on the door of a small, painfully respectable house in Chatham. The lady of the household, a Mrs. Head, cautiously opened the door. Respectable householders in Chatham had as little as possible to do with the soldiery that swarmed in the town, but Mrs. Head, instead of sending for the police, actually asked the strange young man in after a few moments' conversation, so magnetic was his personality. He was about thirty-five years old and spoke with a faint American accent; he introduced himself as James White and talked earnestly and vehemently, "seriously enquiring the way to salvation," as Mrs. Head bitterly described it long afterwards. She and her husband were trustees of the New House of Israel and were eager to gain converts—sufficiently so for Mrs. Head to break a basic code of English respectability and invite a total stranger into her home. The total membership of the New House of Israel, after a series of secessions, schisms and heresies probably did not then amount to more than a score.

Nevertheless, despite their eagerness to spread the gospel, the Heads had no intention of being stampeded into accepting all who asked. Private White wanted to be enrolled on the spot: the trustees insisted that he should think about it and gave him a copy of the Book of Laws, which outlined their faith and indicated what was demanded of the faithful. Two days later White returned, more eager than ever, well rehearsed in the catechism. The Heads were delighted to accept this forceful male convert into a society that was rather heavily weighted in favor of the elderly and female, and they agreed to enroll him. Private White thereupon added his name to the roll of members and, as he did so, glanced at Mrs. Head and said, with great deliberation, "Keep nothing from me, for I mean to make a speedy work."

It was a curious statement which Mrs. Head interpreted as the enthusiasm of the convert. A little over two months later, however, the too-trusting trustees discovered exactly what Private James meant. He announced that he was the appointed Messenger of the Lord and therefore the man intended, by divine command, for the vacant office of Leader. Indignantly, the Heads exerted their authority and announced his immediate expulsion. But during the two months that the eloquent, forceful Private White had been a member he had fascinated, and then completely dominated, his fellow Israelites. He was expelled, but took all the other members with him; the wretched Mr. and Mrs. Head found themselves in the poignant position of being the sole representatives of orthodoxy. Thereafter they drifted plangently from the story, and their late co-religionists barely noticed their going. On December 26, 1875, Private James White was acknowledged as messenger and leader of the New House of Israel.

James White's origins were, and remained, wrapped in deliberate mystery. Probably he was an American: Years later an indignant English review of his mystic books claimed that he could not possibly be English. "There is an Occidental tang to his idioms: moreover, he writes 'rumors', 'savors', 'endeavors' " instead of using the letter "u" like a gentleman should. At one time White claimed to have been a bank clerk on the western coast of America, but on receiving the divine call, he promptly set out to cross the continent without food, money, or transport, relying for his sustenance on the same source as did Elijah. The story was only one of many he spun deliberately to confuse the public. He was fond of referring to himself as "the stranger," and shortly after becoming leader of the New and Latter House of Israel—as he now named the fissioned sect—he finally obliterated his obscure and secular past with a new identity and name. Henceforth, he was to be known as Jezreel— James Jershom Jezreel. The sonorous roll of biblical names certainly better suited his new style of prophet and Messenger of the Lord than did the pedestrian "White," and it was as Jezreelites that the members of his breakaway sect were to be known to history.

For Jezreel-White possessed in full the magnetism of the prophet. Three months after he installed himself as leader, he was drafted to India with his regiment and remained there for nearly six years. Nevertheless, so powerful an imprint had he made upon his followers during those three brief months that, faithfully, they obeyed the instructions he sent to them from eight thousand miles distant. Few prophets have labored under such a very heavy disadvantage as being obliged to fashion their creed by remote control; Jezreel turned it to advantage, wrapping himself in the glamorous aura of distance. His personality reached out to bind one follower in particular, the fifteen-year-old Clarissa Rogers who, with her thirteen-year-old sister Elizabeth, were to form with Jezreel a species of Holy Trinity. Elizabeth died, negating that particular prophecy, but Clarissa remained faithful to the memory of the handsome, fair-haired prophet, and it was her deep, unquestioning loyalty that was, in large part, to launch him as an international figure.

During his brief stay in Chatham, Jezreel had begun to write the copious "sermons" that were to form his scripture and testimony. He continued to write in India, words pouring from him, prolix if obscure. At intervals these sermons would be dispatched on the immensely long searoad back to England, to come into the hands of the faithful little band in Chatham. There they were printed and promulgated as the scriptures of the new religion under the title, *The Flying Roll*—a tortuous allusion to Zachariah Chapter V: "Then I lifted up my eyes and looked and beheld a Flying roll."

The text of *The Flying Roll* is almost unreadable; not the least remarkable aspect of the Jezreelites is how children, as well as adults, could memorize large chunks of this unutterably unmemorable work. It is reminiscent of Joanna's Southcott's writing at its worst, unreedemed by Joanna's occasional pithy observation or explicit prophecy. Jezreel adopted his own punctuation, scorning the use of paragraphs so that the eye hunts dizzily on, searching for a resting point that never comes. But the eccentric punctuation is itself a faithful reflection of the turgid flow of undifferentiated ideas. Quotations from Old and New Testaments are strung together with no apparent relationship except a fancified significance in some word. Interpretations are distorted to grotesque degrees. In reviewing *The Flying Roll*, the highly respectable Church of England periodical, *The Record*, lashed itself into a lather of indignation and contempt: "They [the sermons] have all the inconsequence of dreams: they have no more thread than a dictionary: they have no foundation in fact as prophecy . . . The absurdities are legion: words are used regardless of meaning: texts are torn from their contexts and whole paragraphs have as much consecutive meaning in them as syllables of Abracadabra . . ." [44]

It may, perhaps, have been the very phantasmagoric nature of *The Flying Roll* sermons that accounted for their success: They were, quite literally, occult writings from which almost any meaning could be distilled. There was, however, a detectable framework, for Jezreel adopted the chronology of Revelation. For the concept of the Fall and Original Sin, he drew freely from Joanna Southcott, adding a relish of his own. The Deity was both male and female, he claimed. The Female Immortal Spirit had come down into the world in the person of Eve, but when she sinned, the Spirit had promptly returned to heaven. This Female Spirit had, ever since, been seeking a vessel on earth which it could again inhabit. Jezreel's tumbling style makes it almost impossible to determine whether he believed that the entire body of the New and Latter House of Israel was "the Woman"; whether Jezreel's future wife would be that New Eve, or indeed whether Jezreel himself possessed a dual spirit. But the return of the Woman was an essential prerequisite for the Millennium.

Unlike most millenarians, Jezreel paid little attention to the political economy of paradise. He did, however, have the courage to postulate the physical nature of those who would survive, returning again to the Bible for authority. But in all the Scriptures, there was only one description of a resurrected, physical body, and that was the description of Christ at Emmaus. In seeking to convince his disciples, Christ had said, "Handle me and see, for a spirit hath not flesh and bones, as ye see me have." Blood was not mentioned, and therefore, Jezreel cloudily deduced, blood must itself be transformed before the physical body could enter on eternity. Jezreel described the process as "cleansing the blood" but did not specify the nature of the operation. Others would do that, with scandalous results.

The loyal Jezreelites in Chatham propagated the book with such devotion and diligence, peddling it from house to house, that the name of Jezreel began to be spread through the land. *The Record*, having demolished *The Flying Roll*, thought it worthwhile and of sufficient national importance to launch an attack upon the movement itself: "The doctrine contains in grotesque jumble almost every variety of gnostic error and is a strange tissue of absurdity in which vulgarity is shot with ignorance . . . yet holding the Bible in its hands it displays to the vexed and startled student a *Flying Roll* in which, it is claimed, God sends his message to men, before the end comes." [45]

For that was the central message of the Jezreelites, the prime cause for their sudden rapid growth: The time of the End was at hand. Jezreel addressed his book to "The Gentile churchs of all sects and denominations and to the lost tribe of the house of Israel," for at the very heart of his preaching was the concept of the literal, physical "ingathering of Israel" that must take place before the Millennium. According to Jezreel's calculations, mankind, in this last quarter of the nineteenth century, was living in the third watch of the eleventh hour of the sixth day. Drawing freely upon the calculations of his predecessors, rummaging as freely through the times, allegoric and prophetic, alluded to in the Bible, Jezreel came up with his own chronology for the last days. Using Archbishop Ussher's famous date of 4004 B.C. for the Creation, and adding six thousand years to that date to correspond with the six days in which God labored, it was simple enough to calculate the Millennium as beginning just before the year A.D. 2000. The normal human life span being what it was, it seemed that that date could possess only an academic interest for anyone living in the 1870's. Jezreel's confident eclecticism overcame that difficulty. Those who embraced the Jezreelite faith now—immediately— would be numbered among the 144,000. They would survive throughout the twentieth century, share with Christ the triumph and glory of the Second Coming at or about 1996, and enjoy the terrestrial paradise with him until A.D. 2996. There would then be a resurrection of those virtuous non-Jezreelites who had died before the Second Coming, the Last Judgment would take place and eternity commence.

Such was mankind's destiny as foreshadowed in the cluttered pages of *The Flying Roll*. Despite the growing fame—or notoriety—of its author's name, the little band in Chatham grew with painful slowness in the absence of its prophet. But one of the band had faith enough in the Messenger to take his teaching into foreign parts while he languished in India. In the spring of 1881, Clarissa Rogers, then just twenty years of age, parceled up some dozens of copies of the new scriptures and, quite alone, set sail for America. Her intention was limited and concrete: to gain converts who would provide funds for the new religion. Unconsciously, she was in the vanguard of the great transatlantic movement of cultural cross-fertilization.

Ever since the eighteenth century the millennial dream had possessed a curious potency for the small, predominantly rural communities that sprang up along the eastern seaboard of America and then spread westward. The conservative puritanism that was at the very core of their being, the bright badge of their defiance of a corrupt European aristocracy and priesthood, could only too easily turn into fanaticism and madness. The isolation of the communities under a vast and alien sky ensured conformity among their members, who were, for the most part, unsophisticated, a high proportion of them drawn from the peasant societies of Europe with their traditional preference of the miraculous to the mundane. The New World had dispensed with the tyranny of the established churches, but it had dispensed, too, with the social corrective and balance that a mature hierarchy could provide. The person most likely to place a religious imprint upon the surrounding society would not be a philosopher or theologian but a prophet—the wilder, the more likely to succeed. Some of the cults imported from Europe flourished wildly and then settled down to a serene development. This happened to the Anabaptists, whose turbulent career in Massachusetts in the seventeenth century, with Boston cast in the role of New Jerusalem, was an echo of the furor in Germany. By the nineteenth century, they had evolved into eminently respectable nonconformist sects, such as the Mennonites or the Amish, with their model farming communities.

Most of the imported millennial sects, however, knew a lurid but brief existence, a hectic flowering in the heady new climate of liberty.

In 1771, Ann Lee arrived from Manchester to found the Millennial Church, more commonly known as the Shakers. Whatever belief she privately held regarding her mission in the world, her followers insisted on regarding her as the second Incarnation of Christ—a curious reappearance of that long dead Montanist teaching that Christ had returned to his prophetess Priscilla in the guise of a woman. The members of the Bishop Hill Commune which emigrated from Sweden in 1846 were at least orthodox in that their reincarnation of Christ was a man. He was Eric Janson, who had brought his people to America to build the New Jerusalem but was murdered before work could start. The Rappites followed their leader, George Rapp, from Germany to Pennsylvania and finally to Indiana, confidently awaiting the Second Coming, which was expected to take place in Rapp's lifetime. A good, gentle man, he was as confident, as deceived, as his followers right up to the moment of his death: "If I did not know that the dear Lord meant that I should present you all to Him I should think my last moments had come," were almost his last words.[46] Even the comparatively late doctrine of Christian Israelites already had its following. John Wroe, a strange, savage, part illiterate, part inspired follower of Richard Brothers and Joanna Southcott, had made a missionary journey and added the concept of the ingathering of Israel to the already potent brew existing in New England.

When, therefore, little Clarissa Rogers descended from the boat in New York, anxiously superintending the removal of her baled books, she was not quite so isolated as she appeared to be. Awaiting her in New York was a Miss Easton, a lady who appears to have had private means and who was already a convert to the Christian Israel movement. Her house became Clarissa's headquarters, the lady herself rapidly becoming a devout believer in the Jezreelite version of the Christian Israel teaching after a few days acquaintance with her eloquent, vehement young guest. The two of them rapidly put into motion the technique of "publishing," which had already taken the name of Jezreel throughout the United

Kingdom and was to have such immense success later in the hands of the Jehovah's Witnesses. It was emphasized that one of a Jezreelite's duties was to bear witness to the truth and that the best means to this end was to persuade the unconverted to buy copies of *The Flying Roll*. Receipts probably did not cover costs, but they did help to close the gap, and placing a price on the book helped to ensure that the person who received it would actually read it.

Clarissa and Miss Easton presumably appointed agents, for an impressively large number of copies of *The Flying Roll* was distributed in New York during Clarissa's brief stay. One of the copies came into the hands of a certain Noah Drew, a prosperous farmer from Michigan who was so impressed by the argument that he visited the house of Miss Easton. There he seems to have been even more impressed by the personable Miss Rogers and lost no time in becoming a full member of the New and Latter House of Israel. Clarissa carried back with her to England a most warm and pressing invitation to visit the Drew household near Detroit. The invitation included, Noah Drew added with every indication of sincerity, her future husband James Jershom Jezreel.

For Private James White had just severed his connection with the British army and, returned to Chatham, was there awaiting his bride. Seven days after his formal discharge, they were married. Despite the prolixity of contemporary accounts both by and about the Jezreelites, curiously little has been recorded regarding the personal relationship of Jezreel and his wife. Clarissa had known him personally for less than five months before he was drafted to India. During his six-year absence, when their only means of contact was by mailboat over half a world away, she had passed from girlhood to remarkably attractive womanhood and had kept faith, though his memory must have grown very dim, indeed. Whatever he had said or promised to her during those five months in Chatham must have been very potent to have survived the natural erosion of lengthy separation. Only one clue was provided as to the attraction he held for her. On the marriage certificate, she adopted the name of Esther—the same name as the Jewish maiden who reigned as queen by the will of Ahasuerus and was instrumental in saving her people. From Clarissa Rogers to Queen Esther was a wide step, but not too wide for one who had faith in the Messenger.

But in the early months of their relationship, it was Clarissa–Esther who supported Jezreel, rather than Jezreel who raised up his wife. It was through her that the flattering invitation came from Noah Drew in America, an invitation that not only urged them to come and proselytize in the New World, but also offered them their fares. England seemed to have little to offer an ex-soldier whose character was classed, damningly, as "Indifferent" upon his discharge papers and for some months the newly married couple had pursued a dreary, indeterminate life in and around Chatham. Noah Drew's generous action opened up the New World to them. In April 1882, they set sail across the Atlantic, again accompanied by the precious baled copies of Jezreel's book, and from New York made their way to Michigan. The flame of the New and Latter House of Israel, after guttering almost to extinction, was about to flare into life.

In the early years of the nineteenth century, Michigan lagged behind in the population race. In the closing years of the century it caught up with, and then swiftly passed, the national average—Detroit doubled its population in each of three successive decades. A very high proportion of the people were foreign born, something like a quarter of the state's population of 1,600,000 having immigrated from Britain, Germany, or Scandinavia. The state was relatively remote, two peninsulas of heavily wooded, rolling country jutting deep into the Great Lakes, a rich farming country once the forests had been cleared, but one which encouraged the growth of many small communities, rather than a few large ones. A people which had severed their genetic roots but not yet put out national ones, who were caught up in an exciting, effervescent, but bewildering population expansion, and who were at once isolated and unsophisticated formed ideal missionary material for any faith that could promise an immediate sense of goal and identification. That was the message that Jezreel brought: Whatever their genetic origins, they were now Americans, and Americans were, as honorary Anglo-Saxons, included in the covenant which Jehovah had sworn with Israel.

The Jezreelite headquarters in Michigan was Noah Drew's farm near Fleming, but Jezreel intended a positive, dynamic missionary journey. Noah Drew, dizzy with delight at being chosen as host to the Messenger and his attractive wife, placed both his money and his local knowledge at the service of the missionaries. He and his two sons organized an elaborate wagon train, consisting of a number of covered wagons, tents, food, and sleeping and cooking equipment, and sometime in the late spring of 1882, the cortege set off on the task of converting America, beginning with the state of Michigan.

The Messenger of the Lord received a very mixed reception. In many of the small towns and villages, the Jezreelites were met with delight. Jezreel had already begun to experiment with that mixture of entertainment and Bible-thumping which was to be a hallmark of Jezreelism. Clarissa could play the harp very prettily, and backed up by a couple of fiddlers, a flautist, and a piccolo player, a tolerable orchestra came into being—certainly a much better orchestra than the average Michigan village could boast. The people came in the dozens, crowding into the large tent that sheltered the orchestra, gawking at the foreigners from beyond the Atlantic, listening uncomprehending but impressed to Jezreel's immensely lengthy sermons, joining in the hymns. There were perhaps no lengthy queues to buy *The Flying Roll*, but in most places one or two people would suddenly see the light, acknowledge Jezreel as the Messenger, and take over stocks of the sacred book. Some of them wanted then and there to join the missionaries, to return with them to Chatham for the ingathering, but behind Jezreel's mysticism was a very practical mind. The overenthusiastic were dissuaded; they could best serve the cause by remaining and tilling their fat farms, sending tithes to Chatham until The Day arrived, when they too would be brought in.

So throughout the summer, threading their way through the beautiful, water-dappled landscape, camping sometimes beside the lakes, sometimes deep in the woods, sometimes respectfully enter-

tained to the best by a convert. Not all their contacts were respectful, or even friendly. At Brighton, a mob threatened to wreck the
tent, and there were later rumors that Jezreel had been tarred and
feathered. Noah Drew managed to save the situation through his
local connections, but the police ordered them out before a riot developed. They traveled on northward to Detroit, and there the
missionary journey foundered.

What exactly happened in Detroit in the late summer of 1882
is unclear. They preached successfully and established a small
community, but the relationship between the Drews and Mr. and
Mrs. Jezreel turned sour. Judging by the Jezreels' arrogant later behavior to their followers, the probability is that they made demands upon the Drews which Noah Drew, devout Jezreelite
though he was, could not tolerate. The disagreement developed
into an open quarrel; Jezreel and his wife haughtily departed from
Detroit—leaving the Drews to pay the debts, dismiss the wagon
train, and in general clear up the mess. From Detroit the Jezreels
made their way back to New York and thence to England, while
the Drews returned home to the farm, doubtless bitter against
Jezreel, but still profoundly devoted to the New and Latter House
of Israel. They were to have cause deeply to regret that devotion.

(iii) The Ingathering of Israel

"Hear O House of Israel, the time has now come for each one to be
put to the test to see whether they have gold, silver, or land or
house more than the bones of my body, my bride, my church,
said the Lord. Therefore exhort every bone of the virgin to put
their shoulder to the wheel now. For the command of the Lord is
given to all Israel to assemble in the Land of Joseph." [47]

So the proclamation went out to the scattered members of the
New and Latter House of Israel in July of 1884. Its combination of
bathos and cloudy symbolic language was typical of Jezreel's writing. But typical, too, was the true purpose of the proclamation,
buried within the morass of worn rhetoric. The summons of Israel
into the Land of Joseph was, for the moment, strictly symbolical;

the reference to gold, silver, and land was not. The Lord, through His Messenger Jezreel, had need of money, not for any ignoble purpose but to build the grandiose sanctuary, the Tower of Israel which was to be to the new age what Solomon's temple was to the old. And the money began to come in.

The character of James Jershom Jezreel remains curiously blurred and out of focus, despite the fact that he was the center of attention and speculation of both hostile and reverential observers. It is probably easier to discern the character of Richard Brothers, of Thomas Venner, even—despite the distorting veil of time and language—of Jan Bockelson, than of this ex-soldier who founded his church at about the time that Marconi was experimenting with electronic intangibles. Most contemporaries agreed that he was a very bad public speaker, and posterity is hard put to make any sense at all out of his written work. Yet he had some vital ability, some inexplicable magnetism which could persuade total strangers to place their lives wholly in his care, resigning to him all their worldly wealth as well as the care of their souls.

The activities of Jezreel and his wife for about a year or eighteen months after their return from America in the autumn of 1882 are unclear. Money must have been coming in on a comparatively large scale, for certainly there was enough to pay for a missionary trip to Australia for Jezreel, to maintain Mrs. Jezreel at home in a fair degree of comfort, and at last to establish the nucleus of a community in Chatham. By the spring of 1884, the Messenger and his wife were established in a large and comfortable country house, and the movement owned a number of other houses in the vicinity that were used to accommodate the faithful as they arrived.

For the Ingathering of Israel had begun. Initially the postulants came from the immediate locality, then from further afield in Britain, then from overseas—from France, Australia, and America in particular. Jezreelites who remained in the world were allowed to contribute only the literal tithe to the movement, but those who joined the community were obliged to pass over their entire possessions. The exhortations that brought them there were, with one striking exception, strongly reminiscent of the exhortations that Jan Bockelson had sent to the Anabaptist brethren outside Munster. Jezreel, like Bockelson, urged the faithful to flee the world, to seek sanctuary in the New Jerusalem for the ending of days was upon them. But where Bockelson had exhorted the faithful not to trouble to bring worldly wealth, for they would enrich themselves at the expense of the ungodly, Jezreel wanted cash: "No one must bring furniture or cumbersome luggage with them. But let all convert everything into gold, and bring all they can with them in the way of cash, but no more luggage than is necessary. All these things were to be provided for them here when they arrive." [48]

On arrival, the newcomers turned their money over to Jezreel, were allocated accommodation and drawn into the religious life of the community. But those who expected to pass the interval between their arrival and the commencement of the Millennium solely in praying and hymning were very rapidly disabused. Allied to Jezreel's mysticism was a very strong practical streak and an excellent organizing ability which would have made him a highly successful entrepreneur. Chatham was growing rapidly and there was an ever increasing demand for service industries. Jezreel set about satisfying the demand, establishing a baker, a blacksmith, cobbler's, grocer's, and dairy—advertising their wares with a blithe indifference to incongruity. "Jezreel's Magic Polish! Once Used, Always Used!" the advertisements proclaimed in the robust contemporary manner.

The newcomers found they had entered a community run with the most rigorous discipline. Jezreel was not only priest but king, not only king but treasurer and chancellor. As a matter of course it was he alone who interpreted the divine will down to the smallest detail. As a matter of course he prescribed the form of the hours-long religious services. As a matter of course he presided over the school, grandiloquently known as Israel's International College, whose curriculum was almost entirely based on endless studying of his *Flying Roll.* But in addition, he exercised the same iron control over every trivial detail of the commune's domestic life. If a mother wanted to buy a pair of boots for her son, then it was necessary to approach Jezreel personally with the old, worn boots as evidence. He and his wife lived well, ate well—and drank well; the lower orders ate what they could get and so learned to mortify the flesh.

The control extended over the Jezreelites' costume and personal appearance. The men, certainly, were distinctive, with flowing beards and long hair tidily tucked up under a purple cap. Local legend had it that the Jezreelites believed that, when the time came, they would be pulled up to heaven by their long hair. In fact, it was kept long in obedience to the curious Levitical injunction, "Ye shall not round the corners of your heads, neither shalt thou mar the corners of thy beards." The womenfolk should, logically, have been dowdy, for not only was the Puritan ethos strong in the cult, but Jezreel also taught that celibacy would be a condition of the Millennium. But here he had to reckon with his wife. Whatever the relationship between husband and wife, Queen Esther had not the slightest intention of creeping around like a dusty black beetle, and her flair for clothes established a standard that leavened the usual dullness. Jezreelite children were always proudly on display, smartly dressed in scarlet and gray, reeling off from memory long passages of *The Flying Roll* or even extemporizing lengthy sermons. The spectacle of the prating tots might have been ludicrous, but was certainly no more distasteful than the general contemporary belief that children should be treated as articles of furniture or, at best, docile pets.

But the establishment of a prosperous community whose cowed members were obedient to his slightest wish was not sufficient for the dynamic Jezreel. Throughout the struggling years, when the only evidence of his mission had been the printed copies of his sermons, a titanic vision had taken shape and grown and grown in his mind. The vision was worthy of a pharaoh, for it was nothing less than the intention and desire to build an enormous sanctuary for the Ingathering of Israel. As soon as his community was functioning and he possessed land to build on, he set about turning that vision into reality.

Years later, when the huge yellow-brick structure had survived all but a few dwindling remnants of the sect, legend took over. It was asserted that Jezreel had intended it to reach the very heavens, providing a physical ladder to eternity. Others claimed that he was attempting to build a physical sanctuary or fortress, a place in which the 144,000 of the Elect could retreat during the cataclysms that must accompany the dawn of the Millennium. Considering the exotic claims of the New and Latter House of Israel, the legends of outsiders were not particularly extravagant. Jezreel did, in fact, intend his tower to be a literal, concrete foreshadowing of the New Jerusalem.

Originally he instructed the architects to follow the proportions of the supernatural city as given in Revelation: The building was to be a perfect cube, each side 144 feet in length. The architects objected that this was an impractical proposition, and reluctantly he modified the proportions. But in all other details, from the elaborate emblems and symbols on the outer walls to the stage that could be raised and lowered by hydraulic pressure, Jezreel had his way. What he was designing was, in effect, an enormous combined assembly hall, printing press, and administrative building, and he designed well. Time and death alone were to defeat him.

An assembly hall for five thousand people, a workshop for twelve large printing presses, installation of the magical new means of illumination called gas and electricity, landscaped gardens, workshops, an international college—such was Jezreel's splendid vision. But in the cold nineteenth-century world, visions cost hard cash, and his architects estimated that he would need at least £25,000—perhaps £250,000 or nearly half a million dollars in current prices. Present income only just equaled expenditure, and to build this holy ziggurat a massive fund-raising operation would have to be instituted. Jezreel's thoughts turned, as the thoughts of so many other prophets were to turn, to America, specifically to the fat farmlands of Michigan where he had left loyal—and prosperous—followers. In July 1884, a new edict went out: "I am now instructed by the one Immortal Spirit that it is the will of Shiloh, Immanuel, for Patrick Mihan, wife and son, for Charles Drennan, wife and family, Noah Drew, Job Drew, wife and child to come over to England as soon as possible to settle their affairs." From time to time other Jezreelites in Michigan were singled out by name and exhorted to cross the Atlantic, bringing their wealth with them. Precisely, Jezreel spelled out what each was to do and when: "Let no one come to England to headquarters until they are sent for, until they get a direct call from Heaven. Members will settle their affairs as speedily as possible yet as profitably as they can. They are not to drop everything at once nor yet to sacrifice anything but to sell out to the best advantage that they may do all in their power to bring over with them as much money as they can." The lukewarm and the fainthearted were reminded that they would have little use for worldly wealth in the great and terrible Day of the Lord that was just over the horizon. "They had better realize and make the most they can for they will do better now than when the troubles break out among nations (which they will do shortly). Property is sure to run down in price at a terrible rate so all who mean to realise the better, for shortly they will be only too glad to find refuge in the land of Joseph." [49]

Jezreel evidently believed in miracles, for scarcely four months were allotted to the construction of the great building. He planned to have it ready for a great Jubilee of Nations in January 1885, and such was his energy and will power that the foundations were laid and a sizable height of wall raised by the end of that month. But heavy drinking, overwork, and religious excitement undermined even his robust frame. He fell ill at the end of February; on March 2, the Messenger, the immortal leader chosen by the Almighty to lead the Elect into earthly paradise, died. Ironically, it was only at his death that a portrait of him was sketched in for posterity. An inquisitive reporter from a local paper gained entrance to the death chamber and saw the body lying, in bright spring sunlight, on a massive bedstead:

It appeared simply as if the deceased had fallen back exhausted and was in a deep sleep. He was lying on his back, with his head slightly on one side, his light flowing locks clustered over his shoulders, while his beard came down to his breast. His eyes were carefully closed, and altogether he presented a pleasing appearance. One thing I could not fail to notice was his massive build: he must have measured two feet across the shoulders and was nearly six feet in height.[50]

The death of Jezreel seems to have occasioned not so much sorrow or even astonishment as profound embarrassment to his followers: How was it possible that he, who had promised them escape from death, had himself fallen victim to the eternal enemy? But rationalization saved the faith. Jezreel, after all, had only been the Messenger, not the principal; logically, he could not have been one of the Elect, for if he had, he could not have died. So the customary process began to operate, leaching out doubt and fear. At the same time, the Jezreelites had an immediate and absorbing problem. Who would step into the vacant place? Who would take on the awesome burden of leading the Elect into paradise? It was assumed that the mantle must fall upon the patriarchal James Cummings, one of Jezreel's very first followers. Cummings hastened back from America, where he was engaged upon a missionary tour, to take up the burden, but after some days of discreet but deadly jockeying it was proclaimed that the new Messenger was no grizzled patriarch but the very smart and attractive twenty-five-year-old wife of Jezreel himself. "Queen Esther," as she very soon came to be known, was in the strongest of all positions, for she was on the spot and already had control of the treasury. Cummings protested the impropriety of a woman holding this exalted office, but he was no match for the tough, quite unscrupulous widow, and shortly afterward he returned to America, shaking his head over the destiny of Israel.

Queen Esther inherited a well-founded, smoothly running organization whose efficiency was the product of a tyrannical discipline. She unhesitatingly adopted the system and added refinements of her own. A group of favorites came into being—spies who kept her minutely informed of any disaffection in the commune. Apart from a liking for good food and strong drink, Jezreel had not cared overmuch for physical comforts or appearances. Queen Esther was a very handsome young woman with excellent taste in dress. Now, with the treasury so conveniently to hand, she was able to indulge that taste at considerable expense. She had been born in Chatham in very humble circumstances, and it was perhaps understandable that she should wish to cut a figure in that town. A handsome carriage and pair made their appearance, together with a smartly dressed groom, and in that manner Queen Esther took the air in her native town.

But behind the display, behind the tea parties with the whispering spies, behind the hauteur, was a very real and passionate devotion to the faith that her husband had implanted in her. Jezreel had died in trying to raise his tower; his widow took on the task, throwing herself into it with such energy that, within four months of his death, she had amassed enough capital to give the builders confidence to carry on. In September 1885, the foundation stone was laid and dedicated to the 144,000 Elect.

Esther took the opportunity to produce one of the marathon ceremonies for which the Jezreelites were now famous. It went on for over four hours in which the faithful were entertained by an excellent orchestra, harangued by a succession of holy children, and exhorted by a succession of prophets. Old Patrick Mihan from Michigan announced that the divine plan had at last been revealed with the establishment of Israel's Sanctuary, the vital prerequisite to the Millennium. Another speaker announced that the Christian dispensation was now ending, even as the Jewish had ended, and seemed inclined to identify Esther either with Joanna Southcott, or with the woman in Revelation, or Shiloh, or all three. Esther herself was modest and charming and quite captivated the reporter from the local paper: "She is a young woman under thirty years of age, with a cheerful winsome countenance which is quite pleasant to look upon. She had displayed considerable taste in her toilet, being attired in an elegant dress of dark-green silk, with a white hat. She wore gold ear-rings, rings and bracelets." [51]

But not all were captivated by Queen Esther. In Chatham, Noah Drew and his wife sourly heard of the great work that had been initiated. Far from being inspired by it, a few weeks afterwards they subjected the New and Latter House of Israel to the indignity of a legal action. They wanted their money back.

Noah Drew had been one of the first Americans to respond to Jezreel's exhortation in July of the previous year. He and his wife sold their prosperous farm in Michigan, turned their backs on America, and arriving in Chatham, joyfully handed over all their money to the Messenger. It was a substantial sum, well over £1000, but a small price to pay for a ticket to eternity. Suddenly the value of that ticket became very problematical when James Jershom Jezreel died like any other unredeemed human being. Noah Drew was unable to perform the mental gymnastics of his fellow Jezreelites and promptly left the sect. But having withdrawn from the commune, he needed money and applied to Esther for the return of part at least of his investment. Esther haughtily refused, and Drew promptly took the matter to court. He lost on a technicality, and Esther began a campaign of venomous harassment of the elderly couple that aroused the indignation of the citizens of Chatham. Jezreel had been arrogant enough as shepherd toward his flock, but he conducted himself discreetly with the townsfolk. But almost from the beginning of her reign, Queen Esther seemed constrained to flaunt herself in the public eye, and in the matter of Noah Drew she completely misjudged the popular reaction. The Drews were still living in Jezreelite property—they had no choice, for they had no money—and Esther found one pretext after another to move them into smaller and ever dingier lodgings. Drew was now well over seventy, and the spectacle of the old man and his wife being driven from one wretched bedroom to another, sometimes under threat of force, aroused the mob's indignation. Jezreelite officials were attacked in the town, the police were called in, and it seemed that Chatham was on the brink of riot. Firm handling by the police held the rowdies in check, but the damage had been done to the Jezreelite reputation. Wild rumors spread around the town as to how the Drews had been "swindled out of thousands," the press took up the tale, and Esther was at length obliged to drop her pose of hauteur and publish a lengthy apologia. According to her, Drew, far from being a prosperous farmer, had been bankrupt, maintained in charity at the expense of the New and Latter House of Israel. The explanation, conflicting so obviously with the evidence of Jezreel's own letters, was treated with skepticism, the local press even going so far as to accuse Esther openly of having used the money to keep up her domestic comforts.

Esther was too arrogant, too self-confident to value public relations. She was nevertheless an energetic, intelligent, and skillful administrator, and under her the New and Latter House of Israel achieved its apogee. Single-handed she planned and launched a weekly periodical, *The Messenger of Wisdom and Israel's Guide*, giving it so firm a base that it survived well into the twentieth century. *The Messenger* was Esther's platform, from which she did not hesitate to harangue and attack the great ones of the land. She claimed a circulation of ten thousand for it, and though doubtless she exaggerated, the publication probably paid for itself, for she engaged professional canvassers to push it. The reader was a well-founded suspicion that Esther contributed considerably more editorially than was claimed over her name, including such gems as the letter from a Joseph and Betsy Jane Morgan supposedly seeking instruction from her: "It aint no good at all talkin about doin a thin and never doin of the same as sais i i rites the day sartin for heres me an Betsy Jane a sittin thinkin over this ere book or yourn an lettin the tay git cold nite after nite," [52] the honest fellow was alleged to have written. Given time, Queen Esther might well have made her debut—and perhaps her fame—as a novelist.

In addition to editing (and probably writing) *The Messenger*, Esther greatly increased the range of missionary activities, through them founding daughter houses throughout Britain, in America—particularly in Michigan, and even in Australia and New Zealand. Meanwhile the great work, the task she had inherited from the Messenger himself, went on without pause, and by the summer of 1887 the Sanctuary of Israel towered up seven stories high. The great printing presses were already installed, turning out copies of *The Flying Roll* and *The Messenger;* the huge auditorium with its extraordinary hydraulic platform for speakers was now a reality. The Sanctuary only required to be roofed, painted, and decorated internally to be ready for its thousand-year-long role.

But at this stage of high endeavor, Queen Esther died painfully of a kidney disease at the age of twenty-eight. Work on the tower immediately stopped, and the New and Latter House of Israel began to slide helplessly into decline.

Arguably, Clarissa–Esther White was the true architect of Jezreelism, codifying her husband's wild and whirling teaching, establishing the community on a firm financial basis. On any consideration, she was an extraordinary woman. Born in very humble circumstances, totally lacking any formal education, in her mid-twenties she came to dominate an organization which contained men of maturity and some education, and whose sole purpose was to place its own gloss on biblical scholarship. The building of the great tower was the kind of grandiose concept that became common among wealthy American sects from the 1920's onward. It was an astonishingly high achievement for the England of the 1880's, when nonconformist places of worship usually took the form of very modest one-story brick and tile shacks. Esther not only had to ensure a steady flow of cash, but she had to persuade a succession of jobbing builders, traditionally very wary men, that the money would indeed continue to flow and that therefore they could go ahead and order expensive materials. She was perhaps fortunate in having found, through Jezreelism, an outlet for her formidable talents, for the England of her day offered very few opportunities for someone of her sex and class. Yet in the end, the observer of her life is oppressed with a sense of waste for what she might have accomplished if those energies had been employed in a field less bizarre, less sterile.

(iv) The Coming of Prince Michael

Some few weeks after the death of Queen Esther in Chatham, a prosperous young businessman in Detroit returned home one night to find his wife, Rosetta, in a state of great excitement. An English lady—a Jezreelite missionary called Eliza Court—had visited the house that day and left a copy of *The Flying Roll*. Rosetta was eager to know what her husband would think of this blinding glimpse into the future. He read, made an appointment with Miss Court, and forthwith became an impassioned member of the New and Latter House of Israel.

Michael Keyfor Mills was a pleasant but not particularly outstanding young man. Born in Detroit, he had been brought up in Canada, discovered there that he had a considerable talent for engineering, and at the early age of thirty-one, had just set up his own small factory in Detroit. Nothing in his past gave any indication of the exotic role he was about to claim for himself, although as a youth he had been a reasonably keen Bible student. Judging by what happened afterward between missionary and convert, it does not seem uncharitable to suppose that Michael Mills was initially at least as interested in Miss Eliza Court as he was in Jezreelism. She was, by all accounts, a personable young lady, somewhat reminiscent of Clarissa–Esther during her missionary days.

But whatever reason persuaded Mills to become a Jezreelite, he threw himself into the work of collecting souls for the ingathering with all the devotion of the convert. At first he was content to be simply another missionary, and to carry out his task the better, he sold his business and, with Miss Court and his wife, set off on a protracted missionary journey through Michigan as Jezreel had done just ten years earlier. But soon this was not enough, and the manner in which Mills received his divine call and became at last convinced that he was the prince Michael of the book of Daniel throws a brief but vivid light on the psychosomatic processes that could persuade a man he was under divine control. The revelation happened with startling suddenness. He turned to his wife and, without preliminary explanation, ordered her to pour oil upon his head. Immediately after his anointing, his hands jerked involuntarily above his head and rubbed one against the other. The right arm then shot into the air in the imperial salute, and in a strangled voice he called out, "Prince Michael has come!" Nothing in the contemporary account gives any indication but that Mills was acting quite sincerely and under a weird compulsion.

By the end of 1891, Prince Michael, as he was now known to his followers, had established his own community in Detroit, following the Chatham model whereby recruits were allocated neighboring houses purchased or rented by the House of Israel. Michael, it appeared, was not only the prince whose coming had been prophesied by Daniel—"Michael shall stand up, the great prince which standeth for the children of thy people"—but he was also the seventh and last messenger. By adopting the style, he implicitly branded Queen Esther as usurper and heretic, for Jezreel, according to the canon, had been the sixth messenger in succession to Richard Brothers. In the standard manner whereby cults budded off one from another, Michael rummaged through the teachings of Jezreel, discarding and adopting facets on an arbitrary basis. The doctrine regarding "cleansing the blood" took on great significance for him. He announced to the press that he was now free from the stain of Adam, a purified human worthy to be ranked with the archangels and, as such, marked out as one of the captains who would take part in Armageddon. He also remarked, with an engagingly casual manner, that during the purification process balls of fire were seen to be thrown off by his body, and he was heard to ejaculate "Praise God!" ten thousand times.

The fact that Prince Michael made his announcement to the press was indicative of the respect he accorded it, his canny awareness of the power of the new practice of mass journalism. The great age of the stunt was dawning, and anyone who could provide material for a press hungry for spectacular copy would be ensured of a hearing. The Detroit *Tribune* had already nosed out the Jezreelite community established (with unconscious irony) in Hamlin Avenue, and with a masterly use of the deadpan style, summarized its tenets: "They believe in a male and female deity and by continued obedience to the Levitical laws regarding marital relationship believed pure and sound progeny would be produced and adherence to Matthew Chapter 7 verse 11 would keep them so physically and mentally fit that in the end disease would be banished from the earth. They believed in the immortality of the body and the millennium." Publicity produced more recruits, though the membership of the Detroit "god-house" never succeeded in climbing out of the lower hundreds. The tithes of the faithful, however, proved sufficient to maintain Prince Michael, Prince Michael's wife, and the enigmatic Miss Eliza Court in reasonable comfort—and also, in due course, to buy a transatlantic ticket for the prince. For the Seventh Messenger had decided that the time had come to travel to the sacred city and there take over, as by divine right, the role of leader, vacant since Queen Esther's death. In January 1892, the motherhouse in Chatham saw for the first time the portly figure of the self-appointed prince and prophet. The motherhouse displayed no great evidence of delight. Schism had bitten deep into the community during the four years since Queen Esther's death. She had foreseen the possibility and sought to avoid it by training a young nephew eventually to take her place. But her own sudden death brought to an end an interesting experiment in hereditary succession and left the office of messenger and leader open to whomever could claim it—including an eccentric who proclaimed that both Esther and Jezreel had risen from the dead. Esther's father stepped into the breach as trustee and was certainly not in the least disposed to accept the claims of a loud, confident American, claims that would finally extinguish the Rogers's family chances. Prince Michael, after hanging around Chatham for some weeks vainly trying to raise a following among the leaderless Jezreelites, returned disconsolate to Detroit.

His troubles, had he known it, had only started. The Jezreelite community in Detroit was run on the same autocratic terms as the one in Chatham, but Prince Michael, though an excellent showman, lacked the martinet qualities of Jezreel. The Jezreelites in Chatham proved again and again that they were prepared to close their ranks if need be, even the schismatics refusing to wash grubby linen in public. It was a discipline in which the Detroit Jezreelites were sadly lacking. Rumors began to spread through the town of some curious happenings that were going on in the "godhouse" between the Messenger and the younger female members of his following, and of the somewhat less than spiritual relationship that existed between himself and pretty Miss Eliza Court. His long-suffering wife, Rosetta Mills, decided that there was substance to the rumors and, storming out, subjected the prince to the indignity of divorce proceedings. And as if this were not enough, there appeared at the door of the god-house a new claimant to the crown of Israel—Benjamin Franklin Purnell.

Throughout its colorful life, the Christian Israel movement had attracted equally colorful eccentrics, each of whom contributed a unique twist to the dogma. Some were eccentric to the point of lunacy, some were forceful to the point of tyranny, but Purnell was the only one to have had an actively criminal bent, an intention and ability to make capital out of the delusions of his followers. But even Purnell seems, ultimately, to have been a believer in his own mission, and regarding his career, posterity is reminded of the rather similar character of Jan Bockelson. Born in Kentucky, Purnell's great object in life was to avoid work. He managed to persuade his wife's parents to keep him for some time after their marriage, but when they threw him out, he chose the hand-to-mouth but undemanding role of traveling evangelist. It is unclear whether he encountered *The Flying Roll* before or after his divine call, but once he had done so, he became an energetic missionary of the Jezreelite faith. Jezreel and his wife must have unloaded hundreds of mint copies of their scriptures, for Purnell was able to acquire sufficient to set up in business. In 1887 he was established in Richmond, Ohio, the leader of a flourishing sect of Jezreelites which he called the Flying Rollers, and proclaimed it as the true transatlantic daughterhouse. Then, with what must have been considerable chagrin, he heard of the existence of Prince Michael's group in Detroit. Purnell had the sense to realize that the Detroit group, which could trace its line back to the founder himself, was the natural center of Jezreelism in America, and instead of establishing his own schismatic sect in Ohio, he took the journey north. It was a delicate moment when he, the head of his own sect, stood face to face with Prince Michael, but the two worked out an amicable formula, with Purnell as deputy to the Prince.

Purnell did not have to wait long for the opportunity of grasping the crown. Prince Michael's estranged wife Rosetta was loudly telling the world just what was going on in the Detroit god-house and, with melodramatic suddenness, Prince Michael found himself arrested, tried, and sentenced to five years imprisonment for the debauching of female minors. It appeared that, instead of leaving the ceremony of "cleansing the blood" in decent metaphysical obscurity, he had been interpreting it in his own highly idiosyncratic manner. Gossip spoke of the "brutal and sadistic rape" of girls scarcely at the age of puberty, and Michael's life was in very real danger from the Detroit mob. But judging by the relative lightness of his sentence, he seems to have been able to persuade the trial judge that the partners in his "ceremony" had been quite willing.

With the involuntary withdrawal of Prince Michael, Purnell decided that the time had come for his own takeover of the group. He reckoned without Eliza Court. From his prison cell Prince Michael reached out and transferred his charisma to her. She was now become Princess Michael, vicar apostolic of the absent leader and vested with plentipotentiary powers in all that affected the New and Latter House of Israel as it was constituted in the New World. She was worthy of her charge, and after some bitter infighting, Benjamin Purnell took himself off with a supply of *The Flying Roll*, some dissident supporters, and a new title—King Benjamin. He led his little band through the Michigan wilderness and established his House of David on the shores of Lake Michigan. He was an excellent organizer. By the turn of the century, the House of David was a prosperous community, attracting disciples from Jezreelite communities not only in America but even in England and Australia. Not for the first time in religious history, the rebellious offspring threatened to overshadow the orthodox parent.

Meanwhile Prince Michael had been released from prison, paler and thinner than when he went in but otherwise his ebullient old self. The Detroit House of Israel had dwindled to a bare handful, a pale shadow of the House of David, unworthy of the prince's undivided attention. With the immense confidence that never deserted him, Michael decided that the time had come for him to offer himself again to the motherhouse in Chatham. In March 1906, he, Princess Michael, and a small band of disciples took ship for England. As their vessel stood out from land, the Messenger raised his hands and cursed the New World with the opening line of the Jezreelite hymn: "Woe, woe to this land of the West." Shortly afterwards there occurred the great earthquake of San Francisco and the great fires that ravaged Michigan, the Jezreelite chronicles noted with somber satisfaction.

The mother church of the New and Latter House of Israel was now in a desperate state. Seventeen years after the death of Queen Esther, it still possessed no leader but was divided between itself, as members of the Rogers family fought for control. A large section had hived off and set itself up in London, while the rump in Chatham daily watched their numbers and possessions dwindle. Queen Esther's fiery old father, Edward Rogers, who had taken on himself the role of chief trustee, was forced to leave that handsome country house which was now almost regarded as the family mansion. Few recruits came forward to make good the deaths and defections; more and more of the retail shops and residential houses were relinquished. At last even the great tower, the very badge of Jezreelism, came under the hammer. Over the years desperate financial expedients had enabled the Jezreelites to maintain at least an interest in the building, a complex system of mortgaging allowing them to occupy the ground floor. But at last money ran out, the mortgage was foreclosed, and the Jezreelites were ordered to evacuate the building so that it could be demolished and the materials sold. There was a poignancy and courage about the defense of their temple by these twentieth-century Israelites that earned them, at last, the respect and admiration of their neighbors. The story of how Edward Rogers, a frail old man, "fought like a lion and pummelled a gigantic navvy manfully, although his opponent (was) strong enough to kill him" went the rounds. The tower, too, defied its would-be destroyers and was destined to survive for more than a half century before falling victim to modern technology and land hunger.

But Rogers and his dwindling band were obliged to vacate the lands held by the House of Israel for over a generation. And it was at this stage that Prince Michael bobbed up out of the ocean to plague the declining years of the Jezreelites.

The New and Latter House of Israel had always possessed a

certain somber dignity even in its most extreme and exotic claims. Prince Michael arrived to change that dignity into farce. He had acquired as herald, or press agent, a Scotsman, David Mackay, a man considerably his superior in intellect and education, but who had accepted him wholeheartedly as the prince of Israel. An abiding mystery of the Christian Israel movement, indeed, was the manner in which its more or less preposterous leaders attracted supporters from among people trained to evaluate such claims as theirs. Mackay had studied theology at Edinburgh University, saw the light when a copy of *The Flying Roll* came into his hands, and made the long journey to Detroit to offer his services to Prince Michael. Now, in Chatham, he was engaged in fending off the attentions of the local press which, after a long dull period, welcomed the advent of the remarkable Prince Michael with something like joy. Freely, frankly, Mackay explained how the prince had been traduced and imprisoned on perjured evidence; freely and frankly he explained how it was that Michael Keyfor Mills was the prophet and prince proclaimed in Daniel L2: 1: "At that time shall arise Michael, the great prince, who has charge of your people. And there shall be a time of trouble, such as never has been since there was a nation till that time. But at that time your people shall be delivered, every one whose name shall be found written in the book." The book, of course, was *The Flying Roll*, and Michael Mills had not only been given, by divine providence, the sacred name at birth, but possessed now the divinely granted gift of healing. How was this gift demonstrated? The prince was able to cure Mackay's frequent headaches simply by laying on his hand—a statement which probably told more about Mackay's mental state than Prince Michael's mission.

But it was one thing to provide good stories for newspapers and quite another to persuade the prickly, stubborn Jezreelite rump to accept the new Messenger. Mackay made the attempt with style in a letter that seems deliberately designed to enrage its recipient, so loftily condescending was its tone. "To Edward Rogers, Greetings," it began. "Michael, your Prince, wishes to give an opportunity to yourself and all interested in *The Flying Roll* to come forward and lend their support in the rebuilding of the Sanctuary. It greatly grieves your Prince to see the dismal state in which the Remnant of the former House and Sanctuary itself now lies, but with God's help he believes all can be restored." The letter went on to recite the basis of Prince Michael's claim to the leadership and ended with the warning that the times of the End were fast approaching: "Now, according to the Chronicles of Israel, the month of May is to decide the final destiny of Man, wherefore we exhort you to weigh well what is herein written."

The letter invited, and received, a contemptuous rejection, old Edward Rogers dating it, with a wholly uncharacteristic touch of humor, "Last day of the fatal month in the destiny of Man." That exchange of letters was the opening shot in a sniping campaign that continued for months. Neither succeeded in persuading the other to adopt a subordinate role, but time was on Michael's side. Death at last removed the indomitable old man, a death which seemed to the tiny number of his supporters to be another inexplicable heresy on the part of their leaders. Michael became, by default, leader and very voluble spokesman for the New and Latter House of Israel, now renamed by him the New Eve. For a time he prospered; through judicious management of the Jezreelite shops and trades he raised enough money to acquire Jezreel's old country house, the Vatican, Canterbury, and Jerusalem of the cult. There was even, for a time, money to pay off some of the mortgages on the tower itself, and for a heady period, the Jezreelites occupied their temple. But inevitably money again ran short, and after a squalid wrangle over a sum of scarcely £50, Prince Michael and his Jezreelites were thrown out, finally, of the Tower. At some stage David Mackay seems to have despaired at last and dropped out. The extensive Jezreelite trading concerns dwindled to a little tearoom. But still Prince Michael strode around Chatham in his startling suit of imperial purple, haranguing, litigating, prophesying—and still, it seemed, there were sufficient people to listen and believe and contribute to the upkeep of their prophet and his new wife, for Prince and Princess Michael lived in great comfort in the sprawling old house. For over twelve years, the flame of Jezreelism was kept alive in Chatham, but on a January day in 1922, the Prince and Princess fell ill of a cold and died within three days of each other. Dismayed and stunned by this last heresy, the little band in Chatham was at last dispersed, those Americans who had come over so confidently with Prince Michael in 1905 returning to die in Michigan.

But even now the New and Latter House of Jezreel was not allowed to drift with dignity back into obscurity, mist, and legend; there was still King Benjamin Purnell to place his curious seal upon its ending. The community he had established at Benton Harbor on the shores of Lake Michigan had flourished very well indeed. By 1910 his House of David owned over eight hundred acres of good farming land and had even established a cannery. Converts came from all over America, from the disillusioned, bewildered community in England, even from Australia. They were hard-working, frugal folk, and their devotion to the well-being of the House of David and of King Ben was ensured by Ben's ingenious adaptation of the confessional formula originally ordained by Jezreel himself. Jezreel had ordered all converts to write their sins down upon paper, and at a subsequent ceremony the sheets of paper were destroyed, symbolizing the convert's break with the sinful past. King Ben also insisted on a written account of the converts' misdeeds—but those accounts were carefully filed away, to be pro-duced if their writers proved recalcitrant. By the 1920's, Purnell was probably a millionaire, and the proprietor of a fairground and baseball team, as well as factories, farms, and the expanding can-nery. The Jezreelite ritual was still adhered to; members still waited for the return of Shiloh, for the Second Advent of Christ, for the Millennium, for the Ingathering of Israel that would now take place in Michigan. Newcomers, shown around the well-kept grounds and the prosperous undertakings, had reason to believe that King Ben must indeed be the last of the prophets, the leader who would take them into the Millennium, for did not the Lord look after His own?

At this high point of success, with the lurid melodrama that had attended all the affairs of Israel, King Ben in his turn was in-dicted by a grand jury. There were two distinct charges: Two young sisters swore that he had raped them upon their induction into the House of David and sued him for two hundred thousand dollars. And a disillusioned male, undeterred by the confession in Ben's possession, followed up with a suit for twenty-four thousand dollars, claiming that this represented the sum he had invested in the community in addition to the wages he had waived while a true believer. Local and national newspapers took the matter up with venom and vigor, and Ben thought it best to disappear.

Three years, later, in November 1926, another disillusioned member of the colony betrayed him, and the police were astonished to discover that throughout the three years they had sought him, King Benjamin had been comfortably in hiding under their very noses—in a secret underground room, luxuriously appointed, built under one of the community's houses. His trial in May 1927 was all that a sensation-hungry newspaper could demand. Girl after girl came forward to swear she had been debauched by him, then forcibly married off to one of his cronies; other witnesses deposed how they had gullibly passed over their entire wealth to the community, and thereafter were reduced virtually to the status of slaves working simply for their keep.

But King Benjamin cheated them all. He died before a verdict was passed, and with him died the last effective leader of Christian Israel. Yet, astonishingly, the tough little cult survived. Even in the 1970's, isolated members are scattered about America, England, and Australia, distressed by the deaths of their compeers, yet still hopeful for their own triumphant entry into the New Jerusalem.

•

CHAPTER VII

OCTOBER 1975

(i) The Invisible Kingdom

In the spring of 1879, the first copies of a rather badly printed but splendidly named magazine came off a decrepit printing press in Pittsburgh, Pennsylvania. Charles Taze Russell, a handsome young businessman of twenty-five, owner of the press, editor of the magazine and contributor of most of its contents, watched as the machine thumped out six thousand copies of *Zion's Watch Tower and Herald of Christ's Presence.* After eight years of devoted Bible study, he was at last launching himself as publisher to Jehovah's Kingdom.

A little under a century later, an average printing of the same magazine, now called simply *The Watchtower*, totaled eight million copies in some seventy-four languages. Each issue is distributed throughout the planet by a force of over a million voluntary workers, each eagerly sacrificing leisure hours in order to bear witness to the imminence of the Millennium. The phenomenal growth of the magazine provides an unusually exact yardstick to measure the development of a religious belief: *The Watchtower* is the official mouthpiece of the organization known as the Jehovah's Witnesses.

The origin of the movement was a cry of protest, an instinctive, despairing reaction on the part of human beings who found themselves trapped in a kind of hell. It was born in Pittsburgh in the closing decades of the nineteenth century—and Pittsburgh was a city that had forgotten its past with an almost frightening speed, obliterating it behind clouds of bituminous smoke, sealing it under brick and iron and stone. At the beginning of the nineteenth century, the population of the town had been about a thousand souls, but with the coming of the railroad and the exploitation of rich deposits of coal and iron, the little town on the river became a bloated technological giant. By 1880, the population was 156,000, and by the last decade of the century the urban and industrial sprawl linked together, in one continuous mass, once separate communities housing over a quarter of a million people.

Looking down from the nearby low hills—particularly at night when the lurid fires of rolling mills and glass houses lit up the soot-blackened city, the observer could detect a certain grim majesty about it. Those citizens fortunate and wealthy enough to live in such favored suburbs as Allegheny could console themselves for their smoke-limited horizon by contemplation of their swelling bank accounts. But for the vast mass of people, whether immigrants from Europe or country folk ingested by the gravitational pull of a great and growing city, Pittsburgh was simply another outpost of hell created by the Industrial Revolution. The only way out was up, and churches and chapels flourished exceedingly. The census takers noted that there were 237 houses of worship in the 1880's, divided pretty equally between the great established faiths and the nonconformist leaven that made bearable the squalor of daily life. These were the architecturally recognizable buildings, formal places of worship that clung to the tradition of ecclesiastical architecture even if it was only a barnlike building dignified with an architrave or a couple of exterior pillars. Below them in the social order were huts and shacks and the rooms of ordinary homes where those who had lost contact, or faith, with the orthodox church sought their God as best they might.

Among them were a large number of Second Adventists, people who believed—with considerable justice—that life must have more to offer than the smoke clouds of Pittsburgh. They owed nothing to Jezreelism; that particular version of millenarianism had remained for the most part in the Michigan peninsula, some two hundred miles northwest of Pittsburgh. Here, the line of descent was traced back to an older, more indigenous source, that of William Miller who, in 1833, announced in Low Hampton, New York, that Christ was due to return in a decade's time. The movement, which attracted thousands of followers over the ten years, fragmented after the inevitable disillusionment, but still survived. The fragment which rooted itself in Pittsburgh had neither head, nor body of clear-cut beliefs. It was, perhaps, little more than a corporate hope, the combined voice of little groups of people meeting to speculate prayerfully on the day of the Return. In 1870 young Charles Russell, then just turned eighteen, drifted into one of these meetings in Allegheny and came out a changed man.

Charles Taze Russell was the son of a draper who had grown wealthy with the phenomenal expansion of Pittsburgh. Young Russell entered the family business, and later ran it with such outstanding success that he was able to turn his back on it and devote his time and then considerable fortune to the nurturing of his infant society. For behind the facade of the brisk young businessman was the poignant figure of the bewildered theist searching for meaning, groping for spiritual comfort and aid. None of the existing churches or cults in Pittsburgh satisfied him. After that flash of insight in the Adventist hall, he gathered together a group of like-minded earnest young men for the purpose of studying the Bible, absorbing direct from that most potent source. It was all very informal at first, but in 1875 came an additional revelation that triggered off what was to be the fastest-growing religious organization of the twentieth century. In that year he was in Philadelphia, prosaically enough on a business trip, when a copy of a rather badly printed magazine, *Herald of the Morning*, came into his hands. Much of the text seemed to be the work of its editor, N. H. Barbour, and its key message was that Christ had returned to earth, invisibly, the year before. Fascinated, Russell contacted Barbour in New York and offered to pay all his expenses if he would come to Philadelphia and give instructions in the strange doctrine. Barbour accepted, and Russell, in between selling his bombazines and serges and tweeds, plunged deep into the heady business of the Second Coming. He was already familiar with the recondite calculations that placed the Second Advent in 1874; what particularly intrigued him was the concept of an invisible Return. In explaining that concept, Barbour also introduced the eager young draper to that juggling with the meaning of translated words that was to be a hallmark of his society. The Greek word *parousia*, Barbour explained, was usually translated as "coming" or "advent"—but it could also mean "presence." Therefore it was entirely permissible to argue that the Lord was already in the world, had started collecting His sheep and would take them back to heaven with Him. These would be the Elect, the glorified who would never know death. And when would their glorification take place? Barbour now introduced his pupil to another exegetical technique—that of analogy. The Lord's first ministry had lasted exactly three and a half years after His baptism, and it was therefore logical to suppose that His Second Advent would last as long. He had returned in the autumn of 1874, and the glorification must therefore take place in the spring of 1878.

Charles Russell reacted in precisely the manner an intelligent, earnest young man would react to news of this stupendous nature. Henceforth, everything must take second place to the spreading of this new gospel. He poured money into Barbour's printing works, published a book which outlined the revelation, and acted as unpaid and highly energetic editor of Barbour's magazine. There was an embarrassing incident in the spring of 1878 when a group of believers, bathed and dressed in white robes, waited in an upper chamber for the calculated hour. Nothing happened. No angel appeared to rend the smoky skies over Pittsburgh; no irresistible force drew them up through the roof and out beyond the gravitational pull of earth to their eternal home. Barbour lost faith and even attacked Russell in print. Russell reacted with dignity, withdrawing his financial support and establishing his own magazine, *The Watch Tower*. There had been a miscalculation, no more: Devoted study provided the answer that the Return was actually due in 1914. But the Lord was even now invisibly present and would continue to be so until 1914, when all the kingdoms of the world would end, superseded by Jehovah's Kingdom.

In 1879, Russell finally turned his back on commerce. During his relatively short time as head of the drapery business, he had expanded it from one store into a chain of five which he now sold for over a quarter of a million dollars. And now he turned his formidable energy and administrative skill to the creation of a viable society, establishing that pattern of businessman turned evangelist which was to be America's distinctive contribution to twentieth-century religious life. Already he was known informally as pastor to the little "ecclesias," or millenarian Bible-study groups that had come into being in and around Pennsylvania. They looked to him as teacher rather than leader, a role he was perfectly content to accept. In 1884, however, he formed a legal body which, while in no real sense a church, naturally and inevitably codified the as yet flexible beliefs that had developed among the various Bible-study groups. Zion's Watch Tower Tract Society was essentially a publishing organization, designed not only to print and distribute the magazine *Zion's Watch Tower* but also the increasing number of pamphlets and books produced by members of the Society. And it was in the distribution of this flood of material that Russell was to make his unique contribution to contemporary religious practice. So successful was he that members of the Society were eventually to be referred to as "publishers" and consider it as part of their highest duty to God and man to "publish" news of the coming Kingdom by selling the Society's literature from door to door.

Russell organized his publishing operation as though it were a major—and continuing—sales campaign. He advertised for a thousand "preachers," and though he got less than four hundred, they formed a formidable spearhead for his religious shock battalion. Drawing upon his very considerable experience in advertising and salesmanship, he guided his "preachers" into the art in racy, colloquial English. They were given suggestions and recommendations rather than outright instructions or orders. He suggested that they employ trusty boys or girls, on a commission basis, who would go out and get orders for the publications ("Girls would generally succeed best."). He advised them how to approach the client in his home, how long to spend on each visit—"no more than two or three minutes at each house"; how to shame parsimonious householders into parting with a paltry twenty-five cents for priceless reading matter. The preachers, in fact, were working in a sellers' market: Some quality about *Zion's Watch Tower* satisfied the spiritual hunger of thousands. Unlike the turgid, subliterate flow of such publications as Jezreel's *Flying Roll*, Russell's magazine was written for the most part in a vernacular that might perhaps descend into banality, but was usually at least clear and vigorous. By the turn of the century, there were at least twenty thousand regular subscribers, and though Russell was still prepared to pour money into the organization, it was gradually becoming self-supporting. In 1891, Russell undertook his first round-the-world trip, as a result of which branches were later opened in England, Germany, and Australia; in 1893, the first of the famous Watch Tower Conventions was held in Chicago; in 1908, pressure of work had become so great and the movement so international that the comparatively remote city of Pittsburgh was deemed no longer suitable, and the headquarters were moved to New York.

But though the Society gave the impression of moving effortlessly from triumph to triumph, Russell's personal life meanwhile moved from crisis to crisis, studded with lawsuits. The first and most damaging was his divorce. He had married in 1879, and though he and his wife had been drawn together by their mutual passionate interest in Bible study, there was little happiness in the marriage. They separated in 1897, and nine years later Mrs. Russell instituted proceedings against him, citing an impressive number of grounds ranging from "conceit, egotism and domination" via adultery to an attempt to have her certified as insane. Russell lost the case, with consequent immense, if temporary, damage to the Society, as disillusioned members dropped away in the hundreds. Almost immediately he was involved in a libel action, for he incautiously sued a pamphleteer who mocked his claims to scholarship, in particular his claims to that knowledge of Greek which allowed him to adjust translations as required. Russell seems to have panicked, for he must have known that it was the easiest thing in the world to prove or disprove the possession of a foreign language. As it was, he had to endure the profound humiliation of standing up in court, looking blankly at a page of Greek, and being forced to admit that he could not even transliterate the characters. After that fiasco came the bizarre business of the "miracle wheat." A Virginian farmer had developed a strain which more than trebled the normal yield. Overjoyed, Russell hailed it as the first yield of the Millennium, when each grain of wheat, each cluster of grapes, would yield a hundredfold. Two of his Bible students presented the Society with a quantity of the wheat, which was to be sold for the general funds. Russell sold it, and there was an ambiguity regarding what happened to the $1,800 that resulted from the sale. When the New York *Daily Eagle* accused him outright of embezzling the money, he threw himself into yet another libel action, and yet again lost.

The notoriety of the cases and the tangled subsequent controversy served to obscure Russell's character for posterity. But behind the veil of words can be detected a likable human being, a warm, intelligent, impulsive man who, in his impatient quest for the truth, frequently got himself into untenable situations from which he could not extricate himself without some cost to his reputation. In the matter of the divorce, the objective observer almost inevitably ends as a partisan of the guilty party. Mrs. Russell was a tough-minded woman determined to thrust her way high in the Society. Even if her husband had been prepared to back down in her favor, his followers would have been scandalized, for did not the Bible teach that the woman should be in subjection to the man? The charge of adultery was certainly unfounded, although Russell was undoubtedly incautious in his relationship with their adopted daughter, Rose. The probability, too, is that Russell—a handsome, distinguished-looking man—encountered the usual hazard that threatens a man of God from too devoted, usually unmarried females, and his wife resented it, adding it to her store of complaints.

Outside his marriage the dislike that Russell could arouse in his contemporaries arose from his passionate, unswerving conviction that he really did hold the key to man's stupendous future. Significantly, he liked to refer to himself as a "timelock," and his choice of phrase at once threw light on his essential humility as a man—a mere device to be used for the divine purpose—and his arrogance as a prophet proclaiming and defending that purpose.

But as the fateful year 1914 drew closer, the reader can detect a growing hesitancy in the prophet's published words. In 1889 he could state unequivocally, "We consider it an established truth that the final kingdoms of the world, and the full establishment of the Kingdom of God will be accomplished near the end of A.D. 1915 . . . The beginning of the early phase of the Kingdom in the end of A.D. 1914 will, we understand, consist wholly of the resurrected holy ones of olden time—from John the Baptiser back to Abel . . ." [53] But by 1907 he was obviously beginning to doubt the wisdom of anchoring Zion's Watch Tower in the shifting sands of biblical calculations. How many brave millennial organizations had withered away because their leaders insisted on giving a fixed date for the ending of things, and when that date had arrived. . . . Referring to the complex calculations through which he had arrived at 1914, Russell remarked cautiously, "We have never claimed that they were knowledge, nor based upon indisputable evidence . . . our claim has always been that they were based upon faith." With courage and honesty he faced the problem as to what the Society's position would be "if A.D. 1915 should pass with the world's affairs all serene and with evidence that the very elect had not all been changed." It would indeed be a hard blow—but not a fatal one. "One of the strings of our harp would be quite broken. However, dear friends, our harp would have still all other strings in tune." [54]

But whatever doubts Pastor Russell might be entertaining in the privacy of his mind, he gave every appearance of confidence to those around him. One of his lieutenants, A. H. Macmillan, gave a picture of what happened in the last week of September, 1914. There had been a large and successful convention, and a number of the delegates had been lodged at Bethel—the headquarters building in New York where Russell himself lodged. There was a feeling of Christmas morning excitement that built up to a climax on October 1, "because a few of us seriously thought we were going to heaven during the first week of that October." At breakfast on the morning of October 2, Macmillan and his companions were at the table together as usual, waiting for the pastor. He entered the room, "but this morning, instead of proceeding to his seat as usual, he briskly clapped his hands and happily announced 'The Gentile Times have ended; the kings have had their day.' We all applauded." [55]

Did Russell really believe that the awesome machinery had started, that the prosaic breakfast they were about to eat would be the last they would ever eat because their glorified bodies would never again need earthly food? Or was he whistling in the dark, as much to keep up his spirits as to comfort and sustain his followers? They needed comfort as the hours of waiting became days, the days weeks, and at last the great year of 1914 melted into the past. The feeble of faith fell away, but Russell never doubted. There was disappointment, naturally—bitter disappointment—but God could not deceive his Elect, and therefore there must have been an elementary error in calculation or interpretation. Meanwhile the greatest war in the history of the planet had broken over Europe, and even the unconverted were speaking of Armageddon. So Pastor Russell continued his Bible study with undiminished confidence and began again his long missionary journeys, though he was now an old man in failing health. And it was on a train on one of these journeys, somewhere between California and Texas, that he died on October 31, 1916, confident still in his God and his mission.

And his followers, his fellow members in Zion's Watch Tower, who passionately believed themselves to be witnesses to Jehovah's greatness, but were not yet known as Jehovah's Witnesses, began the search for another pastor who would supervise the vital task of preparing the world for the End.

The story began some six thousand years ago, sometime after the Creator had appointed one of the most glorious of his great angels as warden of earth and guardian of Eden. The angel, envious at last of the continuous praises offered up by Adam and Eve, seduced Eve in the guise of the serpent, persuaded the mortal couple to worship him instead of the distant Jehovah, and even persuaded those lesser angels who formed his own court to worship him now as monarch instead of honoring him as vassal. The angel had become Satan and presented his omnipotent Creator with a problem. The rebellious vassal could be blotted out of existence with a word of power—but, paradoxically, this would be a confession of weakness, an apparent admission that the All Powerful feared the competition of a creature. Jehovah therefore accepted the challenge. Satan was to have total freedom to corrupt mankind in an attempt to win them to his service. He was given six thousand years to do this: If, at the end of that period, he had not succeeded in corrupting all human beings, without exception, then he and all his angels and followers would be destroyed.

Central to the doctrine was the concept of God vindicating His name, that name vilified and traduced by Satan. Russell and his followers turned to Exodus for the foundation of their belief: "For this cause have I raised thee up, for to show in thee my power, and that my name may be declared throughout all the Earth." [56] Enigmatically, Russell turned to the derived rather than the original Hebrew version of that name, and it was the euphonius "Jehovah," rather than the craggy "Yahweh" or "Jahwah," that became enshrined in the movement's title. Russell claimed, and his successors enthusiastically embraced that claim, that the witnesses to Jehovah's name were as old as history itself, ranging down from the unfortunate Abel via every outstanding and godly person, whether he called himself Jew or Catholic or Lutheran. Apart from their shared role as witnesses, they possessed one additional characteristic in common—in particular if they were nominally Christian: They were in rebellion, open or otherwise, against the established religious order of their day. A suspicion amounting at times to a savage contempt of the orthodox Christian churches was one of the badges of the movement. Formal Christianity, from the death of Saint Paul onward, had systematically distorted and obscured the great Truth, Russell proclaimed.

The role of Jesus Christ in this cosmogony was therefore peculiar to the movement. He was, in effect, a substitute for the fallen angel, created by Jehovah to assume the role of guardian and lord of earth, destined to lead the redeemed element of mankind into the earthly paradise at last. He, too, would have His court, for Jehovah decreed that 144,000 virtuous human beings would be resurrected at death to ascend to heaven and there form the "New Heavens" with Christ, in place of the fallen angels who were now Satan's attendant demons. Those who were actually alive at the advent of the Millennium and who were considered worthy to reign with Christ would never know death. Those who were dead, but were also considered worthy, would be resurrected to share in the earthly paradise. All others would experience not an eternity of suffering, as the orthodox taught, but simply nothingness. It speaks much for Pastor Russell's humanity that at a period when the major Christian churches seemed fascinated by the concept of hell—so dazzled, indeed, by its flames that they had difficulty in seeing heaven—he boldly declared its nonexistence. The technique he used in proving his case was his favored one of juggling with translated words. " 'Gehenna' is translated 'hell,' but literally means 'Valley of Hinnom' . . . originally a valley outside Jerusalem's southwest wall, [which] became Jerusalem's dump or incinerator, where the city's refuse was dumped and destroyed by burning. To increase the destructive power of the flames, the Jews added brimstone or sulphur. Occasionally the dead bodies of criminals who were considered too vile to have any hope of resurrection were not buried in a grave but were cast into the fire of Gehenna to be burned to ashes . . . Hence the valley of Hinnom or Gehenna became a symbol, not of eternal torment, but of the place or condition of everlasting condemnation; the flames of Gehenna symbolized the everlasting destruction from which there can be no recovery or resurrection." [57]

At the end of the six thousand years, God would engage Satan in the Battle of Armageddon, bind him, and destroy the world. Russell certainly did not intend it to be understood that the physical world would be physically shattered, burnt, drowned, or in any way brought to term in time and space. Rather he foresaw the end of a condition of affairs, the end of death, pain, and sin, which were the natural corollaries to the rule of Satan. With that end, the Millennium would begin. And just as the Bible had given clear, unequivocal pointers to the development of history, so it provided clear, quite unequivocal means to calculate the Great Day of the Lord.

In order to follow Russell's chronological calculations, the reader ideally should not only be equipped with Russell's exhaustive knowledge of Old and New Testaments, but also be able to follow his dizzy leaps from book to book, to recognize his complete belief in the factual truth of every word together with his ability to select favorite texts while wholly ignoring the unfavorable. At one stage, when the Great Pyramid of Gizeh was arousing great popular interest, Russell even fell victim to the pseudo-science of pyramidology and enthusiastically buttressed his biblical calculations with those based on the pyramid's dimensions.

Essentially, however, his calculations were based on the famous chapter in Saint Luke where Christ enumerates the signs of the End. Christ had warned of the coming destruction of Jerusalem, of how the very Temple would be thrown down. "Master, when shall these things be?" his appalled hearers had asked. "When ye shall see Jerusalem compassed with armies, then know that the desolation thereof is nigh . . . There shall be great distress in the land, and wrath upon this people and Jerusalem shall be trodden down of the Gentiles, until the time of the Gentiles shall be fulfilled." [58] But how long would this "time of the Gentiles" endure? For answer, Russell turned to the horrific story of Nebuchadnezzar's madness in Daniel: "Seven times" passed over the wretched madman's head while he ate grass like a beast in the field. And to find out the length of a "time," Russell took one of his dizzy leaps and landed in Revelation where the woman clothed with the sun escaped from the Dragon and remained hid for "a time, two times and half a time" or "a thousand two hundred and three score years." If three and one-half times equaled 1,260 days, then seven times must logically equal 2,520 days. And finally the accommo-dating Ezekiel provided the information that "I have appointed thee each day for a year," and 2,520 years from B.C. 607 brought the calculations exactly to A.D. 1914. One needed only patience to wait, and a certain skill to reinterpret and recalculate when the longed-for day arrived—and drifted into the past like any other.

(ii) *"Millions Now Living Will Never Die"*

Throughout its long and stormy history, Christianity had seen law-yers, bankers, theologians, and on occasion even soldiers occupying the seats of religious power. On the death of Pastor Russell in 1916, for the first time in history the businessman and advertising executive made his bow in the person of Judge J. F. Rutherford, successor to Russell and the true architect of the new religion. The profound difference between the two men found expression even in their appearance: Russell—handsome, with white hair and beard and dark, lustrous eyes, looked like an Old Testament prophet, while Rutherford—jowled, neatly suited, clean-shaven, icy-eyed— could have been a prototype for the folk-figure of the thirties, the tycoon. Yet though in mind and manner and appearance he was to-tally a product of North America of the boom years, yet in role and instinct he belonged to a far older species, a group which in-cluded some of the world's greatest saints and sinners—those who placed their imprint upon a society after a period of formative chaos. Saint Paul and the little monk Hildebrand (who became Pope Gregory VII), John Calvin and John Knox, Francis of As-sisi and Ignatius Loyola would each have recognized something of their own goals and energy in Joseph Rutherford, even as they would have deplored his manner.

Unlike so many of the leaders of the rapidly proliferating sects and cults, Rutherford was legally and fully entitled to his title, for he was indeed a fully qualified lawyer and had served as judge in Missouri. As he climbed higher in the Russellite movement, he seemed more and more intent upon ensuring that his personal life should be kept secret so that it was not even known for certain whether or not he was married. He was one of five children of a Missouri farmer, a harsh and godly man who regarded his children as free labor granted him by the Almighty. When young Joseph declared that he wanted to become a lawyer, Rutherford senior demanded that his son pay for a substitute to take his place on the farm. The type of childhood this implies would explain adequately enough the type of man that Joseph Rutherford became.

At Russell's death, Zion's Watch Tower Society was run by a president and board of directors. Under Russell, the Society could be described either as a democracy which had freely yielded the direction of its life to its leader, or a benevolent autocracy: Russell's power was complete, but tempered by his own sense of personal limitations. He had given no indication that he had any particular regard for Rutherford; to the contrary, the judge was merely one of the reserves of the editorial committee set up to run the all-important magazine. But during the confused days that followed the leader's death, an energetic and not too scrupulous man could establish himself very firmly indeed. Afterwards, when Rutherford emerged as president, there were bitter charges of chicanery and vote-rigging. The charges were admittedly made by the unsuccessful candidates, but Rutherford's first act as president gave ample evidence that he regarded rules and regulations as aids to his advancement; where they impeded that advance, they were to be ignored or adapted. With the energy of the fledgling cuckoo ridding itself of competitors in the nest, Rutherford set about purging the board of directors of all who opposed him.

There were seven on the board, of whom four were in bitter opposition to him, claiming with justice that he was seeking to impose his will in contemptuous disregard for the beliefs or wishes of the majority. The constitution of the Society was such that he should have been outvoted and, if not deposed, at least forced to limit his actions. Instead, to their astonishment, it was the majority who found themselves dismissed and deposed. The extraordinary result was due in part to Rutherford's very real legal skill in proving, on a completely technical point, that the four directors had not legally been elected to the board. But the pale technicality was given force by the man's violent, autocratic nature. P. S. L. Johnson, one of those expelled with the directors, described the physical assault that Rutherford made upon him. It came at the end of a stormy meeting of the board, with Rutherford shouting his demands. "He ordered me to leave Bethel on pain of legal proceedings. I replied that I had appealed to the Board from that decision and that since I recognised the Board as in control . . . I awaited its decision. If it ordered me to leave I would do so at once. At this he completely lost control. To enforce his order he rushed at me, crying out 'You leave this house.' Grabbing me by the arm he almost jerked me off my feet." [59] In the face of such white-faced, hysterical rage, the bravest man would think it prudent to retire and regroup his forces.

Aided by the impetus of that first resounding victory, Rutherford set about purging the administration of all potential sources of opposition to his will and desires. The moderate element quailed, broke off the engagement, and then broke away all together to form their own splinter groups, each little group claiming to be the true inheritor of the word as preached by Pastor Russell. The great bulk of the movement, however—those ordinary men and women who never personally suffered Rutherford's scathing tongue and scornful eye—gravitated to him because, for all his faults, he was positive and utterly, devastatingly sincere in his beliefs. With America's entry into the war in April 1917, the New World itself was swept up into Armageddon. The End obviously could not be long delayed: "We have only a few months in which to labor before the great night settles down when no man can work," he wrote in October. His re-election to the office of president in January 1918 was almost a formality and, firmly in control of the only organization equipped to face the end of the world, he embarked on an ambitious project of simultaneously undermining the corrupt governments of the world and their priestly supporters, while trumpeting the message of Jehovah to the leaderless, helpless multitude. Rutherford might perhaps be a bully, but he was certainly no coward, being prepared to take on anyone and anything that stood in the way of the "theocratic kingdom" which he was divinely ordained to bring about. The antipathy toward organized religion that Russell had shown became, in Rutherford, a steady scream of hatred. "Religion is a snare of the Devil," he declared roundly, an ancient web of lies designed to entrap the souls of men and, by necessary extension, the priests of the orthodox religion were—wittingly or unwittingly—ministers of Satan. The governments of the world—and specifically, the government of the United States of America—were designed to prop up "the present evil order of things."

Under normal circumstances, such mouthings would have been dismissed as harmless if unpleasant fanaticism. But these were not normal times. The first, terrible, casualty figures were circulating through America. The country was gripped in the ferocious xenophobia and mindless patriotism that characterized every country caught up in the hell of the Great War. Rutherford's contempt for established government, his belief that all soldiers on both sides of the conflict were equally deluded, could very easily be established as treason. As early as February 1918, government agents began investigating the affairs and motives of Rutherford and his followers; in May, warrants were issued for his arrest and for that of most of the administrative body of the Watch Tower Society. In July, seven of the eight men, including Rutherford himself, were sentenced to the appalling term of eighty years in prison. They were charged specifically with inciting the armed services to mutiny, but the savagery of the sentences also reflected the rage of the conservative against an organization that not only proclaimed, but actually behaved as though, the accepted pattern of social life was an empty, meaningless show. It was to be the first of many increasingly venomous attacks upon the Society. In this instance, however, the movement's enemies had overreached themselves, and Rutherford and his followers served scarcely ten months of their sentences before being released in March 1919 on the grounds that the trial had been misdirected.

Confirmed overwhelmingly in the presidency, martyred indubitably if temporarily for his faith, Rutherford was given a free hand to mold the movement into his own image and likeness—and he took the opportunity with total confidence in his rectitude, total indifference to the objections of others. Indicative of the scope and nature of his planned changes was the name he now bestowed upon the Society. The clumsy title of Zion's Watch Tower Tract Society related to its publishing activities and was, in any case, scarcely a stirring rallying cry; the members themselves were variously known as Russellites, Millennial Dawners, and even by the colorless term, International Bible Students. They were all witnesses to Jehovah's name, Rutherford argued, and therefore should adopt that name as banner: From 1931 onwards the succinct, impressive title "Jehovah's Witnesses" was used for the whole movement.

A few days before Rutherford was thrown into prison, he had given a lecture in Brooklyn under the resounding title, "The World has ended: Millions now living will never die." It was a courageous, not to say foolhardy, title to choose considering how the world had so conspicuously failed to end in 1914. But it was all of a piece with Rutherford's ability to remold philosophy to square with reality, an ability which he was to transmit to his revived organization. For despite the lip service paid to Pastor Russell as founder, in sober fact the Jehovah's Witnesses cult was Judge Rutherford's creation. On his release from prison, he ruthlessly set about editing or eliminating large areas of the doctrine as propounded by his predecessor. There is little doubt that Rutherford was totally sincere in those interpretations, but there is equally little doubt but that he interpreted in a wholly ad hoc, intensely personal manner. His was not by any means an original mind; his innovations were shallow, bearing evidence of a narrow, rather mean personality that was entirely self-absorbed. But the second-rate desires and opinions were backed by an immensely formidable will power, so that they achieved instantaneously the status of law as soon as they were enunciated.

The first, and most essential need, was a reinterpretation of the chronological prophecies to explain the disasters and disappointments that had beset the Witnesses over the past few years. By juggling with Revelation, Rutherford was able to prove that the very disasters of the Witnesses were the fulfillment of divine prophecy concerning them. In Revelation the monster had climbed out of the abyss and slaughtered the two witnesses of God. The lifeless corpses had lain exposed to public gaze in the streets of the evil city but, after three and a half days, the corpses triumphantly returned to life, to the amazement of the bystanders, and then ascended to heaven. In exactly the same manner, Rutherford announced, the Jehovah's Witnesses had been "dead" for three and a half years—from the autumn of 1914 when Russell's prophecy had failed to be fulfilled, to May of 1918, when Rutherford and his followers had been imprisoned. The year 1914, in fact, had not been the foredoomed year when Christ would gather up his Elect and usher in the earthly paradise, but was the year in which Christ hurled Satan out of heaven during that great war in heaven foretold in Revelation. Thrown out of heaven, Satan had come to earth and was now energetically seeking to bring it under his rule in the dwindling time left to him. Proof? The terrible war in Europe. Admittedly, the Great War had come to an end of mutual exhaustion in November 1918, but all historians agreed that the world would never be the same again, that 1914–1918 drew a red weal across human history that would never disappear. Unenlightened historians merely noted that the pattern of life had changed: Jehovah's Witnesses were able to state unequivocally that they were living in the times of the End. And when would the consummation come about? In 1925, Rutherford declared firmly and incautiously. It was the last such time he was to commit himself to a date quite so indiscreetly, for when 1925 arrived and departed with no more than the usual load of human misery, he announced that though the time of the End was indeed probably imminent, only God knew the exact day. Rutherford's successors were to prove of tougher fiber, in this matter at least, proclaiming in 1966 that the end of things would come about in October 1975. Presumably an alternate date is being prepared should the sun, after all, arise upon November 1975.

Among the lumber which Rutherford cleared out of the Witnesses' attic was the belief in the Ingathering of the Jews in Jerusalem and the role played in Witness prophecy by the Great Pyramid of Gizeh. The Ingathering had played a constant role, larger or smaller, in almost every millennial organization. Some may have viewed it purely symbolically, as Bockelson and Jezreel had done by transforming their own headquarters into New Jerusalem; others, like Brothers, had insisted that real Hebrews must make the painfully real journey from all the corners of the earth where they had been dispersed, back to the physical strip of land in the eastern Mediterranean. Allenby's entry into Jerusalem during the war had caused immense excitement to the more literal party, but by the early thirties it became evident that the return of Israel remained still in an unspecified future, and Rutherford excised it from the canon. The Great Pyramid theory was thrown out with a similar cavalier disregard for Pastor Russell's posthumous reputation, together with Russell's insistence on the necessity of keeping the Sabbath.

But if Rutherford threw out ideas, he imported or developed others with equal energy. Russell had referred to, without a great deal of emphasis upon, the idea of the return of the "ancient worthies." These were the witnesses to Jehovah who had kept their faith during the long rule of Satan but died before Christ was created to take the place of the fallen angel. Abel, Abraham, Isaac, Ezekiel—all the great prophets and virtuous heroes of Jewry would be resurrected on earth as signs of the approaching Millennium. The concept of a physical return of immortalized bodies to a physical earth having been established, it was logical to enquire how and where these returned ancient worthies would be housed and entertained. Rutherford decreed that a suitable mansion should be purchased in California and furnished in preparation for the return of the heroes. And rather than leave the building with its valuable contents standing empty for an indefinite period, he announced that he intended to live in it himself as its caretaker. From any other person such a statement and action would have seemed a crudely cynical manipulation of public trust for private means. But behind the tycoon's face and administrator's skill was a remarkably naïve mind. In a different generation and milieu, Judge Rutherford could have been the founder of a cargo cult. The difference between a New Guinea native painstakingly laying down an airstrip and hopefully awaiting the coming of the magical aircraft crammed with good things, and Judge Rutherford hopefully awaiting the return of Abraham in his California mansion, seems one of degree rather than of kind.

Rutherford adapted and imported religious ideas, but it was in humdrum organization that he made his true mark. Jehovah's Witnesses was to be truly a theocratic organization with so absolute a hold upon its members' hearts and minds and souls as to make that other theocracy, the papacy, seem sloppily democratic by contrast. By the mid-twenties the movement had been purged of all who differed from him in any degree, and on that soft blankness he placed a permanent imprint. His most important measure was, characteristically, not original. Over half a century earlier, James Jershom Jezreel had equated the demonstration of faith with the energy displayed in selling copies of his scripture, and Charles Russell took the principle a giant step forward when he built his movement around a tract-publishing organization. But Rutherford's genius was personally suited to precisely this task.

It was in September 1919 that he launched a new form of religious activity when, to the missionary, the saint, and the martyr, he added the figure of the advertiser. "Advertise, advertise, advertise the King and his Kingdom," he cried to his fellow Witnesses, and they did. Over the next generation they were to distribute an estimated total of one and one-half billion pieces of literature; over the same period it is probable that every urban domestic dwelling in the English-speaking countries, and a very high proportion of all others in Europe, had at least one visit from an earnest "publisher" who, armed with comprehensive catechism, was prepared to wrestle for the soul of the hostile, indifferent, or simply embarrassed householder facing him. Other religions, cults, or denominations might be content to claim as member any person who was simply too indolent or indifferent to dispute the claim. From Rutherford's day onward, the definition of a Jehovah's Witness included only those who were prepared to "witness"—to trudge endlessly through countless miles of dreary suburbs, encountering rebuffs, laughter, contempt, and actual violence and to spend their scanty remaining leisure in study of their movement's version of the Bible. For this was the second prong of Rutherford's immensely effective double-pronged assault upon the citadel of Satan. It was not enough for the Witnesses to give up their lives to publishing the truth; the truth they published must be, undeviatingly, that handed down from the vicar of God. Rutherford took the concept to its extreme and logical conclusion, employing modern techniques with his usual flair. Witnesses were supplied with a gramophone and a record of the judge expounding the truth; all the Witness had to do was prevail upon his unwilling audience to wait while the machine was switched on, and the judge's deep and thrilling voice would then do all that was required. Rutherford even made effective use of the new means of communication—radio—and eventually operated six stations which, through a nationwide network, took his fifteen-minute sermon to every part of the continent.

Membership of the Jehovah's Witnesses snowballed, literally doubling every decade. Where it had been ignored as a mere group of eccentrics during its early Bible-study days, it was now seen as a threat by church and state alike, as its numbers moved toward a half million and then, inexorably, towards a million. Rutherford's hatred of the established religions was incorporated into the structure of his own movement, and the established religions fought back. They attacked first the Witnesses' desecration of the Sabbath, and in lawsuit after lawsuit Rutherford had to defend his "publishers" against the civil offense of selling literature at the door on a Sunday. This running battle continued throughout the twenties and early thirties but proved to be a mere skirmish compared with what was to follow. For as the world began to lurch yet again toward another titanic war, so the frenetic yells of patriotism began to drown the few moderate voices. As early as 1935 the Witnesses in America were charged with insulting the flag. An organization that awaited the setting up of a divine kingdom perhaps had no choice but to refuse to honor the emblem of an earthly power, but it did nothing to endear them to fellow Americans, and again court case followed court case. With the outbreak of war, insults and judicial fines gave way to judicial imprisonment and mob violence: Later, the Witnesses' archivists calculated that, between 1940 and 1944, 2,500 mob attacks were made upon members of the cult. The Witnesses' refusal to fight had nothing in common with religious pacifism. They had no objection to war as such—to the contrary, they held that their final triumph would be brought about by the bloodiest and most gruesome war in history—but they were trapped in the unbreakable web of their logic. Earthly governments, whether American, Nazi, British, French, or whatever the local variant, were all irrelevant at best, and at worst were delaying the setting up of the ultimate government. They paid very heavily indeed for their steadfast faith. In the democracies, death came to the Witnesses through mob violence; in the dictatorships—Japan and Germany particularly—they became the object of official persecution. Thousands of them were thrown into the concentration camps of Europe where they gained the wholehearted, if slightly sardonic, admiration of their fellow victims. Those who recorded their impressions of the Witnesses in the camps of Buchenwald, Dachau, Ravensbruck, and the rest remarked that the average Witness tended to be ill-educated, narrow-minded, and dogmatic, but also noted that, "Because of their conscientious work habits they were always selected as foremen. Even though they were the only group of prisoners who never abused or mistreated other prisoners . . . S.S. officers preferred them as orderlies because of their work habits, skills and unassuming attitudes. Quite in contrast to the continuous internecine warfare among other prisoner groups, the Jehovah's Witnesses never misused their closeness to S.S. officers to gain positions of privilege in the camp." [60] Such a testimony from hell was one of which any group could be proud.

Joseph Franklin Rutherford died in January 1942 at the age of seventy-two, his successor was chosen decorously, and the Jehovah's Witnesses began that explosion of growth that brought them up to the million mark by 1964. Their enormous conventions, when anything up to one hundred thousand delegates would attend for a week or more, were so efficiently organized that they became models for others to try to emulate. Their printing presses broadcast their message by the million copies; their scholars undertook the notoriously controversial task of attempting their own translation of the Bible; even their film makers threw themselves into the business of bringing the message informatively and entertainingly to a humanity wandering lost down murky byways. Martin Luther, who in his time made similar energetic use of the newly invented printing press to spread his own version of truth, would have envied the media available to the Witnesses, applauded their technique, and regarded with considerable bewilderment what they were so intent upon communicating.

(iii) Armageddon and After

Sometime during the closing years of the present century—and probably during the closing phase of the seventh decade—some million or so people will walk out of whatever shelter they chose while destruction fell upon the world, and look around them. They are "the surviving sheep of the New World Society (who) will go forth to look upon the slain of Jehovah." It would seem that the immediately dominant, inescapable first impression of the terrestrial paradise will be an appalling stench, for the survivors will see scattered around them the two billion or so people who have been destroyed in the war of Armageddon. Natural forces will, however, continue to operate until the planet is cleansed: "Worms will not stop swarming over the millions of bodies until the last body is eaten up. Birds and beasts will also eat their fill of human flesh until nothing is left but white bone." [61] Following the instructions given in Ezekiel, all the survivors will then spend exactly seven months, no more and no less, in burying the bones. Thereafter, pious travelers who come across any bones that have not been buried will set up a notice beside them so that special burial detachments can dispose of them. And after this titanic mortician's operation, the joys of the Millennium will presumably begin.

Pastor Russell had banished hell for his followers; Judge Rutherford substituted the concept of earth as a charnel house. Down the centuries, each millennial group had developed the aspect of the belief which most appealed to them. The majority had concentrated on the problem as to how best to bring paradise about. Few, until the coming of Joseph Rutherford, had troubled themselves overmuch about the actual details of the battle of Armageddon. Even John, the author of Revelation, the man who had created the idea, dismissed it casually in a sentence or two, although the choice of the site where this, the last battle, would be fought betrayed his Jewish culture.

The plain at the foot of Har-Megiddo (the Mountain of Megiddo) some ten miles southwest of Nazareth had been a natural battleground for centuries before John's day and would continue to be a battleground for centuries afterwards. The Pass of Megiddo was a natural route for an army moving northward. In 1479 B.C., Thothmes III smashed a rebellious force of Syrians there; in 1918 A.D., British artillery punched a hole through the Turkish lines in the same place. It was therefore "into a place called in the Hebrew tongue Armageddon" that the writer of Revelation naturally gathered together all the kings of the earth for the final battle after the sixth angel had poured out the bowl of wrath. Considering the lurid and haunting terms with which John could describe the process of destruction, he was comparatively restrained—uninterested, it seems—in this supposedly greatest of battles. Mountains and islands vanished; the "great city" was divided into three parts, and there was a great hailstorm, "every stone about the size of a talent." It was an unimpressive scenario, but other prophets in the Bible could provide facets which, combined, would give a mosaic of appropriate terror and horror.

Rutherford might have been by nature, inclined to give excessive emphasis to the idea of Armageddon, but he was also driven to it by logical necessity produced, in turn, by the very success of the Society. The problem that faced him was, in effect, that outlined by the parable of the laborers in the vineyard: Were the hundreds—the thousands—of converts to enjoy the same privileges in the New World as did those who had labored from the beginning? They could hardly be expected to be glorified, to become part of the saintly elite in heaven itself, and would have to be content with the reward of eternal life in the terrestrial paradise. But this, after all, was precisely the destiny which Pastor Russell held out for all humans who were not transported bodily to heaven. What, then, was the point of becoming a member of the New World Society, of devoting all one's free time and energy, of tramping through endless suburbs, if at the end one would enjoy no more—if no less—than the ungodly? Driven by the same remorseless logic that made even the tender-hearted Saint Augustine claim that the blessed actively rejoiced in the agonies of the damned, Rutherford was forced to the conclusion that all outside the Society were to be destroyed at Armageddon. Nevertheless, Jehovah in his mercy had given the clearest possible signs of the impending End, so that those whose eyes are opened may yet scramble just in time onto the ark.

It is highly doubtful whether any generation of men has ever considered itself wholly blessed, has ever been so wholly contented with its lot that any change must seem change for the worse. Fundamentalist sects, too, of their nature are incurably pessimistic about the present. The past can be viewed as a golden age, despite its bubonic plagues and periodic massacres and famines, because it is lit by the sun of faith. The distant future, when all will have been swept under the wing of the God-favored sect, is also bright. The present alone is murky and threatening. Historical accident, however, enabled the Jehovah's Witnesses to add some very pointed observations regarding the signs of the End, observations over and above those usually relating to the perennially uncertain state of human existence. The destruction of the Old World in 1914, the appalling scope and frequency of worldwide famines despite an almost miraculous improvement in agricultural technology, the frequency and scale of armed conflict resulting in the agonized deaths of untold millions over the past half-century, the sudden nightmare of air, land, and water pollution, and finally the looming, brooding menace of nuclear power have spelled out to the least imaginative that a most ancient pattern of life is irrevocably at an end. For most people, the crises are the products of an enormously expanding population that has also acquired unprecedented technological skills and appetites; for the Jehovah's Witnesses they are the working out of prophecies—a working out so clearcut that, in 1953, the Society was able to publish a work that classified and described the signs of the End under thirty-nine different headings.

High among these signs of impending evil was the formation of the wretched League of Nations and its pallid successor, the United Nations Organization. Neither friends nor enemies of U.N.O. would define its major characteristic as a demonic vitality, but for the New World Society, it is the seven-headed Beast of Revelation because it usurps—or attempts to usurp—the planetary sovereignty that belongs to the Kingdom of God alone. And here, perhaps, the ghost of Nero receives its last and greatest humiliation. Nineteen centuries earlier, the embattled Christians had interpreted that infinitely sinister description of "the beast that was and is not," the head that was dead and yet lived, as the resurrected murderer, the emperor Nero. Over the following centuries, wanly he had dwindled; now, in the twentieth century, he was transformed at last into an incompetent bureaucracy. The Beast that had died and come to life was the international organization that had died but was resurrected as the United Nations. The woman clothed in scarlet seated upon its back—the woman who was "Mystery, the Mother of Harlots and Abominations of the Earth"—was the twentieth-century spirit of organized religion, not least that controlled from Rome. During the Second World War, indeed, Adolf Hitler, Pope Pius XII, and Satan were pictured as being in intimate league with each other.

The changing pattern of world alliances and enmities find faithful expression in the signs of the End. Soviet Russia now occupies the place that once was occupied by Nazi Germany and papal Rome. Other fundamentalist sects have cast Russia in the role of satanic power by identifying it with the mysterious power, Rosh, in the prophecies of Ezekiel. Scorning such simple play on words, the Jehovah's Witnesses turn to the faithful witness of Daniel. There, among the symbols of impending doom, a "king of the north" pushes against "a king of the south" precipitating a terrible general war. Daniel meant nothing more than that the northern king, Antiochus, would attack the Egyptian king, but generations of enthusiastic "interpreters" identified the kings according to their own predilections. For the Jehovah's Witnesses, the king of the north is Russia, he of the south, America, and their lethal jockeying for position ends abruptly when the Russian, goaded by "tidings out of the west and out of the north . . . shall go forth with great fury to take away many. And he shall plant the tabernacles of his palace between the seas in the glorious holy mountain: yet he shall come to his end, and none shall help him." [62] Daniel's rich and chaotic style, with its admixture of religious prophecy, historical summary, and military analysis, yet again allows the interpreter to fish out of the potent brew what meaning he will. For the Jehovah's Witnesses, the tidings which goad the Kremlin to fierce and final action is the existence of the New World Society, the knowledge that it scorns and rejects all earthly governments—including that of the U.S.S.R. It is not the first time that the Society has claimed how Satan manipulated his forces in order to obliterate the great center of opposition to his power. In World War II, the demons who controlled the actions of the pilots of the aircraft of the Luftwaffe launched attack after attack upon Bethel, the headquarters of the New World Society in London.

The Russian–Satanic attack upon the New World Society will trigger off the heavenly defense which will, in turn, produce Armageddon. This will not be simply a military engagement in the plain of Har-Megiddo. Presumably this would not be sufficient to eliminate the hundreds of millions of humans who must be removed from the planet in favor of the godly, and natural forces will be summoned up as auxiliaries to the heavenly slaughterers. Flood, rain, fire, and earthquake will take their millions, and plague will remove the rest in a process described in meticulous detail:

> Their flesh shall rot while they are still on their feet: their eyes shall rot in their sockets: and their tongues shall rot in their mouths . . . Eaten up will be the tongues of those who

scoffed and laughed at Armageddon. Eaten up will be the eyes of those who refused to see the sign of the "time of the end"! Eaten up will be the flesh of those who would not learn that the living and true God is named Jehovah. Eaten up while they stand on their feet.[63]

Such is the plan that the ever-loving Jehovah God has in store for his creatures, according to his Witnesses—in a book, intended primarily for children, entitled with unconscious irony *From Paradise Lost to Paradise Regained*.

> When the storm of Armageddon finally passes, the rumble of its thunder fades away and the earth stops shaking under the impact of divine fury expressed against the nations, we will come out from wherever Jehovah God has seen fit to preserve us and we will rejoice in the morning of a new day. When we gaze round, possibly all that will meet our eyes may be rubble and ruin—but, if so, it should look *beautiful* to us. Why? Because then we can say from the depths of our hearts "Thank God, finally the old order . . . is gone for all time." [64]

The Witnesses turn their attention to the physical conditions existing in the terrestrial paradise. The earth will again be an eden—parklike. There will be an abundance of food and drink as promised in Isaiah: "a banquet of well-oiled dishes, a banquet of wine kept on the dregs, of well oiled dishes filled with marrow." Conscious, perhaps, that a diet of strong wine and marrow bones will appeal less to twentieth-century Europeans and North Americans than it did to Palestinians in the sixth century B.C., the Witnesses elaborate on other advantages. Death will not only be banished, but all forms of physical disability as well—blindness, deafness, lameness, leprosy. Sexual congress will continue, but the power of reproduction will be reduced or removed so that "God's earthly family comfortably fills, but never outgrows its home." Unlike the Fifth Monarchists, the Witnesses make no provision for the policing of the Millennium, for crime and sin will, like disease, come to an end: "You will never again need to lock your door or fear for the safety of your loved ones. Not hidden electronic listening devices or concealed television cameras, but God's spirit will be the deterrent for wrongdoing then." Some thought has also been given to the problems facing a generation that has come to associate civilization with technological devices—in particular, those concerned with communication.

> With mail, telephone, telegraph and radio systems gone, how could there be any unified direction of activities, as by an earthly governing body serving under the heavenly kingdom? How will people know where to live? Will it be a case of everyone just picking out the area where he likes and settling there, as was done in the days of the "frontier west" of the United States? If not, how and by whom will the land be assigned out? When the clothing or shoes one is wearing at the time of survival wear out, where will new ones come from . . . Will electric stoves, electric washing machines and similar devices be available? Questions like these are multiple.[65]

And the reader scans on eagerly, whether in skepticism or faith. For the first time in nearly two thousand years, the prophets of the Millennium have lowered their eyes briefly from the titanic events about to unfold in the sky to consider the humdrum but very real facts of life, of conditions in the terrestrial paradise. But though the questions might pour out, the answer they receive is short and distinctly dusty: "God's word, the Bible, does not say and so we do not know." [66]

CHAPTER VIII

•

THE TECHNOLOGICAL DISPENSATION

In June 1895, young Guglielmo Marconi set up an apparatus which succeeded in ringing an electric bell at a distance of three feet. The following year, an improved version of the apparatus sent a signal winging nine miles across the Bristol Channel. In 1898 warships of the Royal Navy were communicating with each other, via Marconi's invention, at a distance of over seventy miles, and in 1901 human beings separated by over three thousand miles were able to communicate instantaneously with each other.

The miraculous nature of the wireless served to raise men's eyes from the surface of the planet to look out, with speculation, into the depths of deep space that had, until now, been the exclusive field of mythology and religion. Marconi himself gave a direct boost to the process in 1921. In September of that year, the London manager of the Marconi Wireless Telegraph Company arrived in New York with the sensational news that Marconi had received signals emanating from Mars or some other point in the solar system. The report was inconclusive, but taken sufficiently seriously for a worldwide listening watch to be set up three years later when

Mars came to its closest point to earth. In 1930 the indefatigable Harry Price, ghost hunter extraordinary and highly skilled self-publicist, announced a plan for sending a light signal to Mars by igniting tons of magnesium on the highest point of the Bernese Oberland. An even more elaborate variation was the proposal to outline Pythagoras's theorem in an enormous system of electric lights; intelligent observers on Mars, it was calculated, could not fail to supply the proof and so initiate communication.

All such proposals were still-born because of the enormous costs involved. Far more practical, and therefore impressively widespread, were the plans to maintain listening watches on the rapidly increasing number of wireless receivers. In 1950, Byron Goodman, the assistant technical editor of *QST*—the official magazine of the American Radio Relay League, Inc.—recorded an encounter with a wireless operator who claimed that ever since the 1920's he had been in wireless communication with extraterrestrial intelligences. Goodman inspected the man's equipment, listened to an exchange of signals, and though he suspected a hoax, could not fault the story, and he thought it worthwhile including in the otherwise austerely technical pages of *QST*.

Throughout the twenties and thirties, newspaper editors faced with a dull page learned that they could always titillate their readers' imaginations with a popular speculative article on life on other worlds. The immense flood of science fiction still lay in the future; apart from the work of the tiny handful of respectable practitioners such as H. G. Wells, science fiction was anonymous and lumped together with the occult in the pages of pulp magazines. But it was contributing steadily to that climate of opinion which resulted in the astonishing scenes of panic when Orson Welles's radio version of *The War of the Worlds* was broadcast in 1938. By the time the Second World War started, the general public was accustomed to the idea—if still couched in openly fictional form—of extraterrestrial interference with worldly affairs.

The cataclysm of Hiroshima gave a new and dramatic twist to the idea. The destruction of the two Japanese cities accelerated the end of the war in the Far East and so tended to obscure the reality of exactly what had happened in the skies above Japan in August 1945. Thereafter the euphoria brought about by the end of the World War, followed by the domestic problems of millions of people trying to pick up the threads of ordinary life in a deeply disturbed world, pushed the horrific problem into the background. It was brought into the foreground, brutally, by the stage-managed explosion on Bikini Atoll on July 1, 1946. The mushroom cloud became a symbol of a huge force, unprecedented in the history of the planet, that was inimical to all life. The fear developed swiftly and logically into the hope, and then the belief, that human beings could yet be saved from themselves by a species of elder brother possessed of vastly superior but benevolent intelligence. Within a fortnight of the Bikini explosion, the mechanistic angels of the new dispensation made their bow. On July 19, a French newspaper, *Resistance*, carried the first report of a wave of mysterious lights and aerial objects that had been seen over Sweden and Finland. Over the following month, most of the other French newspapers, including the magisterial *Le Monde*, carried similar reports, followed by the British and other Europeans. With the memory of the war still vivid, it was inevitable that quasi-military terminology and motives were applied to the objects—ghost rockets, shells, flying bombs being the most common terms, followed by meteors and fiery spheres.

The wave, whatever its source, died down, but it proved to be merely a harbinger. Eleven months later, on June 24, 1947, an American, Kenneth Arnold, was piloting a private aircraft near Mount Rainier when he reported seeing ten huge, shining discs speeding around the peaks of the mountain. In attempting to describe their motion, Arnold chose an unfortunate, if vivid, analogy: They moved like saucers skimming through the air, he reported. The world's press promptly dubbed the mysterious objects "flying saucers," and the term, with its somewhat flippant overtone, was rapidly adopted by believers and skeptics alike. Later, the more exact term "unidentified flying object" came into use. In the current fashion, the initials of the three words produced a noun, UFO, which in turn produced such grammatically unforgivable but semantically useful terms as ufology, ufologist, and even ufo-nauts for the supposed crews of the supposed vehicles.

In groping for a phrase to describe the objects, Kenneth Arnold had quite unwittingly chosen the same word "saucer" that a Texas farmer, John Martin, had chosen to describe a flying object that he had seen in January 1878. For one solid fact was to emerge from the tens of thousands of words and the endless heated controversies that followed the Mount Rainier sighting: Such objects had been seen again and again in the sky over many centuries. Enthusiasts even combed the pages of the Bible seeking to identify the enigmatic visions of the prophets with the flying machines of an unknown race. The vision of Ezekiel, in which the author seemed to be struggling to describe a mechanical object in terms of a pastoral vocabulary, was a prime favorite for such a treatment. That "whirlwind which came out of the north" with its internal fire, revolving wheels, and wings which made a rushing noise "like the noise of great waters" could become, without too much difficulty, a circular craft, crowned with a transparent dome and resting upon four legs. The rich field of Revelation was yet again worked over, this time by those in search not of prophecies and visions, but mechanical devices of unexplained origin and purpose. The enormous angels moving between heaven and earth in searing light and thunderous noise could also, like Ezekiel's whirlwind, be cast in the role of unidentified flying objects without too much distortion of the available evidence.

Erich von Däniken makes the point explicit in his book *Chariots of the Gods.* "Was God an astronaut?" he asks, and develops the plausible argument that the destruction of Sodom was the result of a nuclear explosion, deliberate or accidental, Lot's wife falling victim to the radiation. Elsewhere in his book, whose enormous popularity argues a widespread hunger for such assurances, he cites the enigmatic artifacts and sites revealed by modern archaeological techniques. Unsurprisingly, the riddle of the Pyramids bulks large, and he adds yet another calculation to the thousands already made for the Great Pyramid: its height, multiplied by a thousand million, is approximately the distance between earth and sun.

Scattered throughout the secular chronicles of earlier centuries are sporadic references to enigmatic objects in the sky which were quite distinct from the chroniclers' noting of astronomical phenomena, such as comets, that were taken as signs and portents. In A.D. 776 the Annales Laurissenses recorded how two large, reddish discs (shields = *scutorum*) hovered, apparently watching a fight between pagan and Christian Saxons. In A.D. 840, Agobard, archbishop of Lyons, related how he encountered a lynch party in Lyons engaged in murdering a group of foreign-looking people who had unwisely admitted to descending from a "cloudship." Flodoard, the chronicler of Rheims, recorded that in March 927, "fiery armies" were seen in the sky. Guicciardini, first of the great Italian historians, set down in his sober history details of crosses, wheels, and "armies" seen in the sky in his day; he assumed, by hindsight, that they were divine portents warning of the traumatic French invasion of 1494. The recording of the phenomena which appeared over Nuremberg in April 1561 provided invaluable additional information for posterity, for a drawing was made of the event. The artist was a highly skilled man, for the skyline of Nuremberg shown in the bottom left-hand corner was exquisitely detailed, but the objects he was depicting in the sky were so wholly outside his experience that they became almost arbitrary symbols in his drawing. Yet they were symbols which the more precise recording of the twentieth century were to render familiar—in particular, the cylindrical objects containing a number of discs or globes which, in UFO terminology, became the "mother ships" with scout crafts on board.

The number of reports of mysterious aerial objects increased spectacularly during the nineteenth century, appearing now not only in imprecise terms in general chronicles and popular broadsheets but also in the learned journals of the innumerable societies that sprang up, so confidently, to observe and resolve all mysteries of nature. The documentation of the sightings was so exact that, for the first time, it proved to be possible to prepare graphs of the incidents showing that, for example, there was a peak of activity in the early 1880's and again in the late 1890's. The incidence declined during the first half of the twentieth century and then soared spectacularly between 1946 and the early 1950's.

Until the 1940's, the general opinion regarding the aerial phenomena was that they were either divine portents placed in the sky as warnings, or imperfectly understood natural phenomena, owing their origins to meteorological or astronomical causes. The tense military and political situation in the immediate post-war years, coupled with the war-engendered habit of expecting governments to take the lead in research, led to the formation by the United States Air Force of a survey project to investigate the new wave of phenomena. The Project came into existence in September 1947 and lasted for twenty-two years, being terminated in December 1969. Beginning as an honest attempt to record and analyze objectively, by the end of its existence the Project had succeeded in turning the entire subject into one of mockery, a music-hall turn into which professional astronomers or airmen entered with the greatest reluctance, if at all.

J. Allen Hyneck, the astronomer who was co-opted into the Project initially to sift out sighting reports that had an astronomical explanation, described the effect the Project eventually had upon his professional colleagues. "During an evening reception of several hundred astronomers at Victoria, British Columbia, in the summer of 1968, word spread that just outside the hall strangely maneuvering lights—UFO's—had been spotted. The news was met by casual banter and the giggling sound that often accompanies an embarrassing situation. Not one astronomer ventured outside in the summer night to see for himself." [67] In his book, *The UFO Experience*, Hyneck outlined the problem with lucid detachment, surveyed the work of the Project, and attempted to give an explanation for the unscientific technique of prejudgment adopted by its scientific members. The technique was admirably summed up in the notorious memo which passed between members of the committee before the reorganization of 1966: "The trick would be, I think," wrote the Project coordinator, "to describe the project so that, to the public, it would appear to be a totally objective study but, to the scientific community, would present the image of a group of nonbelievers trying their best to be objective but having an almost zero expectation of finding a saucer." [68] Hyneck made his own position clear, speaking in the name of a sanity that rejected alike the visions of fantasts and the blindness of savants: "I cannot presume to describe what UFO's *are* because I don't know; but I can establish beyond reasonable doubt that they are not *all* misperceptions or hoaxes." The waters had been so muddied by the Project that scientists of the status of Hyneck entered only at peril to their reputation. But meanwhile others, less troubled by pedantic quibbles regarding the nature of cause and effect, plunged enthusiastically in, bringing some very queer fish to shore.

The 1950's wave of sightings was declining when C. G. Jung turned his formidable intelligence to the problem. The subtitle of his book, "a modern myth of things seen in the skies," seems to indicate his opinion succinctly enough, but again and again he returned to that aspect which particularly intrigued him, the seeming reality of the objects in physical terms: "The only thing we know with tolerable certainty about UFOs is that they possess a surface which can be seen by the eye and at the same time throws back a radar echo." [69] With becoming hesitancy, he speculated that the objects "are real material phenomena of an unknown nature, presumably coming from outer space," that had for centuries been visible to human eyes but only achieved their twentieth-century significance because of humanity's desperate need for reassurance. "The present world situation is calculated as never before to arouse expectations of a redeeming, supernatural event." [70]

Flying saucers as Parousia, as a physical expression of the spiritual Second Coming which mankind had been awaiting for nearly two millennia, seemed as bizarre as any theory that had been advanced by the wildest of the cultists. Yet the established church itself seemed reluctant to relinquish the idea of a physical Return which, in a technological age, inevitably aroused speculation regarding the vehicle. In 1971 the bishops of the Anglican Church engaged in a decorous controversy in the columns of the *Times* of London. Bishop F. R. Barry had contributed an article, "Why

Christ Has No Need of a Second Coming," in which he argued that "Parousia is a word that has no plural. There is only one Coming" [71] —a continuing condition that was an inescapable factor of Christ's abiding presence. The letters that followed were overwhelmingly critical, overwhelmingly in favor of accepting the traditional, literal return of Christ, defending and maintaining their position even at the cost, as a skeptical colleague pointed out, of being prepared to admit that the returning Savior could be picked up in space by radar and tracked down to the earth's surface like any other body moving through the skies.

If logic could force high-ranking churchmen to maintain such a concept, there was small wonder that those who yearned for a spiritual answer but were nevertheless free of ecclesiastical discipline, should in time evolve even lusher fantasies. During the peak period of the UFO sightings between 1946 and 1950, the fantasies began to develop away from the pattern established, pre-war, by H. G. Wells and his followers. Then it had been assumed that extraterrestrial creatures would be hideous in appearance and wholly inimical to humanity. So deeply ingrained was this idea that the shorthand term "B. E. M."—bug-eyed monsters—could be used, only partly flippantly, to designate the species. But in the post-war years, the picture began to soften. The monsters disappeared from the "contact" stories, and in their place began to appear beings who were at first merely quaint, but who gradually became angelic in form, manner, and motive. The angels of the technological dispensation, however, differed in one important characteristic from the long line of their supernatural forebears: They were held to be of the same order of nature as the people they had come to save.

The scriptures for the new teaching are a heterogeneous mass of newspaper and magazine articles and hastily produced books, mostly American in origin but also supported by a substantial number of British and French productions. They came into being in direct response to the public hunger for information regarding the mysterious objects, for the cautious, sober press releases put out by the official agencies merely whetted the appetite. The

American Project Sign merely collected reports, weeded out the 90 percent or so which could be attributed to natural or known mechanical causes and labeled the tiny residue "unknown" or "unidentified." A generation or so earlier, the label would probably have been taken at its face value, as a purely negative classification to hold uncertain material pending fuller information regarding it. But throughout the 1930's and 1940's, the natural tendency to skepticism had been steadily undermined, as wonder after wonder came pouring out of laboratories and workshops. A public which, in five short years, had accepted the concepts of radar, stratoplanes, frogmen, rockets, and the mind-bending implications of the atomic bomb was well on the way to accepting the possibilities of interplanetary movement by alien beings. In hundreds of popular articles and books, the label "unknown or unidentified" was torn off the classification, and the writer's own predilection offered as fact. Some could be dismissed as the rather pathetic fantasies that they were—the accounts of passionate love affairs with beautiful Venusians, the stories of titantic powers granted to the narrator by some grateful demiurge from outer space. But others again retained sufficient link with reality, garnishing their stories with all the panoply of sworn affidavits and circumstantial evidence, so as to present a coherent development. Over some twenty years, as one followed the other, drawing upon its predecessor and manufacturing additional details for its successor, a complex faith evolved. The disciple or passive believer in one story frequently appears as the leader or hero in the next, creating an impression of continuity.

The development of these "contact" stories was quite different from that recorded by Hyneck. He included the classification "Close Encounters of the Third Kind—those in which the presence of animated creatures is reported" with reluctance and distaste: "To be frank, I would gladly omit this part if I could without offense to scientific integrity . . . unfortunately one may not omit data simply because they may not be to one's liking or in line with one's preconceived notions." [72] But a prime characteristic of the contact stories that Hyneck admitted was their uniqueness to the observer, in spectacular contrast to the evolving cultist stories where the observer or narrator was sought out again and again by the extrater-restrial intelligence for the imparting of cosmic secrets. Rich in de-tail, confused in purpose, the contact stories neverthless share definite characteristics, so that the evolution can be traced as it broadens down from something closely resembling a straight-forward science fiction story to something closely resembling a religion.

George Hunt Williamson's book, *The Saucers Speak*, de-scribed itself in the subtitle as "a documentary report of interstellar communication of radiotelegraphy." The slender, unpretentious little work, first published in 1954, purported to contain the record of wireless transmissions that took place between a group of seven or eight people in Arizona, and identified, extraterrestrial in-telligences transmitting from one or other of the planets or from spacecraft approaching the earth. The transmissions took place be-tween August 1952 and February 1953, and despite the subtitle of the book, most of the communications were received by what was described as telepathy but more closely resembled the traditional occult technique of automatic writing. The wireless messages were received and transmitted on behalf of the group by a certain Lyman Streeter, a radio operator for the Santa Fe railroad who played a leading but enigmatic role in the proceedings.

The story, as it developed through the medium of the trans-missions, was of a group of superhuman intelligences forming a universal tribunal established on Saturn, who were hastening to earth's aid before she destroyed herself. The author calmed his readers' fears that the actual end of the world was approaching by emphasizing that the Millennium must take place on the physical earth itself. "A new Golden Age is about to be ready to be born on the Earth and the planet beneath our feet will have to be here if we are to reap the glorious benefits of such a New Age." [73] Neverthe-less, the earth was in great danger, the greatest it had been in dur-ing the seventy-five thousand years that the universal tribunal had been keeping it under observation. The tribunal's major purpose in contacting the earth at this point in time was because the nuclear explosions had alerted the inhabitants of other planets to the danger that the third planet represented for all solar life. Elaborate arrangements were made for the Arizona group to rendezvous with a spaceship. It was never made explicit what actually the occupants of the spaceship intended to do in order to avert earth's impending calamity, and owing to an apparent misapprehension on the part of the radio operator, terrestrials and extraterrestrials never did meet. It was understood that a flight of Martian spacecraft would arrive in 1956. In the 1963 edition of the book, the author speculated that the flight may, in fact, have arrived as promised—but in secret, a curious echo of Charles Russell's belief that Christ had arrived in 1874—invisibly.

The lengthy telepathic messages were a mishmash of chattiness, religious uplift, and "scientific" information, the whole forming a species of ufologian salmagundi that was to act as a very useful source book for Williamson's successors in the technico-religio-occult field. Among the bits and pieces of information conveyed was that the sun was a cool body; that the inhabitants of Neptune ate Macas, a species of hornless cattle with very big ears; that earth had a second, dark, moon called Fowser; that Elala was planet fifteen of solar system 22, whose former name was Wogog. The extraterrestrials lived for hundreds of years, powered their spacecraft by magnetism and, at home, enjoyed idyllic circumstances. All these enviable qualities were available to the inhabitants of earth if they would show a change of heart. Ponnar, a Universal Head from the planet Hatoon, held out lively hopes that the change would come about: "There are now many young people in your world who understand our message. They will accept it quickly for they are of the New Age. The Great Awakening is here." [74]

The supposed radio communications occupied very little space in the book, but they at once served as link with the older tradition of "space communication" which had begun with Marconi, and acted as model for those who wanted to give a technological gloss to their revelations. In the 1954 edition of *The Saucers Speak*, the identity of the radio operator was concealed by the pseudonym "Mr. R." The second edition revealed his identity as Lyman

Streeter and told an elaborate story as to how he had been threatened by a mysterious government agent that if he did not prevent publication of the work he would lose his license. Lyman Streeter, however, had died shortly after publication of the first edition, and the author felt free to disclose his real name, together with the government conspiracy to prevent news of the contact with the extraterrestrials.

The story is, admittedly, confusingly told, but the reader is left with the very strong impression that Lyman Streeter was a practical joker of some skill and dedication. He was the only member of the group to understand Morse code and was therefore free to interpret the signals as he wished. He was the only person to be entrusted with the information regarding the rendezvous point with the extraterrestrials, and he succeeded in separating himself from the rest of the group before arriving at the point. And he was the only person to be contacted by the mysterious Bill Clark, agent of the Civil Aeronautics Administration, and warned that the book *The Saucers Speak* must on no account be published. Streeter certainly made a determined attempt to prevent publication, and the reader is again left with the strong impression that he realized that his joke had been only too successful and, sensibly, was trying to put a term to it.

But whatever deliberate role Lyman Streeter played in the Arizona group, his presence gave its communications an added dimension: The story of the government conspiracy confirmed the objective reality of the communications—for otherwise why should authority wish to halt them? Streeter's skill as radio operator gave a twentieth-century polish to the somewhat tarnished claim to telepathic communication and, most dramatically of all, Streeter revealed that his real name was Kanet, that he was of extraterrestrial origin and had been born upon earth to assist the space confederation's program. This had been revealed to him when he had been taken up in a trance to the tribunal on Saturn. Each of the three points—official hostility, technological gloss, and occult wanderings were major characteristics of the new pseudo-religion.

In his entry for November 20, 1952, Williamson noted baldly

that he and his wife, together with two friends and three other unnamed and unidentified people, observed a cigar-shaped mother
ship and made personal contact with the crew of a flying saucer in
the California desert. The entry was curiously pedestrian considering the high drama of all that led up to it and also that one of the
unnamed three people was George Adamski. For this meeting
which took place 10.2 miles from Desert Center was perhaps the
most famous "contact" of all, the meeting between George
Adamski and the occupant of a Venusian scout ship.

George Adamski's seminal *Flying Saucers Have Landed* was published a year before Williamson's book, although the events it de-
scribes were either contemporary with, or actually later than, the
events described by Williamson. Considering the notoriety that
Adamski was to gain through this book, its contribution to ufology
is, quantitatively, small: Of the 281 pages of the 1970 edition, only
forty-eight pages are by Adamski or, indeed, relate directly to his
experience. The bulk consists of a very lengthy preamble by Desmond Leslie which attempts to trace "flying saucer" stories back
through history in a variety of cultures and literatures and to explain their mechanics. Leslie's viewpoint is demonstrated accur-
rately enough by his emphatic statement that the first flying saucer
arrived from Venus in the year B.C. 18,617,841. But though this
"ridiculous accuracy" as Sir Bernard Lovell described it, relied
heavily upon such suspect or unspecified sources as the records of
Atlantis and "ancient Brahmin tables," Leslie's conspectus also
drew upon the reports of astronomers, newspapers, and eminently
respectable nonsecular sources such as the Hindu scriptures. In
collating such outwardly disparate sources and looking for the common denominator in their reports, Leslie performed a signal service
for the still infant study of UFO's. Thereafter, even those who
were thoroughly skeptical of his conclusions adopted his technique
if only to modify it, preparing the way for the broad, sober analy-
ses such as Jung's and Hyneck's.

But though Leslie's work added substance to Adamski's vision, it was the description of what happened in the California
desert on that November Thursday, together with Adamski's dra-

matic if enigmatic photographs, that accounted for the book's immense and enduring popularity. Adamski described himself as "philosopher, student, teacher and saucer researcher" without going into any great detail about his career. Overenthusiastic friends added a further gloss by claiming that he was a professor of astronomy at Palomar Observatory, possessor of the great two hundred-inch telescope, the world's largest. "Actually," Donald Keyhoe noted caustically, "Adamski operates a refreshment stand on the road up to Palomar and his astronomical experience seems to be confined to a small telescope mounted on the roof." [75] Keyhoe was being less than fair. Adamski had admittedly dabbled in the occult in the past and frankly stated that he had no particular professional qualifications, but he was a dedicated amateur astronomer with some experience of photographing celestial objects through a telescope. It was this latter talent which was to bring him a degree of fame or notoriety, depending on the assessment of his character.

As he tells the story, he was moved by impulse, presumably telepathic, to go into the desert and did so, accompanied by four members of the Arizona contact group, among others. He went to considerable trouble both to name and identify the four from Arizona, a courtesy which was not returned in Williamson's own book, where Adamski, acknowledged hero of his contact story, is dismissed simply as one of "three other people." Even more curiously, Adamski's detailed account of the occasion makes no mention whatsoever of the copious messages which had been passing between Williamson's group and the extraterrestrials and were presumably the cause of this desert meeting.

The meeting took place shortly after noon on a bright day, in a stony valley or depression not far from the road. Adamski was the only one actually to make the contact, the remainder of the party standing respectfully some considerable distance away. The reader is irresistibly reminded of that other contact with extraterrestrial beings, generally known as the Transfiguration, when the witnesses also remained at a respectful distance. The extraterrestrial—a Venusian—arrived at the contact point in a small bell- or dome-shaped scout craft, and he and Adamski conversed through the medium of telepathy, eked out with sign language. Adamski's description of the Venusian seems to owe something to Williams's description of the Neptunian ZO who telepathically transmitted the information that, "I am five feet seven inches tall and I weigh 148 pounds. I have auburn hair. I am what you would call twenty-five years old." [76] Adamski's Venusian was five feet six inches in height, weighed about 135 pounds, was about twenty-eight years old, and had beautiful, long sandy hair. Adamski's published account carried a sketch showing a rather pretty, long-haired young man, who yet seemed capable of infusing his interlocutor with religious awe. "The beauty of his form surpassed anything I had ever seen. And the pleasantness of his face freed me from all thoughts of personal self. I felt like a little child in the presence of one with great wisdom and much love, and I became very humble within myself for from him was radiating a feeling of infinite understanding and kindness, with supreme humility." [77]

Despite the limitations of language, Venusian and Terrestrial engaged in a long conversation of abstracts, touching on the nature of God, the propulsive force of the UFO's, and the reason for their interest in the earth. Adamski's Venusian confirmed Williamson's Martian: The inhabitants of all other planets were becoming alarmed by the terrestrial tinkering with nuclear power. A great future was opening up for earth—provided it continued to survive. As a natural corollary, Adamski asked his visitor whether extraterrestrials still suffered death. In a manner of speaking, was the reply. The speaker himself had once lived on earth but had been translated into space. The meeting ended with mutual expressions of esteem and goodwill, and the spaceman took with him a roll of film which he promised to return. Three weeks afterwards he did indeed return, dropping the roll from his hovering ship. Examination proved that the film roll contained an enigmatic drawing together with symbols in what was apparently the Venusian language.

Adamski's story had sufficient verve and circumstantial detail—including the sworn depositions of the witnesses, to ensure it wide circulation. But it was the photographs that he took through his telescope that attracted popular interest. Instead of the usual blurred light or uncertain distant shape of most supposed UFO photographs, they included close-up photographs of a flying machine, showing such details as portholes, power coils, and landing devices. Whatever the origin of the forms, their shape—disc in plan and double dome in profile—became the standard for all imaginative or conjectured representation of UFO's. This was George Adamski's concrete, measurable contribution to the new humanistic religion.

Far more diffuse, far less measurable, but probably far more important, was the contribution he made to its philosophy or dogma—a contribution so potent that, the day after his death in California, believers held that he appeared in a spaceship in Devon, England. There was nothing particularly original in his contribution; his followers, indeed, appear to be somewhat embarrassed by the full display of its threadbare banality in his second book, *Inside the Spaceships*, and prefer to concentrate their gaze and admiration upon the more plausible story of the first contact. Vague exhortations to virtue; uncritical, unbounded admiration of the vastly superior qualities of "our space friends"; fairy tales of bosky groves on the moon and conferences on Venus—individually, these were common enough elements in the daydream. But in his character, Adamski had the same magnetism and persuasiveness of Brothers, Joanna Southcott, and J. J. Jezreel; the skeptical paused when faced with such confidence, and those in need accepted the message undiluted. In their turn, they propagated the wonders, adding to them. Adamski died in April 23, 1965: on April 24 Arthur Bryant, a gardener, encountered a spacecraft at Scoriton, Devon, one of whose three occupants was a youthful-looking person who called himself Yamski. Was this indeed the resurrected amateur astronomer? The faithful asked and debated the question with all the passion of those who debated the reality of an earlier resurrection.

Whatever Adamski's followers were inspired to proclaim about him after his death, he himself never claimed to be anything but a recorder and observer of essentially natural events. But the ufologian, as occultist, makes no valid distinction between science, religion, and philosophy. Conversation between terrestrials and extraterrestrials is as likely to touch upon the motive power of the UFO as upon the nature of God or the best way for human society to achieve economic balance and spiritual happiness. Nevertheless, until the 1960's, most ufologists were humanist in bias, their written products more closely resembling science fiction than they did religious tracts. But extraterrestrial beings who were consistently described as possessing superhuman powers, beauty, and benevolence were typecast to take over the role of the angel, now being increasingly relegated into the realms of myth and folklore. And, correspondingly, contacts with the extraterrestrial beings took on the nature of religious ceremonial, though remaining "scientific" in its overt details. The International Evangelical Crusade, which came into existence in California, took the process to its logical conclusion and, through the generous Californian laws, sought and found recognition as a church, legally capable of ordaining ministers. Flying saucer doctors of divinity are now among the curiosities of the late twentieth century, joining that long line of eccentrics from the main body of Christianity which began at Wittenberg in 1523.

The Reverend Doctor George King, born in Shropshire, England, in 1919 but resident in California since 1959, was one of those who owed his title of D.D. to the Crusade. Despite the considerable amount that George King has written or caused to be written about himself, little has been publicly made known about his background. According to the British branch of the Society he founded, he served as a leading fireman with the Auxiliary Fire Service in Britain during the Second World War and afterwards seems to have been either a chauffeur or a racing driver. Like Adamski, he possessed one talent which was to bring him a fair measure of publicity and some hundreds of disciples. Adamski's talent was visual—the ability to photograph and reproduce pictures of mysterious flying objects; King's is vocal—the ability to produce the voices of beings claimed to be extraterrestrial in origin, who speak, through King, from outer space. With that talent George King has been able to erect an incredibly convoluted and eclectic religion, a genuine ecclesia of the technological dispensation proclaiming salvation by flying saucer instead of fiery chariot and appealing to Venusians, Martians, and Jupiterians instead of angels, archangels, and cherubim. It is concerned with the same problem as that with which Daniel and John grappled—the impending translation of things—and while its literature lacks something of the sonorous majesty, undeniably it paints a more cheerful future for the human race than that viewed through Greek and Hebrew eyes.

The new era began in May 1954 when an etheric voice announced to George King: "Prepare yourself. You are to become the voice of Interplanetary Parliament." Shortly after this announcement, King was taken on a guided tour of Venus where he was shown, among other wonders, the Temple of Solace in the Valley of the Sun, a building which plays a vital role in the Venusian economy, for the inhabitants draw their sustenance direct from the sunlight passing through the temple. Later, Doctor King took part in an interplanetary war, playing a leading part in the defense of Mars against an evil intelligence from Garouche in deep space. On his return to earth, King began to prepare for his great work, assisting the cosmic masters in the primary initiation of the planet earth into her cosmic heritage, an initiation which would change the very nature of the planet and immeasurably benefit mankind— if mankind reformed in time. To help him in his work, he founded the Society of Aetherius, named after its primary guide, the 3,456-year-old Venusian called Aetherius. Other cosmic masters include the master Jesus, someone or something calling itself Mars Sector Six, and another called Jupiter-92, Saint Goo-Ling, and an entity successively identified with Hercules and Samson.

The central teaching of the Society is that the earth is a self-aware goddess who nobly renounced her cosmic heritage in order to act as refuge for mankind. Something called Karmic Law, however, forbids a Great One to suffer deprivation indefinitely, and on July 8, 1964, the cosmic masters duly charged earth with the necessary spiritual energies, collecting them and discharging them via a system of spaceships acting as relay stations. Nothing outwardly has changed on the planet, but Armageddon, in fact, began on that July day. When the time comes for the goddess Earth to enter into her glorified heritage, she will take the redeemed element of mankind with her. Those who have not been so transformed will suffer what appears to be death but is, in fact, simply a translation to another planet lower in the evolutionary scale.

George King's major role is that of Primary Terrestrial Mental Channel, the only authorized means of communication between the cosmic masters and sinful man. The Aetherius Society owes much to George Adamski with his concrete development of the UFO into a godly chariot; it owes even more, perhaps, to Williamson and his discovery of an Interplanetary Council on Saturn communicating, via telepathy, with earth. But in turning the act of communication into a semireligious rite, the Aetherians have contributed their own unique impress to the ufologian liturgy. The Aetherian temple is part church, part meeting hall, part laboratory. An altarlike desk occupies the traditional place in center front, but where the observer expects to see tabernacle or crucifix there is, appropriately, a microphone. Most of the Society's scriptures are in tape-recorded form, the permanent recording of the communication made by the Masters via their Primary Terrestrial Channel. The content of the communications is mystical, but their form is severely technological. A typical transmission will open with some such phrase as "This is Mars Sector Six reporting from Satellite Number 3, now in Magnetization orbit-Terra." Various subordinate intelligences will manipulate the etheric screens that protect Doctor King from malevolent beings during the transmissions, and each intelligence will report to the cosmic master making the transmissions. All such interruptions are included in the trance speech uttered under the control of the master by George King.

Whatever the origins of the voices, there is no doubt but that King has a very distinctive talent, an ability to differentiate quite clearly between the voices. Thus Mars Sector Six and Mars Sector Eight both speak with deep voices that obviously emanate from the same man, but are subtly different from each other. The voice uttered by the master Jesus is singularly effective and singularly unpleasant, a "nice" voice, the aural equivalent of the washed, groomed, prettified repository portraits of Christ. All voices speak in a monotonous singsong with long pauses between the words and a long-drawn-out *mmmmm* sound after many words. The pauses may be there to allow the speaker to think of the next part of the transmission, but even under ordinary circumstances, the delivery is at least as good as that of professional impressionists. Uttered in the total silence of a religious atmosphere, to people hungrily awaiting revelation, it can be startlingly dramatic.

George King abandoned Britain for America in 1959, setting up his headquarters in Los Angeles. The official reason for the move was that his presence was vital near the San Andreas fault if the world is to survive. But though the Society maintains a flourishing branch in Britain, it has expanded in the more congenial atmosphere of California, taking on an American coloring. In common with all other millennial cults, the Society of Aetherius has moved away from the anarchic to the monarchic. It is Doctor King who designs the electronic equipment with which he gathers together spiritual energies or uses as a weapon against malevolent discarnate entities, and who journeyed to the center of the earth to speak with the Flame Lords. The Cosmic Masters insist that he is their only channel to earth, and it is only to him that they appear in the flesh. His immediate family, however, share something of his charisma, for his wife also has the title of Reverend, and his mother was picked up by a Martian scout craft and taken to a mother ship where the master Jesus blessed the copy of his Twelve Blessings that she brought with her. The implication of change is made specific in the books published by the Society. All bear George King's name as author, but in the later works he is referred to in the third person and in terms of increasing adulation. This is particularly notable in the book entitled *The Five Temples of God* where Aetherius gives instructions to the faithful for the one thousand years after the translation of George King. The Aetherians are comforted with the information that their leader will eventually return, but that even the sufferings of Christ had a mortal end; they must therefore prepare to continue their titanic struggles without the direct aid of the being known as George King.

Aesthetically, the long-haired Venusian descending in his flying saucer to put mankind aright is a poor substitute for the white-robed angel beating his great wings across eternity. The technological Millennium, too, suffers by contrast with its great forebears. The awesome figure of the revealed Christ presiding over a paradisaical world while the legions of hell gather beyond the ramparts for the final battle has been edged aside by a niggling socialism controlled by egotistical pedagogues from outer space. The Interplanetary Tribunal on Saturan, as recorded by George Williamson, can offer only a vague internationalism and good health. Adamski's Venusians exhort vaguely to peace and love without any indication as to how either are to be achieved. The Venusian Aetherius does promise his followers a touch of color: The world's oceans will become iridescent, mountains will gleam like crystals, and permanent music will be heard. It seems little enough but the paucity of the rewards reflects, perhaps, the problem of any millenarian society in an industrial democracy which, with all its manifest defects, does give its members a high standard of personal freedom and physical comfort. Bockelson preaching to citizens tyrannized by the bishop of Munster, Venner leading his enthusiasts against a vengeful and dissolute king, even Brothers proclaiming the end of fratricidal strife had an easier task to project the details of an earthly paradise.

EPILOGUE

•

THE
METAMORPHOSIS
OF ANTICHRIST

In 1830 the Reverend S. R. Maitland, during the course of a poly-syllabic controversy regarding the reality of the visions of Daniel and John, summed up the belief regarding Antichrist that had prevailed for centuries. Christians had always accepted, he insisted, that "at some period or other an Apostacy should take place, promoted and headed by some person or power who is variously described in Scripture as The Little Horn, the Beast, the Man of Sin and who has been commonly known to the Church as Antichrist." At one period, he noted, members of the reformed church had been led so far astray as to employ the name "Antichrist" as a mere term of abuse, instead of accepting him as a horribly real person whose portrait was so clearly painted in scripture. But Maitland was able to end his essay on a hopeful note. "These more ancient doctrines have of late years revived and, I thank God, are spreading." [78] People of the Western world were again becoming convinced not only of the reality of the Man of Sin, but of his distinct identity quite separate from any other force of evil.

That was in 1830. In the 1960's, young men stalked the streets

217

of London and Chicago dressed in flowing sacerdotal robes of black, spreading their new gospel in pubs and bars. The uniform seemed commonplace enough even down to the gleaming pectoral cross of stainless steel. But worn at the throat was a medallion bearing the face of Lucifer. The geometrical simplicity of the symbol of Christianity could not be affected and cheapened, but the face of the entity whom generations of men had been taught to regard as the ultimate enemy might have been designed in the studios of Walt Disney. It was the comic-strip Lucifer with the characteristic horns, arched eyebrows, neat beard, and saturnine good looks.

The wearers of this extraordinary mélange proclaimed themselves members of the Process Church of Final Judgment, come to announce a deity composed of Christ, Satan, and Lucifer. Over in San Francisco, a certain Anton LaVey ran a highly successful organization known as the Church of Satan. "The Satanic Age started in 1966," he announced. "That's when God was proclaimed dead, the Sexual Freedom League came into prominence, and the hippies developed as a free culture." [79] At about the same time, George King descended to the region once known as hell, found there only benevolent entities known as the Lords of the Flame, and returned to announce to his Aetherian disciples that "Satan is dead." By the closing decades of the twentieth century, therefore, Antichrist had not only become merged into Satan, but Satan himself was merged into God, and rich confusion reigned where once there had been logical order, worked out so patiently and clearly by the early fathers of the Church.

It had happened before. Even the author of Revelation himself seemed not quite certain of the relationship between Satan and Antichrist and their respective followers and adherents. He was not, after all, defending a legal brief, and his seven-headed beast, scarlet woman, and horned monster from the sea blended one into the other and resumed separate identities as art rather than logic demanded. During the first millennium, while the world moved on to the significant year A.D. 1000, men turned again and again to that letter of Saint Paul where he argued that Christ could not return until after the "lawless man" had appeared. The lawless man obviously could not be Satan; therefore he had to be a distinct entity in his own right, whatever name might be bestowed upon him. The year 1000 arrived and passed. The tendency today is to play down the once fashionable view that all Europe dwelt in terror as the end of the first millennium drew nearer. Undoubtedly most Europeans continued to jog along much as they had done over the past one thousand years, the ordinary cycle of war, famine, and plague being sufficient to occupy most men. But there were many, indeed, who looked upon A.D. 1000 as something considerably out of the ordinary. "Seeing that the end of the world is approaching" is a fairly common formula in tenth-century legal texts. Wandering friars took the theme of the imminence of Antichrist as ideal material for their hellfire sermons. There was even a date assigned for the end—when the Annunciation (March 25) should fall upon Good Friday. The great artistic theme which appears again in stone, paint, or on vellum is the Apocalypse. And when it was all over and the new millennium was forty years old, a little French monk called Brother Raoul—nicknamed the Bald—turned his attention momentarily from chronicling the wars of kings to note a cultural phenomenon, the sudden upsurge of great abbey churches. "It seemed as though all the world were throwing off its slumber to clothe itself anew in white sanctuaries. Everywhere, people began to restore the churches, and though many were in good condition, they vied with each other in erecting new buildings, each one more beautiful than the last." [80] Those beautiful buildings which dazzled Raoul Glaber about the year 1040 had been planned or commenced at the turn of the millennium, strong enough evidence of a highly charged emotional atmosphere. Glaber at least linked their appearance with the sense of relief that the world had not been destroyed.

But if it had not been destroyed, neither had it been renewed. Deep down in the forgotten—and unknown because undocumented—stratum of society, despair must have been an almost permanent condition of mind, a constant emotion relieved only by the anodyne of fatigue and the stimulant of religious fervor. Their pagan ancestors in the East had had nothing much to hope for in this world or the next; their ancestors in the North had Valhalla for a favored few. But Christianity had promised not only the possibility of eternal bliss in a spiritual heaven, but of bliss in a physical paradise on earth—today, tomorrow, next week, next year, perhaps, but certainly at some point in real time; in the very "twinkling of an eye" as the apostle himself said, the earth itself must change. It was a most potent promise to dangle before a highly gifted race—a race talented enough to create those beautiful "white sanctuaries" of Glaber and fill them with superb artifacts and who were yet condemned to live day by day in windowless hovels built of sods or wood at the same level as their domestic beasts, subsisting for the most part on root crops and niggardly cereals washed down with sourly fermented drink, rotted by plague, shriveled by famine, scourged with endless wars. Any change could not but be for the better, and when prophets rose to lead them into that earthly paradise whose existence Holy Church herself guaranteed, they found a ready-made following.

But as the passionate hunger for and belief in the earthly paradise developed, the figure of Messiah and his necessary forerunner and counterpart, Antichrist, began to fade. Frederick Stupor Mundi was the last, true messiah–Antichrist. For a period, the pope was satisfactorily cast as Antichrist, first for anti-papists and then for the vigorous founders of Protestantism. Melchior Lorch's caricature of the pope endowed him with satanic attributes, but also with the attributes of the man of sin, the beast of Revelation. In England, particularly in the sixteenth and seventeenth centuries, there was a revival of Antichrist, but it was a pale, scholarly shadow of his once appalling self. By the sixteenth century, the protean monster that John had seen arising out of the Aegean had flickered into extinction—or rather, changed its form, for in that same century, the monster's awesome master himself arrived on earth. It would seem that matters had been progressing unsatisfactorily in the diabolical kingdom, and Satan now personally took over his lieutenants' task, ably supported by an enormous cortege of witches and wizards.

The causes of the rise of witchcraft in the sixteenth century are tantalizingly obscure and self-contradictory. Looking back down the long vista of time from the Renaissance to the fall of the Roman Empire, almost any period can be picked that would more logically have given birth to the supposed cult of satanism. But the long agony of the Black Death, the recurrent bouts of famine, the mounting threat from Islam produced instead a passionate religious fervor. It was during the dawn of enlightenment, when men were not only examining the very structure of the universe but, with the discovery of the New World, were breaking free of the claustrophic confines of Europe that the irrational cult of demons and ghosts took final form. Paradoxically, it was the Christian Church which, seeking with all its powers to combat the practice of satanism, gave that same practice a form. It was necessary to define witchcraft in order to combat it, and by so defining, the Church gave shape to what had been little more than folklore. Most of the elements that eventually went to make up witchcraft had long been abroad in Europe, but for centuries the Church had been content to dismiss them as mere fantasy. The legend of the woman who flew by night came in for particular scorn. "Who is such a fool that he believes that to happen in the body which is done only in the spirit?" Such sturdy common sense was forced to give ground at last to a rising tide of fanaticism. In 1458 the ancient ban of the Church on such beliefs was broken by an inquisitor in Germany, who argued that a new sect had grown up which even the fathers of the Church had been unable to foresee. Twenty-six years later Pope Innocent VIII, alarmed at the alleged increase of the cult of witchcraft in Germany, opened a formal crusade against it and appointed two inquisitors, Kramer and Sprenger, to examine the whole structure. The pair devoted five years of labor and produced at last their textbook on witchcraft—the *Malleus Maleficarum*—upon which the whole obscene structure was to be erected.

The *Malleus* was cast in the form of a scholarly disputation; the case for each phenomenon was stated, the objections examined, and the conclusion made. It is difficult to perceive clearly the character of Sprenger, the principal author. He was a man of considerable learning and genuine, if conventional, piety, who seemed indeed to be intent upon the eradication of what he deemed a damnable cult. But he was also obsessed to morbidity with that sexual aspect of witchcraft which dominated the judgment of his contemporaries, discussing at great length and detail whether infants may be generated by demons through human beings. It was Sprenger, too, who was responsible for one of the great slanders upon women. Witchcraft, he asserted, was more natural to them than to men because of the inherent wickedness of their hearts, and because of their greater love of carnality. That conclusion was to bring about the agony of untold numbers of women, most of them old and feebleminded. Men were to burn in the hundreds, but women burnt in the thousands.

The demonology which obsessed Europe for over two centuries was built up partly by deduction but mostly from the confessions of witches themselves. Ideally, the witch should confess spontaneously; yet Sprenger maintained that "it is lawful at times to proceed on the strength of the indubitable indications and conjectures." In other words, if the witch proved unforthcoming with vivid details, then the prosecutor could supply them from the wealth of scholastic studies at his disposal, adding other details as his imagination dictated. The witch nearly always confessed to the most preposterous accusations, and another body of picturesque detail was added to the store. Torture was an inherent and legal part of the proceedings, and few people could accept the prospect of suffering which would end only in death. Counsel, if allowed, was chosen by the prosecutor, but he was himself liable to be charged with witchcraft if he showed himself overzealous in defense.

The questions of the inquisitors naturally fell into a pattern, for they commenced with a preconceived idea; equally naturally, the answers followed a similar pattern so that it did in fact appear that a new cult, complete down to the last horrifying detail, had sprung up all over Europe. Spain alone declined to persecute witches, being already sated with the blood of Jews and *moriscos;* all other countries contributed their national predilections to the growing mythology. The Germans emphasized the peculiar horror of the witches' sabbath, the French and Italians contributed the blasphemy of the Black Mass, England introduced the concept of the animal familiar, Sweden the concept of the human steed, shod like a horse, which conveyed witches to the sabbath.

It was around the sabbath that the great legends of witchcraft were woven. As a matter of common practice, any group of people who wished to meet in secrecy could do so very easily by going a mile or so from the community where they lived. Civilization stopped at the village or city limits; at night time the country beyond was a black wilderness, covered still with primeval forests in many parts of Europe. The occasional traveler would be in no mood to linger and investigate strange lights or sounds, for the very earthy fear of robbers would be as great a deterrent as fear of supernatural beings. Nevertheless, popular fancy believed that the sabbath was held at some unspecified but distant place to which thousands of witches traveled by supernatural means. Much learned attention was given to this problem of nocturnal flight, and most scholars agreed that it was achieved by means of a magic salve. Ingredients of the salve differed from place to place. At a witch trial in Burgundy, the witch confessed that she used the following mixture: stolen consecrated wafers were fed to toads which were then burnt and the ashes mixed with powder obtained from the bones of hanged men together with the blood of newborn infants. By smearing this mess over her body she was whisked high in the air to arrive at exactly the spot fixed on for the sabbath. The Devil was invariably present and took many forms: the traditional, with horns, tail and talons, the human, and most frequently, the goat. Descriptions of the activities of the sabbath itself varied with the imaginative power of the witch or her accusers—cannibalism, obscene dances, blasphemous rites, all found their place. The food and wine were disgusting and were served in filthy vessels.

The *Malleus Maleficarum* was the solid foundation upon which demonology was built, but the Gothic details of the vast mansion of horror were added by the witches themselves. Although most of the details were torn from the wretched creatures by the armory of obscene torture at the disposal of the inquisitors, astonishingly much was yielded voluntarily. Posterity is forced to accept the fact that people—women in particular—freely confessed to the most preposterous actions, including flying by night and association with demons from hell, in the knowledge that the confession would earn them an atrocious death. But there are ample parallels outside the cult of witchcraft: the citizens of Munster who cried out that they saw God the Father descending from High; George King, who described the Temple of Solace on the planet Venus; Joanna Southcott, who became pregnant though a virgin in her sixties; even, perhaps, Frederick Hohenstaufen, who acted as though he were the Messiah; in regarding them, the observer is left again and again groping for the impossible, a test of the reality of another person's visions.

Viewed from the confident nineteenth century, the Renaissance outbreak of witchcraft was an aberration, a mere halt in that ineluctable process of betterment which is the destiny of the human race. The twentieth century is considerably less certain, not least because the outward appearance, at least, of witchcraft has returned. The sixteenth century, like the twentieth, was fragmenting under the pressure of its explosive growth. The Church that had been a symbol of the unalterable will of the Omnipotent, unchanged from century to century, was undermined from within and seemed tottering to its final destruction, carrying with it the hopes of tens of thousands of defenseless, near inarticulate people. Witchcraft was millenarianism gone sour. The residual energy of a thousand years of faith enabled the bulk of the people to cling to the religion of their fathers even if it was in a reformed shape. Those Christians who had the inconvenient habit of assuming that words meant what they said and that Christ was indeed going to return to the distracted planet, sensibly went off and began their preparations for His reception. But those who had tired of waiting, who had been disappointed just once too often, turned at last to the entity whose actual existence their church so passionately affirmed and who had demonstrably never left the planet, much less failed to return.

The last execution of a witch took place in the late eighteenth century, in Central Europe, where it had all begun. The whole business sank into the decent obscurity of the past along with corn kings, haruspex, druids, and the rest of the quaint lumber of the unenlightened centuries. And then, inexplicably, it returned under the blaze of gaslight in the century of common sense and technological enlightenment. It began innocently enough with a party of scholarly eccentrics setting up their occult society, the Order of the Golden Dawn, in the 1890's. In part, it was little more than playacting, scholarship putting on cap and bells. But in part, too, it sprang from the same recognition of the fact that humanity was paying a very heavy price for industrial civilization that impelled William Morris to try to turn the clock back. Morris was content to try to re-create the artist as craftsman; the Golden Dawners were more ambitious—they wanted to re-create the sage, the magi. They wanted to bring back to an earth that was stifling under industrial smoke, strangled by roads and railways, deafened by noise and crushed by the excess of population, something of the quietness, the instinctive contact with nature that they supposed had once existed. The fact that a poet of the stature of Yeats was a member of the circle was testimony both to its scholarship and its ideals. And out of that association was born his sinister poem, "The Second Coming," which voiced the nightmare of those who had waited for so long and now not merely felt themselves betrayed but actively feared, for what might the longed-for Parousia bring in actuality?

> *And what rough beast, its hour come round at last,*
> *Slouches towards Bethlehem to be born?*

Out of the Golden Dawn, too, came Aleister Crowley, whose antics over the next half-century were to delight the circulation managers of innumerable popular newspapers, who was nine-tenths showman and charlatan—but possessed also some quality, some faculty not measurable by the normal senses and was prepared to shape his life to it.

A few pondered on the nature of that faculty, but with the

end of the 1930's, there ended the leisure and the desire for such investigations. Real devils were stalking the planet between 1939 and 1945, and after they had been exorcised—or at least chained— there was the belief and the passionate hope that it was possible to turn the clock back and regain a familiar world. It was to be a world cleansed of its grosser abuses, but still recognizable—a species of secular New Jerusalem with comforting links with the old— and it seemed at first as though the hope might be achieved. As it so happened, 1950 marked one of the quarter-century jubilees of the Roman Church, and for a year the world witnessed one of the great Ingatherings of Christianity. Tens of thousands of pilgrims streamed to make their obeisance at the ancient hub of the world, affirming, it seemed, the indestructible continuity of things.

But even here, at the traditional heart of Christianity, there was a disturbing new note—new to the modern world, that is, for earlier centuries would have had no difficulty in recognizing it. In Fatima, Portugal, in 1905, an apparition of the Madonna was supposed to have appeared to a group of children, and later several thousand people undoubtedly witnessed some extraordinary celestial phenomena. In the early 1950's, a persistent rumor arose that the apparition had left a vital sealed prophecy concerning the end of the world with the children, and that ever since, the prophecy had been locked away in the Vatican. The Vatican, following its ancient and well-tried policy, said nothing; the rumors died away—and received a vigorous resurrection when semiofficial announcements were made that Pope Pius XII had been granted a vision very similar to that which had been seen in the skies above Fatima.

The search for the bones of Saint Peter, which took place beneath the basilica in Rome at about the same time, gave a dramatic emphasis to the story. Why else should the successor of Saint Peter undertake such a search so late in the second millennium after his death? The search was, in fact, somewhat inconclusive, archaeologists identifying only the site of the tomb, and that with some hesitation. The miracle of Fatima faded out of the public consciousness—suffering, indeed, a sea change, for ufologists were to claim it as simply a UFO sighting. But it also marked a moment of profound change. Sometime during the 1950's, a vast qualitative change took place, the product of an ever increasing number of minor quantitative changes. A social pattern that had been developing since the Renaissance—the pattern which affirmed the superiority of reason over emotion, began to collapse. But because that pattern was itself a temporary product, in its collapsing it revealed something of the essential continuity of the human psyche, century by century.

A generation ago, the activities of Jan Bockelson in Munster tended to be regarded either as simply criminal or lunatic. To find analogies, the observer either had to examine contemporary primitive races or prospect back further and further into the mysterious origins of the human spirit. Mass murderers were common enough in every land and every period, but murders committed in a state of controlled trance and virtually as a religious act had disappeared from civilized society. They returned in the 1960's as, hidden behind a smokescreen of pseudo-occultism, a vein of genuine evil developed. In a suburban house in Yorkshire, a young man and woman slaughtered children to the accompaniment of Christmas carols; in California a gang of adolescent, self-proclaimed devil-worshippers murdered a woman and sacrificed parts of her body to Satan; in the Rhineland, two young women murdered those with whom they bedded.

In October 1969 the *San Francisco Chronicle* carried a dramatic story, relating how a major police operation—taking place, appropriately enough, in Death Valley—had rounded up a band of some twenty-seven male and female nomads, most of them nude or nearly so, living together with a number of undernourished children, a quantity of stolen goods, and six dune buggies which allowed them to move swiftly and freely, dodging their pursuers through the desert. The nomads were the "family" of Charles Manson, an undersized, half-educated illegitimate ex-convict who, together with a number of his female followers, was later convicted for the mass murder at the Polanski home.

Manson was Bockelson restated in a twentieth-century setting.

Like Bockelson, he was able not merely to dominate a large number of people—some of them his physical and mental superiors—but also to instill in them something very like worship. In claiming that he was both Christ and Satan, the twentieth-century American went further than the sixteenth-century Dutchman, but ultimately he drew upon the same tradition. Bockelson turned to the concept of the New Jerusalem in Revelation; Manson, roaming Death Valley, subject to hallucinations, at one stage equated himself with the angel in Revelation 9, to whom was given "the key to the shaft of the abyss"—the abyss being a sinister declivity to which he gave the name of the Devil's Hole.

"I am Frederick the Hammer, the Doom of the World," the Hohenstaufen had boasted, and no one knew for whom he wielded the hammer. "I am the Beast 666," Crowley claimed, conjuring yet again the monster of the feverish Judaeo-Christian dream, but not specifically allying himself with it. "I am Satan and Christ," Manson cried. Only the witches of Renaissance Europe had previously specifically saluted the enemy and made common cause with him. Many—perhaps most—of those who identified themselves as satanists did so in the spirit of adolescents joining exotic cults in order to boost their egos. "In modern devil cults," the theologian John Navone argues sardonically, "the Devil is more often a type of magician playmate, the product of a *Playboy* culture, rather than the malign personal being found in Scripture. These cults tend to use the Devil for a type of arcane amusement, whereas the unamusing Devil that appears in Scripture manages to use men for his dark purpose." [81] Certainly the lushly nubile girls cavorting in suburban covens bear little resemblance to the wizened, stinking crones of the Renaissance outbreak. But the Devil, as Saint Anthony knew, for one, comes in many forms.

The millennial dream persists, if flickering wanly, metamorphosized into science fiction fantasy or a dreary biblical fundamentalism. Antichrist, the herald, is gone, but his master remains, coming to the fore again as he did five hundred years ago. And perhaps for the same reason.

. . . things fall apart; the centre cannot hold;
Mere anarchy is loosed upon the world,
The blood-dimmed tide is loosed, and everywhere
The ceremony of innocence is drowned;
The best lack all conviction, while the worst
Are full of passionate intensity.

Surely some revelation is at hand;
Surely the Second Coming is at hand.
The Second Coming! Hardly are these words out
When a vast image out of Spiritus Mundi
Troubles my sight: somewhere in the sands of the desert
A shape with lion body and the head of a man,
A gaze blank and pitiless as the sun,
Is moving its slow thighs. . . .
The darkness drops again; but now I know
That twenty centuries of stony sleep
Were vexed to nightmare by a rocking cradle,
And what rough beast, its hour come at last,
Slouches towards Bethlehem to be born.[82]

SOURCES
OF QUOTATIONS

1. Josephus
2. Rev. 18:10–17
3. Eusebius
4. Ibid.
5. Ibid.
6. Paul: 2 Thessalonians
7. Bousset, p. 78
8. Procopius, III, p. 22
9. Quoted in Gregorovius, I, p. 445
10. Quoted in Bousset, p. 176
11. The full text in Haskins, p. 64
12. Kantorowicz, p. 585
13. Ibid., p. 593
14. Paris, I, p. 313
15. Kantorowicz, p. 553
16. Paris, II, p. 242
17. Gardner, p. 36
18. Quoted in Janssen, V, p. 36
19. Ibid., p. 50
20. Kerssenbroek, p. 265
21. Gresbeck, p. 41
22. Janssen, V, p. 40
23. Gresbeck, p. 119
24. Quoted in Loffler
25. Harleian Miscellany, VIII
26. Abbot, III.
27. Ibid., III.
28. Thurloe, IV, p. 343
29. The unofficial narrative in Rogers, E.
30. Thurloe, III, p. 144
31. Quoted in Burrage, p. 240
32. Pepys, 1660, Oct. 13
33. Ibid., 1661, Jan. 9
34. Hist. Mss. Commission
35. Brothers, p. 39
36. The whole letter published as Appendix in Brothers

37. Brothers, II, p. 46
38. The *Times* report verbatim in Coggan, p. 33
39. Ibid., p. 4
40. Brothers, II, p. 24
41. Ibid., p. 38
42. Halhed, p. 41
43. Southcott, p. 14
44. *The Record*, Dec. 11, 1885
45. Ibid.
46. Smith, p. 37
47. The whole letter in *Chatham and Rochester Observer*, July 14, 1884
48. Ibid.
49. Ibid.
50. Ibid., Jan. 7, 1885
51. Ibid.
52. *Messenger of Wisdom*, May 14, 1887
53. Russell, IV, p. 625
54. *Zion's Watch Tower*, Jan. 10, 1907
55. Macmillan, p. 48
56. Exodus 9:16
57. Watchtower Society: *Hope*, p. 20
58. Luke 21:7–19
59. Johnson, p. 81
60. *The Watchtower*, Aug. 1, 1963
61. Watchtower Society: *From Paradise*, p. 210
62. Daniel, 11:40–45
63. Watchtower Society: *From Paradise*, p. 207
64. *The Watchtower*, June 6, 1973
65. Ibid.
66. Ibid.
67. Hyneck, p. 6
68. Quoted by Hyneck, p. 8
69. Jung, p. 149
70. Ibid., p. 21
71. The *Times*, November 2, 1971
72. Hyneck, p. 138
73. Williamson, p. 150
74. Ibid., p. 78
75. Keyhoe, p. 158
76. Williamson, p. 60
77. Leslie, p. 210
78. Maitland, pp. 1, 19
79. Quoted in Lyons, p. 1
80. Glaber, p. 25
81. Quoted in *Time*, June 19, 1972
82. Yeats, "The Second Coming," quoted by permission of W. B. Yeats and Miss Ann Yeats.

BIBLIOGRAPHY

ABBOT, W. C. *The Writings and Speeches of Oliver Cromwell.* Cambridge, Mass.: 1934–47.

ARCHER, H. *The Personal Reign of Christ on Earth.* London: 1642.

ASPINWALL, W. *A Brief Description of the Fifth Monarchy.* London: 1657.

BALDWIN, R. A. *The Jezreelites: The Rise and Fall of a Remarkable Prophetic Movement.* Orpington: 1962.

BALLEINE, G. R. *Past Finding Out: The Tragic Story of Joanna Southcott and Her Successors.* London: 1956.

BANKS, C. E. *Thomas Venner.* Boston, Mass.: 1893.

BAX, E. B. *Rise and Fall of the Anabaptists.* London: 1903.

BIRCH, T. *A Collection of the State Papers of John Thurloe Esquire.* Vol. II, London: 1742.

BOUSSET, W. *The Antichrist Legend: A Chapter in Christian and Jewish Folklore.* Keane, trans., London: 1896.

BOWMAN, J. W. *The Drama of the Book of Revelation.* London: 1955.

BROTHERS, RICHARD. *Revealed Knowledge of Prophecies.* London: 1794.

BURRAGE, C. "The Fifth Monarchy Insurrection." *English Historical Review*, October 1910 (contains Venner's Journal).

CAPP, B. S. *The Fifth Monarchy Men.* London: 1972.

COGGAN, C. *A Testimony of Richard Brothers.* London: 1795.

COHN, NORMAN. *The Pursuit of the Millennium*. New York: 1970.
CORNELIUS, C. A. *Berichte der Augenzeugen über das Münsterische Wiedertäufer-reich*. Munster: 1852 (contains Gresbeck's account of the uprising).
DIXON, HEPWORTH. *Spiritual Wives*. London: 1868.
DOLLINGER, J. J. *Prophecies and the Prophetic Spirit*. Alfred Plummer, trans., London: 1873.
EUSEBIUS. *The Ecclesiastical History*. Kirsopp Lake, trans., Loeb Classics, London: 1959.
FOX, R. J. *The Finding of Shiloh*. London: n.d.
GARDNER, E. G. *Joachim of Flower and the Everlasting Gospel*. London: 1912.
GLABER, RAOUL. *Chronique*. Paris: 1824.
GREGOROVIUS, F. *History of the City of Rome in the Middle Ages*. Vol. I.
GRESBECK, H. *Summarische* etc. in Cornelius, q.v.
HALHED, NATHANIEL BRASSEY. *A Calculation on the Commencement of the Millennium . . . Together with a Speech Delivered to the House of Commons*. London: 1795.
HARLEIAN MISCELLANY. *A Warning for England. . . .* Vol. VII, London: 1642.
———*Mock-Majesty: Or the Siege of Munster*. Vol. VIII.
HASKINS, CHARLES HOMER. *Studies in the History of Medieval Science*. Cambridge, Mass.: 1924.
HEYMAN, F. G. *John Ziska and the Hussite Rebellion*. Princeton: 1956.
HORSCH, JOHN. "The Rise and Fall of the Anabaptists of Munster." *The Mennonite Quarterly Review*, ix: 1935.
HUILLARD-BREHOLLES, J. L. A. *Vie et correspondance de Pierre de la Vigne*. Paris: 1856.
HYNECK, J. ALLEN. *The UFO Experience: A Scientific Enquiry*. London: 1972.
JANSSEN, JOHANNES. *History of the Germanic People:* A. M. Christie, trans., London: 1903.
JEZREEL, J. J. *Extracts from The Flying Roll . . . Being a Series of Sermons Addressed to the Lost Tribes of the House of Israel*. Chatham: 1879 (reprinted 1970).
JOHNSON, P. S. *Epiphany Studies in the Scriptures*. Vol. V, Philadelphia.
JOSEPHUS, FLAVIUS. *Antiquities of the Jews*. Whiston, trans. London: 1875.
JUNG, C. G. *Flying Saucers: A Modern Myth of Things Seen in the Skies*. R. F. C. Hull, trans., London: 1959.
KANTOROWICZ, ERNST. *Frederick the Sound: 1194–1250*. E. O. Lorimer, trans., London: 1931.
KERSSENBROEK, HERMANN VON. *Anabaptisti fuoris Monasterium . . .* in Detmer, *Die Geschichtsquellen des Bisthums Munster*. Munster: 1851–1913.
KEYHOE, DONALD. *Flying Saucers from Outer Space*. London: 1954.
KING, GEORGE. *You Are Responsible*. London: 1961.

KNOX, R. A. *Enthusiasm: A Chapter in the History of Religion.* Oxford: 1950.

LA LUMIA, I. *Studi di storia Siciliana.* Palermo: 1870.

LESLIE, DESMOND and GEORGE ADAMSKI. *Flying Saucers Have Landed.* London: 1970.

LÖFFLER, K. *Die Wiedertäufer zu Munster.* Jena: 1923.

LYONS, ARTHUR. *Satan Wants You.* London: 1971.

MACMILLAN, A. H. *Faith on the March.* New Jersey: 1957.

MAITLAND, S. R. *An Attempt to Elucidate Prophecies Concerning Antichrist.* London: 1831.

MUNZ, P. *Frederick Barbarossa: A Study in Medieval Politics.* London: 1969.

NEWTON, ISAAC. *Observations upon the Prophecies of Daniel and the Apocalypse of St John.* London: 1733.

NORWICH, JOHN JULIUS. *The Kingdom in the Sun.* London: 1970.

PARIS, MATTHEW. *English History from the Year 1235 to 1273.* J. A. Giles, trans., London: 1853.

PEPYS, SAMUEL. *Diary.* Lord Braybrook, ed., London: 1869.

PLINY THE ELDER. *Letters.* William Melmoth, trans., Loeb Classics, London: 1927.

PORTEOUS. N. *Daniel: A Commentary.* London: 1965.

ROGERS, E. *Some Account of the Life and Opinions of a Fifth Monarchy Man.* London: 1867.

ROGERS, P. G. *The Fifth Monarchy Men.* Oxford: 1966.

——*The Sixth Trumpeter.* Oxford: 1963.

ROGERSON, ALAN. *Millions Now Living Will Never Die: A Study of Jehovah's Witnesses.* London: 1969.

RUSSELL, CHARLES TAZE. *Studies in the Scriptures.* Vols. 1–6, 1886–1904 (Originally published as *The Millennium Dawns*).

RUTHERFORD, J. F. *Prophecy.* New York: 1929.

SANDERS, ED. *The Family.* New York: 1971.

SCHNUR, HARVEY C. *Mystic Rebels.* New York: 1949.

SCOTT, E. F. *Book of Revelation.* London: 1939.

SMITH, HANNAH WHITALL. *Religious Fanaticism.* Extracted from the Papers of HWS, Ray Strachey, ed. London: 1928.

SOUTHCOTT, JOANNA. *Book of Wonders.* London: 1813–14.

STEVENSON, W. *Year of Doom 1975: The Inside Story of the Jehovah's Witnesses.* London: 1967.

THRUPP, S. L., ed. *Millennial Dreams in Action.* The Hague: 1962.

THURLOE, JOHN. *See* Birch.

VARLEY, F. J. *Highgate Episodes: The Insurrection of Thomas Venner.* London: 1938.

Watch Tower Bible and Tract Society. *You May Survive Armageddon into God's New World.* 1955.

————*Babylon the Great Has Fallen!* . . . 1963.
————*Hope for the Dead, For the Survivors in a Religious World.*
————*From Paradise Lost to Paradise Regained.* 1958.
WILLIAMSON, G. H. *The Saucers Speak.* London: 1963.

INDEX

Abel, 185
"abomination of desolation," 4, 8
Abraham, 185, 186
Adam, 176
Adamski, George, 208-211, 212, 214
Agobard, Archbishop of Lyons, 200
Aldegrever, Heinrich, 80
Alexander the Great, 3, 30
al Kamil, Sultan, 44
Allenby, Viscount Edmund, 185
American Project Sign, 204
Amish, 141
Amos, 5
Anabaptists, 64-86, 101, 104, 109, 141,
    148
Annales Laurissenses, 200
Anthony, Saint, 228
Antichrist, ix-x, 30, 59
    Cromwell as, 93-102
    Frederick II as, 52-58, 59
    as Jew, 28
    metamorphosis of, 217-229
    Nero as, 15-17, 26, 94
    as parody of Christ, 16, 17, 29

Paul of Tarsus on, 16, 26, 218-219
personality of, 29
pope as, 42, 88, 220
Rome personified by, 17-18, 26-27,
    28
Second Coming preceded by, 16, 26,
    29, 218-219, 220
Antiochus IV, King of Syria, 3-4, 5, 6,
    8, 13, 16, 89, 94, 193
Antipapists, 42, 220
Antoninus, Arrius, 27
Apocalypse of Saint John, see Revela-
    tion of Jesus Christ
apocalypses, 13
Aquinas, Thomas, 40
Archer, Henry, 89-90
Armageddon, 158, 175, 178, 181,
    189-194, 213
Arnold, Kenneth, 198, 199
Aspinwall, William, 92
astrology, 40, 47, 56
Atlantis, 208
atomic bomb, 197-198
Augustine, Saint, 191

237

Babylon, 5-8, 9, 17-18, 96, 110, 115
Babylonian exile, 4, 9
Babylonians, 16
Barbon, Praise-God, 93
Barbour, N. H., 170-171
"Barebones Parliament," 93
Barry, Bishop F. R., 202-203
Beard, Thomas, 88
Beast 666, xi, 17, 88, 228
Behemoth, 13
Belisarius, 28
Belshazzar's feast, 6
Benedict, Saint, 28
Bethel (Jehovah's Witnesses headquarters), 175, 181, 193
Bishop Hill Commune, 142
Bockels, Jan, see Bockelson, Jan
Bockelson, Jan (Jan van Leiden, Jan Bockels), 61, 66-86, 101, 147-148, 160, 185, 216, 227-228
Brief Description of the Fifth Monarchy, A (Aspinwall), 92
Brothers, Richard, 110-130, 131-132, 133, 142, 147, 158, 185, 211, 216
Bryant, Arthur, 211

Caesar-worship, 11-12, 17
Calvin, John, 179
Catherine of Siena, 67
Chariots of the Gods (von Däniken), 199
Charlemagne, 32, 40
Charles I, King of England, 87-90, 104
Charles II, King of England, 102, 104, 108, 117
Chatham, Kent, Jezreelite community in, 135-166 passim
Children's Crusade, 40
Christ, see Jesus Christ
Christian Church, satanism and, 221
Christian Israelite movement, 132, 142-166 passim
Christians, early, millennium awaited by, 11-12
Church of Satan, 218
Civil War, English, 90, 92, 93
Clark, Bill, 207
"cleansing the blood," 139, 161
Coggan, C., 120, 122
communism, holy, 65
Constance, Germany, 39
Constance, Queen of Sicily, 31-33, 34, 36

Constantine, Emperor, 27
Constantinople, 125, 127
"contact stories," 203-212
Cosmic Masters, 215
Cott, Frances, 128-129
Court, Eliza (Princess Michael), 156-157, 159, 161, 164-165
Creation:
  date of, 140
  duration of, 121
Cromwell, Oliver, 88, 90-101, 108, 109
Cromwell, Richard, 102, 104
Crowley, Aleister, 67, 225, 228
crusades, 40, 43-44, 56
Cummings, James, 152
Cybele, 22-23

Dan, tribe of, 28
Daniel, Book of, ix-xii, 3-10, 15, 110, 157, 163, 178, 192-193
  author of, ix, 5, 8-10, 11, 13, 16, 213
  calculations of millennium in, 8-9, 41, 89, 90, 121
  hero of, 6-7, 8, 10
  interpretations of, x-xi, 89, 90, 92, 117, 123
  visions in, 6-7, 17, 89, 116, 217
Dante, 49
death, 24, 194
della Vigna, Piero, 48, 55-56
demonology, 222
Detroit, Jezreelite community in, 157-165 passim
Deuteronomy, 97
Devil, 223
  see also Satan
devil cults, modern, 228
Dialogue with Trypho, 21
Diaspora, 112, 131
Dionysius, 47
Domitan, Emperor, 11
dragon myths, 15-16
Drennan, Charles, 150
Drew, Job, 150
Drew, Noah, 143, 144-145, 146, 150, 153-154
Dusentschur, Johann, 78, 79

earth, invasions of, 197
Easton, Miss, 142-143
Ecologue, Fourth, of Virgil, 29
Eden, 176

Edict of Milan, 27
Elders of Munster, 74-75, 76
Eldon, Lord, 130
Elect, x, 14, 19, 21, 29, 114
    and Christian Israelite movement,
    133-134, 139, 140, 150, 151
    Jehovah's Witnesses as, 170, 175,
    177, 184
    as Rule of Saints in Munster, 61-86
    "sealing" of, 133-134
    Taborites as, 60
Elijah, 137
Emperor of the Last Days, myth of,
    29-30
Enzio, son of Frederick II, 49, 50, 56
Epistle of Peter, Second, 121
Erskine, Thomas, 129, 130
Esther, Queen, see Rogers, Clarissa
Eve, 139, 176
Ezekiel, xi, 5, 19, 179, 185, 189, 192,
    199
Ezzelino da Romano, 50

Fall, concept of, 139
Fatima, Portugal, 226
Feake, Christopher, 93, 94, 97, 100,
    109
Female Immortal Spirit, 139
Fifth Monarchy, 87-109
Fifth Monarchy Men, 92-109, 127, 194
Final Dispensation, 41-42, 57
Finlayson, John, 126-128, 129-130
Five Temples of God, The (King), 215
Flame Lords, 215
Flodoard, 200
Flying Roll, The (Jezreel-White),
    138-141, 143, 145, 148, 149, 155,
    156, 160, 161, 163, 172
Flying Rollers, 160
flying saucers, 198-216 passim
Flying Saucers Have Landed (Adamski),
    208
Foggia, Italy, 45-46, 56
Francis of Assisi, 42, 179
Frederick Barbarossa, Emperor, 32, 58
Frederick II Hohenstaufen (Stupor
    Mundi), 31-58, 59, 94, 224, 228
    as Antichrist and Messiah, 52-58, 220
    rise of, 31-40
French Revolution, 111, 117
From Paradise Lost to Paradise Regained,
    194

Gardiner, John, 97
Gehenna, 177-178
Genghis Khan, 51
George III, King of England, 111, 117,
    123, 124, 129-130
Germany, Nazi, 192
Gillray, James, 114, 124
Glaber, Brother Raoul, 219-220
Godfrey of Viterbo, 33
Gog and Magog, tribes of, 30, 51
Goodman, Byron, 197
Grasse, Heinrich, 83
"great hallelujah," 51
Great Pyramid of Gizeh, 178, 185, 199
Great War, 182, 184
Greek empire, 7
Greeks, persecution of Jews by, 3-4, 8
Gregory VII, Pope, 179
Gregory IX, Pope, 43, 44, 45, 50, 52
Gresbeck, Heinrich, 69, 71, 73, 74, 81,
    85
Guicciardini, Francesco, 200

Halhed, Nathaniel Brassey, 120-122,
    125-126, 127
Har-Megiddo, 190
Harrison, Major General Thomas, 92,
    100, 103, 121
Hastings, Warren, 121
Head, Mr. and Mrs., 136-137
heaven, 19, 220
    war in, 184
heavenly Jerusalem, 19, 23
Hebrews, Prince of (Richard Brothers),
    110-130, 131-132
hell, 14, 48, 177, 216
Henry, son of Frederick II, 49, 53
Henry VI, Holy Roman Emperor, 32,
    33
Herald of the Morning, 170
Hildebrand (Pope Gregory VII), 179
Hinnom, Valley of, 177
hippies, 218
Hiroshima, destruction of, 197-198
Hitler, Adolf, 192
Hohenstaufen, house of, 32, 36-37, 38,
    44
Holy Ghost, 25, 41
Holy Land, 40, 41, 43-44
Holy Roman Empire, 52
Holy Trinity, 138
Horsemen of the Apocalypse, 13

House of David, 161, 165-166
Hugh the Iron, 40
Huss, John, 60
Hyneck, J. Allen, 201-202, 204, 208

Ingathering of Israel, 142, 146-156
Ingathering of the Jews in Jerusalem, 185
Innocent III, Pope, 34, 36-38, 43
Innocent IV, Pope, 52, 56, 57
Innocent VIII, Pope, 221
Inside the Spaceships (Adamski), 211
International Bible Students, 183
International Evangelist Crusade, 212
Interplanetary Council on Saturn, 214, 216
Isaac, 185
Isabella of Jerusalem, 43
Isaiah, xi, 5, 90, 123, 194
Islam, 29, 30, 44, 45, 53
Israel, 4, 8, 13
  Anglo-Saxon descendants of, 131-132
Israel's International College, 148

Janson, Eric, 142
Jehovah, 176, 182, 191
  covenant of, 131
Jehovah's Witnesses, 143, 168-195
  doctrine of, 176-179
  origins of, 168-169
Jeremiah, 9
Jerusalem, 177, 185
  destruction of, 13, 21, 178
  Emperor of Last Days in, 30
  Ingathering of Jews in, 185
Jerusalem, Latin Kingdom of, 43, 44-45
Jerusalem, New, see New Jerusalem
Jesi, Italy, 30, 31, 50
Jesus Christ, 10, 36, 41, 53, 214-215, 216, 228
  at Emmaus, 139
  false, 17
  Jehovah's Witnesses and, 177
  New Jerusalem and, 20, 22, 23, 98, 99
  Second Coming of, see Parousia
Jews, 177, 222
  dispersal of, 112, 131-132
  of Europe, Messiah and, 51, 117, 127, 131
  Fifth Monarchists and, 99
  Jehovah's Witnesses and, 185

in Judea, 3-5
in Roman empire, 11
Jezreel, James Jershom, see White, James
Jezreelites, 137-166 passim, 169
Joachimite prophecies, 41-42, 57, 90
Joachim of Flora, Abbot, 32, 41-42, 57, 59, 90, 121
Joan of Arc, 67
Joel, 5
John (author of Revelation), ix, 10-11, 12-13, 14, 26, 27, 41, 51, 69, 80, 127, 190, 213, 217, 218, 220
John, the Apostle, 10, 21, 26
John, Saint, Gospel of, 10
Johnson, P. S. L., 181
Josephus, 9
Judaea, 3-5
Judah, tribes of, 131
Judaism, 3-5
Jung, C. G., 202, 208
Justinian, Emperor, 25
Justin Martyr, 21-22, 121

Karmic Law, 213
Kerssenbrek, Hermann von, 64, 73, 76
Keyhoe, Donald, 209
King, Rev. Dr. George, 212-215, 218, 224
Kingdom of God, 7, 174
  as Fifth Monarchy, 89-109
Kingdom of the Two Sicilies, 49
Knipperdolling, Bernhard, 65-66, 68, 71, 74-83, 85-86, 121
Knox, John, 179
Krechting, Bernard, 85-86

Lamb, 12, 13, 14, 20, 80, 109, 127
Last Judgment, x, 110, 140
Laud, William, 88
LaVey, Anton, 218
"Lawless Man," Antichrist as, 26
League of Nations, 192
Lee, Ann, 142
Leslie, Desmond, 208
Leviathan, 13
Little Horn, 8, 89, 94, 217
London, as city of sin, 110-111, 115
Lorch, Melchior, 220
lost tribes of Israel, 117, 131-132
Loughborough, Baron (Alexander Wedderburn), 124
Louis IX, Saint, King of France, 56

Louis XVI, King of France, 117
Lovell, Sir Bernard, 208
Loyola, Ignatius, 179
Luke, Saint, Gospel of, 178
Luther, Martin, 60, 66, 92, 189
Lutheranism, 62, 63, 67, 71

Maccabees, 7, 9
Mackay, David, 163, 164
Macmillan, A. H., 175
madness in millenarianism, 60-61, 64, 68, 69, 82, 115, 119, 123-126
Maitland, Rev. S. R., 217
Malleus Maleficarum, 221-222, 223
Manfred, son of Frederick II, 58
Man of Sin, 217, 220
Manson, Charles, 227-228
Marconi, Guglielmo, 196
Mars, Martians, 196-197, 206, 213, 215
Martin, John, 199
Martin of Tours, Saint, 29
Massachusetts, Anabaptists in, 141
mass hallucination, 66, 68, 74
Matthew, Saint, Gospel of, xi
Matthys, Divara, 66, 76
Matthys, Jan, 66-73, 74
Maximilla, 23-25
Medes, empire of, 7
Mennonites, 141
Merlin, 32, 57
Messenger of Wisdom and Israel's Guide, The, 155
Messiah, x, 5, 15, 27, 42, 59, 220
  Bockelson as, 78-86
  "great hallelujah" and, 51
  as interchangeable with Antichrist, 54-55, 57-58
  Prince of Hebrews (Richard Brothers) as, 110-130, 131-132
  see also Jesus Christ; Parousia
Michigan, Christian Israelites in, 144-166
Midas, King, 22
Mihan, Patrick, 150, 153
millenarianism, 169
  madness and hallucination in, 60-61, 64, 66, 68, 69, 74, 82
  witchcraft and, 220-225
  see also millennium
Millennial Church (Shakers), 142
millennial cults, 60-61, 141-142
Millennial Dawners, 183
Millennium, x, xi, 20-25, 58

in Anabaptist Munster, 64-86, 101, 104
in Apocalypse, 13-15, 19, 25
calculating date of, 8-9, 17, 19, 41-42, 57, 88-90, 111, 117, 121-122, 140, 170, 174-175, 178-179, 183-184, 185, 219
catastrophic portents of, x, 7, 13-15, 17, 18-19, 29, 85, 150, 178, 191-194
celibacy as condition of, 149
Emperor of Last Days and, 30
Evening and Morning State in, 98
extraterrestrial intelligences and, 205, 212-216
Jehovah's Witnesses and, 167-195
Jezreelites and, 137-166 passim
nationalism and, 60
nonfulfillment of prophecy of, 59-60, 102, 183
as physical paradise, 220
in Puritan England (Fifth Monarchy), 87-109, 127
Southcottian sect and, 135, 139
see also Messiah; New Jerusalem; Parousia; prophecies
Miller, William, 169
Mills, Michael Keyfor (Prince Michael), 157-165
Mills, Rosetta, 156-160
Milton, John, 88
Mohammed, 29, 36, 53
Mongols, 44, 51
Monk, General (Duke of Albemarle), 109
monsters:
  in Apocalypse, 15-19, 29, 117, 184, 218, 220
  in Daniel, 8, 10, 15, 16, 89, 94, 117
Montanus, 22-25, 142
Morris, William, 225
Moses, 36, 53, 126
Munster, Westphalia, Rule of Saints in, 61-86, 104, 224
Munzer, Thomas, 60
mysticism, 67, 145

nationalism, 60
Navone, John, 228
Nebuchadnezzar, King of Babylon, 5, 6-7, 178
Neptune, 206
Nero, 11, 12, 15-17, 26, 27, 94, 192

New and Latter House of Israel, 137-166 *passim*
New Guinea cargo cults, 186
New House of Israel, 135-137
New Jerusalem, 5, 226, 228
  Anabaptist Munster as, 61-86, 101, 185
  descriptions of, 19-20, 23-24, 98-99, 127
  designs and plans for, 98-99, 115, 127-128, 129
  England as, 92-109
  Jews in, 99
  of Jezreelites, 141-166, 185
  prophecies of, 20-25, 98-99
Newton, Sir Isaac, 88
New World Society, 189, 192, 193
Nuremberg, UFOs over, 200

Order of the Golden Dawn, 225-226
Original Sin, concept of, 139
Otto of Brunswick, 36-38, 39-40

Paine, Tom, 124
Palermo, Sicily, 33-35, 37, 42
paranoia, 74
Paris, Matthew, 51-52, 54
Parliament, British, 93, 94, 111, 120, 122, 125-126
Parousia (Second Coming of Christ), 11-12, 19, 24-25, 98, 225
  in Anabaptism, 65
  Antichrist as forerunner of, 16, 26, 218-219
  Antichrist's return as parody of, 16, 29
  Christian Israelites and, 140, 142
  flying saucers as, 202-205
  as precondition for Millennium, 26
  timing of, 60, 90, 92, 140, 142, 170
Patmos, island of, 12, 21, 69, 80, 102
Paul of Tarsus, 12, 16, 26, 179, 218
Peasants Rebellion (1525), 62
Pepuza, Sicily, 22, 23-24
Pepys, Samuel, 103-104, 106-107, 108
Persians, empire of, 7
Personall Reign of Christ Upon Earth, The (Archer), 89
Peter, Saint, 83, 226
Peter of Boreth, Brother, 30
Peter of Eboli, 32
Pitt, William, 113, 120, 124-125, 129

Pittsburgh, Jehovah's Witnesses in, 168-169
Pius XII, Pope, 192, 226
polygamy, 76-77, 81
pope, papacy, 36, 93, 192, 226
  as Antichrist, 42, 88, 220
  Frederick II and, 34, 36-38, 43-45, 50, 52-57
Powell, Vavasor, 93, 94
Prester John, 30
Price, Harry, 197
Primary Terrestrial Channel, 214
Priscilla, prophetess, 22-25, 142
Process Church of Final Judgment, 218
prophecies, 12, 220
  in Daniel, 6-10
  of Jehovah's Witnesses, 174-179, 183-184, 189-195
  Joachimite, 41-42, 57, 90
  nonfulfillment of, 59-60, 102, 183
  of Prince of Hebrews (Richard Brothers), 110-130
  in Revelation, 19-20, 25
  Southcottian, 133-135, 138-141
  in Virgil, 29-30, 32-33
Protestantism, 62, 63, 64, 65, 220
psychosomatic processes, 157
Puritans, 87-109 *passim*, 118, 141, 149
Purnell, Benjamin Franklin (King Benjamin), 160-161, 165-166

Rainer of Viterbo, Cardinal, 52-54
Rapp, George, 142
Rappites, 142
Record, The, 138-139, 140
Reformation, 60-65, 88
Reformed Church, 88
religious persecution (ancient), 3-4, 8, 11-12
Restoration, English, 91, 102-109, 117
Revealed Knowledge (Brothers), 112, 115-116, 117, 120, 123-124
Revelation of Jesus Christ (Apocalypse), ix-xii, 10-20, 27, 89, 110, 119, 153, 199
  Antichrist in, 15-20, 26, 51, 218
  author of, 10-11, 12-13, 14, 26, 27, 41, 69, 127, 190, 213, 218
  calculation of millennium in, 17, 41, 89, 121, 179
  Elect in, 14, 19, 133-134

interpretations of, x-xi, 41-42, 89,
110, 115, 117, 123, 184
New Jerusalem in, 19-20, 69, 127,
228
visions in, 13-15, 217
Ribeau, George, 119-120
Richard, Earl of Cornwall, 46
Richard, son of Frederick II, 56
Rogers, Clarissa ("Queen Esther"), 138,
141, 142-156, 157, 158, 159, 162
Rogers, Edward, 162, 163-164
Rogers, Elizabeth, 138
Rogers, John, 91-97, 101-102, 109
Roman empire, 11, 27, 90
Rome (city), 115
Antichrist as personification of,
17-18, 26-27, 28
destruction of, 17-19, 28
Rothmann, Bernt, 61, 63-65, 68, 71,
75, 77, 78, 80, 83
Rowlandson, Thomas, 124
Rule of Saints, 61-86 passim
Russell, Charles Taze, 167, 169-179,
183, 184, 185, 186, 189, 191, 206
Russell, Mrs. Charles Taze, 172-173
Russellites, 180, 183
Rutherford, Judge Joseph F., 179-191

Sabbath, 185, 187, 223
Saladin, 44
Salimbene, 59
salvation, by flying saucers, 212-216
Sanctuary of Israel, 149-151, 153,
155-156, 162, 164
Satan, x, 12, 13, 15, 17, 19, 27, 72, 80,
87, 177, 182, 185, 187, 192, 193,
220, 228
and Antichrist, relationship of, 15,
16, 17, 26, 218
in Armageddon, 178
as merged with God, 218
in war in Heaven, 184
satanism, cult of, 221
Saucers Speak, The (Williamson), 205,
206-207
Saxons (sons of Isaac), 131
Scott, Michael, 47-48, 56
Second Adventists, 169
Second Coming of Christ, see Parousia
Shadrach, 9
Shakers (Millennial Church), 142
Sharp, William, 114

Sheridan, Richard Brinsley, 121
Shiloh, 134-135
Sicily, 32-34, 36-37, 43
Society of Aetherius, 213-215
Sodom, 115, 199
Southcott, Joanna, 67, 132-135, 138,
139, 142, 153, 211, 224
Southcottian sect, 135
Soviet Union, 192, 193
Spittlehouse, John, 92
Strabo, 8
Streeter (Kanet), Lyman, 205, 206-207

Taborites, 60
Temple in Jerusalem, 3-4, 5, 9, 15, 117,
178
ten-horned beast, 8, 15, 89, 94
Thessalonians, 16, 26
Thomison, 24
Thothmes III, 190
Thurloe, John, 95, 97-98
Tiamat, dragon myth of, 16
Tilbreck, Herman, 77
"time, two times and a half a time," 8-9,
17, 41-42, 179
Totila, 27-28
Trypho the Jew, 21-22

UFO (unidentified flying object)
198-216 passim, 227
UFO Experience, The (Hyneck), 201
United Nations, 192
Ussher, Archbishop James, 88, 140

Vane, Sir Henry, 109
van Leiden, Jan, see Bockelson, Jan
Venner, Thomas, 97-109, 147, 216
Venusians, 204, 208-211, 213
Virgil, as prophet, 29-30, 32-33
von Däniken, Erich, 199
von Straten, Hans, 85
von Waldeck, Bishop Franz, 62-63, 67,
70, 71-73, 75, 77, 78, 83, 84, 85

War of the Worlds, The (broadcast), 197
Watchtower, The, 167-168, 171
Watch Tower Conventions, 172
Welles, Orson, 197
Wells, H. G., 197, 201

White, James (James Jershom Jezreel), 136-140, 143-156, 158, 172, 185, 186, 211
Williamson, George Hunt, 205, 206, 207-208, 210, 214, 216
William the Pig, 40
witchcraft, 220–225
World War II, 188, 192, 193, 197, 212
Wroe, John, 142

Yahweh, 4, 6, 176
Yeats, W. B., 225, 229

Zachariah, 138
Zion's Watch Tower, 171, 172
Zion's Watch Tower and Herald of Christ's Presence, 167, 171-172
Zion's Watch Tower Tract Society, 171-183